D1566740

TRIAL AND PRACTICE SKILLS

IN A NUTSHELL

THIRD EDITION

By

KENNEY F. HEGLAND
James E. Rogers Professor of Law
University of Arizona

WEST
GROUP

A THOMSON COMPANY

ST. PAUL, MINN.
2002

Nutshell Series, In a Nutshell, the Nutshell Logo and the West Group symbol are registered trademarks used herein under license.

COPYRIGHT © 1978, 1994 WEST PUBLISHING CO.
COPYRIGHT © 2002 By WEST GROUP
            610 Opperman Drive
            P.O. Box 64526
            St. Paul, MN 55164-0526
            1-800-328-9352

TEXT IS PRINTED ON 10% POST
CONSUMER RECYCLED PAPER

To: Barbara and Ben,
     Robert, Caleb, Alex, and Sarah

Remembering:

    Gary Bellow, and
    Tom Hall

       Lawyers, teachers, and friends

*

PREFACE

Hi!

I'm the guy who (hopefully) sold you your very first Nutshell, *Introduction to the Study and Practice of Law*. You loved it. And I'm the guy who will (hopefully) sell you your last Nutshell, this one. You'll love it as well.

This book introduces the new lawyer to all the varied and wonderful things lawyers do all day: solving legal problems, conducting cross examinations, making closing arguments, taking depositions, negotiating contracts, and counseling clients.

I also write for students in *trial advocacy* courses and those in *clinical* courses. This book can be used either as a text or as a supplement to the many fine texts in these fields.

Another book on the *same* subject?

What makes for the best doctors? Doctors in one community were extensively interviewed and asked who were the best physicians in town. Excellence was not particularly correlated with the prestige of the medical school attended nor with the grades the doctors received. The strongest correlation was with a continuing *interest* in medicine; the best doctors read more medical journals.

The best trial lawyer I know attends every trial workshop he can, even introductory ones. "I always learn something, and the more I know, the more I learn."

Read widely, we have different takes on our subjects, and different insights; try out different approaches and see what works for you; it's your career and people are counting on you.

Sure, another book on the same topic.

Why will you love this one?

It's funny. It's short. It's serious.

Like virtue, funny and short would seem to be their own rewards. Only a law school professor would feel the need to justify them (we are, after all, the folks who brought you the Rule Against Perpetuities).

Funny

I want you to *read* this book; I want to involve you with the choices you will have to make; I want to excite you about law practice. I can't accomplish that if the book sits on the shelf like *Puff,* waiting.

Fred Rodell, a law professor at Yale, wrote an article. It had a spiffy title: *Goodbye to Law Reviews.*

> *There are two things wrong with almost all legal writing. One is style. The other is content. That, I think, covers the ground.*
>
> *Readers like a dash of pepper or a dash of salt along with their information. They won't get*

> *any seasoning if lawyers can help it. Lawyers*
> *would rather be dignified and ignored.*

I won't be ignored. This book will help make you
a better lawyer. Pass the lamp shade.

Short

I have chapters while others have books. Books
are dandy. But books on discovery, negotiation,
counseling, fact investigation, and trial practice,
break up what is in reality a fluid process. You interview witnesses with an eye on discovery, negotiate a contracts with a view to possible litigation, and
counsel clients in light of how they would do at trial.
In a sense, you need to know everything before you
can understand anything.

Brevity means basics. That's okay. Understanding the basics, you can move beyond. Dr. Steven
Rosenberg, the Chief Surgeon of the National Cancer Institute and a leading cancer researcher, wrote
of his early days:

> *Even if I lacked the specific skill to perform par-*
> *ticular operations, such skills can be readily de-*
> *veloped if one knows the basic techniques.*

Then Dr. Rosenberg added:

> *Judgment is harder to develop.*

This book tries to help you on that score too.
Yours is not to memorize basic techniques; yours is
grapple with them, to challenge their philosophical
assumptions, to question their psychological truths,

and to tease out their ethical implications. It is never enough to know the basic techniques; you must know why they work, when they don't, and what gets in their way. That's judgment.

Serious

Despite funny and short, this is a serious book. I treat you as a serious student of your profession and I treat my topic, lawyering, as one of serious intellectual interest. Sure, the Rule Against Perpetuities is complicated, Antitrust is tough, and Law and Economics profound; but none of them hold a candle to what *you* will do all day.

Your daily tasks: discovering truth, teaching, solving heated and complex problems, telling engaging stories, understanding human motivation, and deciding what action is ethical. Law school, and the Bar, are child's play.

The questions you will have to answer are not the stuff of narrow professional interest nor of checklists; they are great questions of the Humanities: of poets and novelists, of philosophers and historians, of sociologists and psychologists, and of physicians and scientists. In the pages that follow I rely on their insights, not to make a dull subject interesting, but because you will face, tomorrow, in your office, the same problems they struggled with. Their insights *help*.

Because we are lawyers, we have a focus that we lacked as undergraduates. All of the classic questions and all of the classic works take on new urgency. As the years go by, and you get better and better at your trial and practice skills, feel no guilt when you go home and relax with a good novel (or poem, or biography, or history, or philosophy or science). You're merely getting ready for tomorrow.

* * *

KENNEY HEGLAND

Tucson, 2002

*

ACKNOWLEDGMENTS

Writing is both solitary and communal. Sitting alone, hacking away, you are surrounded by friends and family, students and colleagues, whispering insights and encouragement. Sometimes, when you are struggling with a thought, one will somehow emerge: "That isn't very clear;" "Well, that's true but not always;" "Not that old joke again!"

I owe major debts to two friends who are no longer with us. Gary Bellow was my supervisor in my first law job, as a staff attorney for California Rural Legal Assistance, a statewide legal services program representing poor folks. CRLA was about to open an office in Delano; one of my first jobs was to find out if we would have to buy a business license. After two or three days, I produced a twenty page memo: yes, Delano's Ordinance did require a $20 fee, but no, we did not have to pay it because it was unconstitutional, for pages and pages of reasons. I was, after all, "law review."

Gary read my memo. My first feedback!

"Do this again, you're fired."

Common sense, it developed, has something to do with the practice of law. Gary taught me so much that a lot of this book is really "Gary recalled."

ACKNOWLEDGMENTS

When I first started teaching Contracts, I assigned *The Merchant of Venice*. Tom Hall was a senior member of the faculty, also teaching Contracts. I knew he would disapprove. He was, after all, older. When I reluctantly fessed up, he smiled broadly, "What a wonderful idea."

Tom taught me to trust myself even when I was a tad off-center. After he had read something I wrote, Tom told me; "Never change your style, Kenney, even if it means getting published."

This book is in its third edition. Those who helped in the first two include Gary and Tom, Mike Sacken, Charles Ares, Sylvia Lane, Barbara Atwood, Kay Kavanagh, Bill Boyd, Toni Massaro, Sherina Cadnum and my parents, writers both.

As for this edition, my clinical colleagues, Paul Bennett, Zelda Harris, and Andy Silverman, gave generously of their time and knowledge. Paul once said, "I tell my students that in trial they are simply telling stories." This led to an entire new chapter. Jamie Ratner, Ana Merico-Stephens, Jean Braucher and Lori Peterson, sent me back to the drawing boards on several occasions. Stephen Golden edited the manuscript and was terrific. George Gross, my marvelous mentor since high school, read most of the book, sharping the literary allusions, offering commas, and an occasional bad joke. Devon May and Sandy Davis were always cheerful in helping with the manuscript and finding the keys to my office. My wife, Barbara Sattler, read as I wrote and offered insights, suggestions and support. Finally, thanks to my youngest, for suffering through a long, hot, summer of "No, Ben, you can't use the computer."

Finally, the Acknowledgment War, Professor David Binder and Professor Paul Bergman versus me. Two against one, not fair; it was *never* fair. Still, I believe I held my own. Until their last book: their acknowledge of my contributions was so clever, so pointed, so devastating, that, in defeat, all I can do is to echo Jack Benny:

"Professors Binder and Bergman, you guys wouldn't dare say those things about me if my writers were here."

KENNEY HEGLAND

Tucson, 2002

*

OUTLINE

Part Two: Practice Skills

OUTLINE

OUTLINE

*

RESEARCH REFERENCES

Key Number System: Attorney and Client ⇨77 –
103, 105 – 129 (45k77 – 45k103, 45k105 – 45k129);
Evidence ⇨355(6) (157k355(6)); Jury ⇨38 – 56,
83 – 42 (230k38 – 230k56, 230k83 – 230k42); Pretrial Procedure ⇨11 – 500 (307Ak11 – 307Ak500);
Trial ⇨31, 106 – 133 (388k31, 388k106 –
388k133); Witnesses ⇨224 – 416 (410k224 –
410k416)

Am Jur 2d, Constitutional Law § 834; Criminal Law
§§ 1085-1091, 1116, 1117, 1280-1282; Damages
§§ 140, 612; Habeas Corpus and Postconviction
Remedies § 254; Negligence §§ 1098, 1971, 2032;
New Trial § 184; Trial §§ 1 et seq.

Corpus Juris Secundum, Constitutional Law §§ 768-
776; Criminal Law §§ 445-468; Federal Civil Procedure §§ 380-383, 528-531, 621-624, 915-932; Juries
§§ 268-282, 340-345; Trial §§ 1 et seq.

ALR Index: Closing Argument; Opening Statement;
Post-Trial Proceedings or Matters; Trial

ALR Digest: Appeal and Error §§ 570, 648, 911-918;
Trial 1 et seq.

Am Jur Pleading and Practice (Rev), Appeal and
Error §§ 556, 557; Continuance §§ 6-16; Dismissal,
Discontinuance, and Nonsuit §§ 261-275; Trial
§§ 1 et seq.

79 Am Jur Trials 285, Premises Liability-Trip and Fall; 76 Am Jur Trials 127, Jury Selection and Voir Dire in Criminal Cases; 68 Am Jur Trials 503, Hidden and Multiple Defendant Tort Litigation; 63 Am Jur Trials 127, Efficiently and Effectively Defending Employment Discrimination Cases; 61 Am Jur Trials 1, Considering Appeals; 59 Am Jur Trials 395, Presentation and Proof of Damages in Personal Injury Litigation; 55 Am Jur Trials 443, Dealing With Judges and Court Personnel; 53 Am Jur Trials 1, Evaluation and Settlement of Personal Injury and Wrongful Death Cases; 52 Am Jur Trials 1, Commonsense Principles of Civil Litigation; 51 Am Jur Trials 337, Civil Consequences of Criminal Conduct; 51 Am Jur Trials 1, Managing Litigation; 50 Am Jur Trials 407, Litigation under the Freedom of Information Act; 49 Am Jur Trials 407, Use of Jury Consultant In Civil Cases; 41 Am Jur Trials 349, Habeas Corpus: Pretrial Rulings; 40 Am Jur Trials 249, Using or Challenging a "Day-in-the-life" Documentary In a Personal Injury Lawsuit; 30 Am Jur Trials 561, Jury Selection and Voir Dire In Criminal Cases; 27 Am Jur Trials 1, Representing the Mentally Disabled Criminal Defendant; 22 Am Jur Trials 1, Prisoners' Rights Litigation; 22 Am Jur Trials 347, Child Custody Litigation; 20 Am Jur Trials 441, Motion In Limine Practice; 5 Am Jur Trials 921, Showing Pain and Suffering; 5 Am Jur Trials 577, Use of Blackboard and Related Visual Aids; 5 Am Jur Trials

505, Mapping the Trial-Order of Proof; 5 Am Jur Trials 331, Excluding Illegally Obtained Evidence; 5 Am Jur Trials 247, Selecting the Jury-Defense View; 5 Am Jur Trials 143, Selecting the Jury-Plaintiff's View; 4 Am Jur Trials 441, Solving Statutes of Limitation Problems; 3 Am Jur Trials 553, Selecting the Forum-Plaintiff's Position; 2 Am Jur Trials 585, Selecting and Preparing Expert Witnesses; 1 Am Jur Trials 1, Interviewing the Client

58 POF3d 395, Challenges for Cause in Jury Selection Process

21 POF2d 645, Expert Testimony at Sentencing; 9 POF2d 407, Discrimination in Jury Selection-Systematic Exclusion or Underrepresentation of Identifiable Group; 5 POF2d 267, Ineffective Assistance of Counsel

Use Westlaw® to Research the Law Governing Trial Practice

Access Westlaw, the computer-assisted legal research service of West Group, to search a broad array of legal resources, including case law, statutes, practice guides, current developments, and various other types of information. Consult the online Westlaw Directory to determine databases specific to your needs.

Searching on Westlaw

With Westlaw, you can use the Natural Language search method, which allows you to describe your legal issue in plain English. For example, to retrieve cases that discuss whether a court has discretion to allow leading questions, access the State Case Law database (ALLSTATES) and type the following Natural Language description: **court discretion to allow leading question**

You can also use the Terms and Connectors search method, which allows you to enter a query consisting of key terms from your issue and connectors specifying the relationship between those terms. For example, to search for the term *exclude, excludes, excluded, exclusion,* or *excluding* in the same sentence as the term *gender* and the phrase *peremptory challenge*, type the following Terms and Connectors query: **exclu! /s gender /s "peremptory challenge"**

Use KeyCite® to Check Your Research

KeyCite is the citation research service available exclusively on Westlaw. Use KeyCite to see if your cases or statutes are good law and to retrieve cases, legislation, and articles that cite your cases and statutes.

For more information regarding searching on Westlaw, call the West Group Reference Attorneys at **1-800-REF-ATTY** (1-800-733-2889).

*

TRIAL
AND
PRACTICE
SKILLS

IN A NUTSHELL

THIRD EDITION

*

PROLOGUE:
ON ADVICE, TEACHING YOURSELF, INSECURITY AND LIVING GREATLY

My best advice, when it comes to advice, is just don't follow it.

That's good advice, but it's impossible to follow. Do, and you don't; don't and you do. Like "All generalizations are false," it turns and consumes itself.

A note on style. I love logical loops, philosophic puzzles, and bad jokes. I entertain myself as I sit here, hacking away. Some folks resent distractions and might wish that I would simply get directly to my point, no matter how dull, no matter how obvious.

If you are one of these folks, you have picked up the wrong book. As Shakespeare asked in *Twelfth Night*:

> *"Dost thou think, because thou art virtuous, there shall be no more cake and ale?"*

This is a book about what lawyers do all day and, as any lawyer will tell you, a day without loops, puzzles, and bad jokes is a day without sunshine.

1

This Prologue is a smorgasbord of topics that cut across what lawyers do: giving and receiving advice, learning from experience, dealing with insecurity, being themselves, and living greatly in the law.

Advice

This book contains a lot of advice, and as a lawyer, you'll give a lot too. A friend comes to you:

> *"I have a problem and need your advice about what to do. But before I get to my problem, I'm concerned with whether I should seek advice at all. In what ways can it hurt me? Would it be better if I figure things out myself?"*

You already know a great deal about advice; over the years you have received and given globs. What advice can you give about advice, particularly as to its limits? Before you read what I have to say, spend a few minutes, perhaps with pencil in hand, responding to the question.

This exercise would have been extremely helpful. But you have already skipped it.

"That sounds like an interesting idea, but I'm only on the second page and I want to get through the chapter before dinner." We measure our lives in coffee spoons, in chapters read and sentences underlined. So here's my advice on the problems with advice.

Seeking advice too early, people deprive themselves of their own insights. Second, what worked once or twice, for particular people in particular circumstances, becomes a rigid rule, such as the "Seven Rules of Successful Living."

Seek advice only after you have grappled with the problem. Figuring things out yourself is always better than underlining. That's why I asked you to think about advice *before* reading my thoughts on the topic. Before you seek advice, ask:

1. *What do I already know about the topic?*

2. *What else do I want to find out?*

For example, before reading my chapter on client interviewing, take a few minutes to ask yourself what you already know about interviewing. Even if you have never been in a lawyer's office, you know a great deal. You have been interviewed by employers, doctors, teachers, and a host of others I am polite enough not to mention. What made you comfortable? What led you to trust the interviewer? What do you want to find out about *legal* interviewing. What problems do you envision? Should you discuss the attorney/client privilege? What if you don't know the answer to a legal question? What if the client cries?

Once you have thought hard about interviewing, *then* read my chapter. You'll find that we agree on many points. Those points you will understand, appreciate, and remember because you didn't merely underline them, you *developed* them. You'll also find that we disagree on some points; well and good, as this will force you to figure out who is right, and hence you will come to a deeper appreciation of both of our points.

You've been lawyering all your life. You have already negotiated deals, if only as to who gets to be Top Hat in Monopoly; you have already engaged in discovery, if only to prove a sibling a liar; and you have already done your share of appellate advocacy, if only to get the car Friday night.

When I was starting out, a lawyer told me, "If you like ideas, you'll like law; if you like people, you'll love law." Our profession is about people, their passions, their fears and their hopes. Our central concern is understanding people. Studies, statistics and novels help; so too reflection:

> [W]hosoever looketh into himself, and consider what he doth, when he does think, opine, reason, hope, fear, etc., and upon what grounds; he shall thereby read and know, what the thoughts and passions of all other men, upon the like occasions.

> Thomas Hobbes, *The Leviathan* (1651)

To understand your client, your adversary, the judge and the jury, put yourself in their position: what would you feel, fear and hope? After all the statutes, all the cases, and all the techniques; what lawyers do, day in, day out, is to deal with people and apply common sense. Don't overlook all you already know.

A Brief Aside: Is there Law Review in Heaven?

Once you get into practice, no one cares where you went to law school and no one cares if you made Law Review. What people care about is whether they can trust you and whether you have common sense. It's that's simple. But it's harder than making Law Review.

As to my advice on advice, access your own knowledge before looking elsewhere. I repeat myself. So be it. In fact, bravo! Information theory teaches that *redundancy is a virtue*. Communication is "iffy" at best. The first time out, the message might have been garbled because it relied upon obscure analogies, quoted long-forgotten verse, or was simply lost in some crude joke the author found more pressing than message. Even if the message was clear and sharp, the readers/listeners/viewers, jurors/judges/clients might have been resistant to the message, or might have been distracted, what with miles to go before they sleep.

Advertisers tell us it takes at least three times.

Images work. Before doing empirical research, Piaget, the great child psychologist, would take long walks, deep in thought, figuring out what his research would establish. I see an elderly gentleman in white frock, hands behind his back, head bent forward, walking next to an Alpine lake. Before putting pen to paper, Agatha Christie would soak in her bubble bath, eating apples, plotting.

Before seeking advice, take a walk or sit in the bathtub. Then there's the matter of reducing advice to a series of *rules*.

Once upon a time, after a dark and stormy night, a lawyer completed a long and complicated jury trial. He (I'm sorry, but I'm sticking to the historical record here) rose to deliver his closing argument. Suddenly it struck him how much he liked the jurors and how much he appreciated the time and effort they had already put in enduring the tedious presentations.

"Ladies and Gentlemen of the Jury, I would like to thank you for all the time and thought and consideration you have already put into this case."

Bingo! Hard faces softened and the judge glanced up from his papers, clearly impressed, and gave a paternal nod.

That was then and this is now. Movement, life, spontaneity collapse into advice!

"Always thank the jury."

"Ladies and Gentlemen of the Jury, I would like to thank you for the close attention you have given this case. Hey, you jurors in the back, wake up!"

All is movement, change, chaos. You cannot step into the same river twice, the flight of a butterfly in Beijing affects the weather in New York, and life cannot be reduced to seven rules. Control forever eludes our grasp, and yesterday's brilliant turn of phrase becomes today's cliché.

Ask of advice *ideas*, not *scripts*. Ask that of this book as well.

When it comes to *your* turn to give advice, remember that the other person has a lot of knowledge and insight.

> *"What advice would you give someone in your situation?"*

And remember that the lessons you have learned were learned in particular circumstances, and that the best advice triggers ideas and approaches, not rules to follow.

Learning from Experience

> *"Why did that witness get away from me on cross?"*

Most of us are too busy, too depressed, or too elated to go back and to do the hard work of learning from our experiences. Give me another cup of coffee and shoot me down the highway.

When we do reflect on our experiences, we generally focus on our mistakes. Here you should consider not only *what* you did wrong but *why* you did wrong. It is usually fairly easy to define good practice; it is more difficult, but more profitable, to figure out why people don't always follow good practice. They aren't idiots. There are usually psychological or situational reasons that compel bad practice; by identifying the causes, you can deal with the symptoms.

But don't focus exclusively on your mistakes. If something went well, *ask why*. The goal is not to come up with a rule to be applied every time. It is to become sensitive to the host of factors that come into play.

Among my other chores, I teach legal writing. Having adequately trashed the first few pages of some timid first year's creation, I said, "These next several paragraphs are good" and started to turn the page.

"Stop. Why are those paragraphs good?"

Previously I'd been content with "I know it when I see it."

"Well, let's see. I guess the main point is that these paragraphs are easy to follow. How did you accomplish that? You seem to start each paragraph with a strong introductory sentence that links the discussion from the last paragraph and makes clear how the point you are discussing fits into your overall legal analysis. You make good use of words of contrast, ('on the other hand,' 'however,' 'even if'). Finally you stay on point and do not veer off onto other legal points."

Insecurity

Law school is not wildly supportive. The limits, vagueness, and contradictions of legal doctrines are our daily meat. Assumptions are identified and challenged: the camera stays out of focus.

First-year skewering is probably a good thing. Pride is sin, humility is virtue. Matters of truth and justice are most difficult. Black-white viewpoints and easy solutions won't produce the society we want nor the lawyers we need. Like omelets, tolerance and mental discipline may require breaking some eggs.

Yet there is a cost to all of this: insecurity. The worst lawyers to oppose are new lawyers: they're so afraid of making a mistake, they will agree to nothing.

Here's some good news about insecurity:

You are not alone. Everyone is insecure. (Maybe that should read, "Most people are insecure," or perhaps, "Some people are insecure," or, better still, "Insecurity is always a theoretical possibility.") Perhaps it has something to do with being born tiny or having supportive parents ("You're not going out looking like *that*, are you?"). I think it has a lot to do with viewing the world from the inside. You *feel* your nervousness; you *see* your opponents' calm. But they live on the inside too; they *feel* their lips quiver, all they *see* is your dashing presence. Students watching their videotaped performances almost always remark on how they look much less nervous than they felt.

Preparation defeats insecurity. Know your stuff and you're the Rock of Gibraltar. Watch Moot Court: you can always tell when the student knows the answer (probably because she anticipated the question) and when she is simply hacking away.

The major trick in combating insecurity is to *silence the internal voice of doom*. When you are on the tennis court, it shouts, "Oh no! It's coming to my backhand, and that's my worst shot!" The little voice helps when we get back to the office. "When the client stops talking, she'll want an answer and I don't even know the topic."

You might try asking the little voice, "Who are you?" Carl Sagen, the astronomer, did. It fired back, "Who wants to know?"

Two devices to silence the little voice:

Shift your focus. Force it from how you are performing. In tennis, watch the ball, actually see the seams as they turn. In the office, focus on the client's story. In court, focus on your opponent's arguments. *Take notes* even if you don't intend to use them.

Second, pretend you're Clarence Darrow. "That's not *me*," and, if Clarence makes a mistake, well, that's his problem. If things are going very badly for you, pretend that you're your best friend.

On Being Yourself

"Be yourself" is the worst advice you can give to some people.

Mark Twain

Unless Twain was talking about you, there is nothing wrong with being yourself; there is no ideal personality type for the practice of law. Gerald Williams, in his fine work on negotiation, has concluded that there is no "best" style. Hardball negotiators and problem solvers seem to have equal success and equal failure.

Second, there is nothing wrong with trying out different personas; it does not entail existential suicide. I assume that there is a "core self," something independent of our roles and of the expectations of others; there is some "thing" to "be" when we are being ourselves. I have a sense of self across various roles and back though time. I am, in some sense, the same person I was in high school. At least I don't dress any better. *However,* not every one of my unfortunate quirks is my essential self. I teach. Whether I stand behind the podium and talk softly or run around the room ranting is not an issue that implicates my essence.

Many students are uncomfortable because they believe that to succeed in law one must be loud, arrogant, and aggressive. Again, no one personality type is required. However, it occasionally helps to be loud, arrogant, and aggressive. (Occasionally it hurts to be loud, arrogant, and aggressive. Unfortunately, students who are loud, arrogant, and aggressive lack the existential angst of their fellows.)

Try out different styles to get comfortable with them: occasionally play Iago, with gusto.

Living Greatly

Viewing people we admire most, be they politicians, poets, or parents, we often lament, "I could never be that good. I could never speak that well; I could never write so well; I could never be that compassionate and insightful."

William Blake had a marvelous phrase: *"Mind-forged manacles."*

When your little voice tells you you can't do something, say, "Thanks for sharing; I appreciate your concern. But I've got to get started."

Justice Holmes saw in the practice of law the possibility of "living greatly." In today's trendy cynicism, we don't talk about that. We stake out modest goals; we talk of partnership and BMWs. The idea of doing something significant, of making an important contribution, brings snickers. And shivers.

The French philosopher, Montesquieu, in the preface to his great work, *Spirit of the Laws*, speaks of his fear of publishing his work, of writing in a field dominated by so many intellectual giants.

> *"I have been lost in admiration but I have not lost courage. I have said with Correggio, 'I too am a painter!'"*

You, too, are a painter. Let's get our brushes.

CHAPTER 1

LEGAL PROBLEM SOLVING

Your first client. You are nervous but ready. This
is what you are told:

> The client, a single father with two elementary
> school children, has been served with an unlaw-
> ful detainer complaint. Three months ago, he
> lost his job and found it impossible to pay the
> rent of $800 a month on the two-bedroom apart-
> ment. He explained this to the landlord, who
> was sympathetic: "Pay me as much as you can
> and you can stay until you find work." The
> client, based on this understanding, made
> monthly payments of $725, $700, and $750.
> Suddenly, and without warning, he got a Notice
> to Pay Rent or Quit. He attempted to contact the
> landlord, but the landlord refused to talk to
> him. Yesterday a process server handed him the
> complaint.

You find this an interesting human tale, not
without pathos. You sit there, mulling it over. Slowly, you become aware that the client has stopped
talking. It suddenly hits you: he expects you to DO
SOMETHING!

But what to do? All you have been trained to do is
write little things in bluebooks. That won't do. Why

is he bothering you, anyway? Sounds like he has a legal problem. Maybe a lawyer could help him. You are about to suggest this, but somehow you regain composure. With boldness, command, and, you are pleased to note, a certain professional air, you say, "I'll straighten this out, I'll phone your landlord's attorney right now."

Have you done well? Do you pass or fail?

Lawyers solve problems. They figure out how to *do* things.

> —*How can I best negotiate this?*

> —*How can I best set up this transaction?*

> —*How can I most effectively cross-examine this witness?*

Lawyers get stuck. They seize upon the first solution they see. It might not be the best solution; indeed, it might not be the right problem. This chapter will help you get unstuck:

1. Realize that there are many ways to define the problem, and that some are easier to solve than others.

2. Appreciate the danger of premature labeling, and be aware of your glasses.

3. Unlock your creativity with play: brainstorm or write.

Finding the Easiest Problem

What you take to be the client's problem will determine the range of solutions you will explore. If you characterize the problem as "Unlawful Detainer," you will think in terms of defeating the complaint, reading the applicable statutes, looking for procedural and substantive defenses.

But have you correctly defined the problem? The client's root problem is that unless something is done, he and his family will soon be without adequate housing. Stated in this fashion, the problem opens itself to another solution: rather than defeat the landlord, help the family find alternative housing. Maybe this would be easier.

Each characterization of the client's problem lends itself to various solutions:

Problem: *How to Defeat the Unlawful Detainer Complaint*

Solutions:

1. Find substantive and procedural defenses to the complaint;

2. Convince the landlord to drop the suit, perhaps by working with her to overcome her financial problems;

3. Help the tenant find more money to pay the rent; perhaps he was improperly fired, perhaps he needs more job training, perhaps he is eligible for welfare.

Problem: *How to Help Find Alternative Housing*

Solutions:

1. Put the tenant in touch with a referral agency;

2. Help increase the supply of low-cost housing by organizing political groups to pass local ordinances prohibiting housing discrimination against children and to pass national legislation funding public housing;

3. Build your client a house. (Bear with me; this might not be as fanciful as it seems.)

These lists can be expanded almost infinitely. The point is this: the client's situation has been caused by the concurrence of many factors, and each of these factors may be taken as the "problem to be solved." Take an example from medicine. In *Mirage of Health*, René Dubos, a medical researcher who helped develop wonder drugs, wrote:

> *The incidence of malaria in a community can be reduced by drugs that attack the parasite, by procedures that prevent mosquitoes from biting man, by insecticides that poison mosquitoes, or by agricultural practices that interfere with their breeding.*

"Just Do It!" is a great slogan but bad advice. It's not simply a question of trying one solution, such as working on a drug, and, if it doesn't work, trying another, working on agricultural practices. Selection of one alternative tends to foreclose others: once you are invested in an approach, you will not likely give it up.

The problem was to design a machine to pick tomatoes. Because tomato skin is quite fragile, the initial solution was to design a very sensitive machine. When a particular design failed, the response was to tinker with it further. The more the people invested in a particular solution, the more difficult it became for them to back up and see the better solution: raise tomatoes with tougher skins. ("Better," unless you're a farm worker, or happen to like tomatoes.)

Another problem with "just do it" is that, in our profession, the field shifts once you begin to act; the problem does not stay constant. The options in the landlord-tenant case will be affected by your call to the landlord's lawyer. Maybe it would be better to write a letter that would invite a more considered, less off-the-cuff response. Maybe it would be better to do additional investigation before your adversary knows you are involved.

An Aside: On Bluffs

Part of the practice of law is bluff. Before you contact the other side, know the strengths and weaknesses of your case. With thought, you can deal with the weaknesses; if you can't, then the case is no good. However, it is devastating to the bluff value of a case to learn the weaknesses from your opponent. You call the landlord's attorney and wax eloquent on the character of your client and the cuteness of his children, only to learn, "Did he tell you about the toxic dump he put in the back yard?"

Returning to the problem of the "first solution," even if it was lousy, soon we will believe it super. So says the theory of *cognitive dissonance*. Should you buy the PT Cruiser or the New Beetle? You test drive both, talk to friends, and consult a consumer guide. You compare mileage, price, resale, design and so forth. You become confused and, quite likely, irritable. The issue is very close and you can't say which is the better car. After much anguish and cold sweat, you eventually decide.

Once you drive it off the lot, you find that you like it better than you thought you would. Slowly you realize its great superiority to the "other car." You have made a decision and you'll be darned if it was a foolish one. All of the factors pointing to your shrewdness crowd in and push out those pointing the other way. You soon forget, for example, that you were ever concerned with either economy or good taste.

By the way, the New Beetle, particularly in Cyber Green, is *objectively* far superior.

Obstacles and Liberators

In the landlord-tenant problem, why didn't you consider going out and building your client a new house? This would solve the problem quite nicely. You cannot defend yourself by claiming that the solution is absurd or impractical. These are reasons why one may *reject* a possible solution, but you didn't even think of it.

What are the obstacles to finding the easiest problem and the best solution? Labeling, your own predilections, and, alas, a lack of playfulness.

Labels

To deal with the blooming confusion of life, we label. But notice what happens when we do.

Once we label, we overlook other labels that might be better. Call it a "contract" problem, and we overlook tort doctrines. The history of the common law is written by creative lawyers who are able to leap the chasms that separate legal categories. The blackletter is that one cannot generally recover damages for mental suffering in an action for breach of contract. Poof! Characterize the breach of a contractual obligation as a tort and land safely. We need to remain flexible and spry.

Once we label a thing, we stop looking at its underlying characteristics. Given a metal ball, a string and a nail, test subjects were asked to construct a pendulum. No problem. They used the metal ball as a hammer. The experiment was then repeated, this time with the metal ball labeled "Pendulum Ball." This stumped many. Looking at the ball, they saw "pendulum ball," not "potential hammer."

We have already seen this in our landlord/tenant problem. The label "Unlawful Detainer" flags certain underlying facts; the label "Need Housing" triggers others.

Conceptions shape perceptions.

We call something "mental illness" and hence look at the medical profession for cures. What if we called it "mentally out of shape?" We know what happened when we called it "madness" and "possessed by spirits." And is drug addiction a "criminal problem," a "medical problem," or a "social problem?"

Scribbles on the tabula rasa

In my unceasing effort to relate law study to undergraduate education, and law practice to the rest of life, recall John Locke and his famous tabula rasa. He believed that people were born with no innate ideas but rather learned everything from sense perception; at birth, the mind was blank, a tabula rasa.

Whether the theory is correct or not, it has led to a misconception about the nature of knowledge: that the mind is a passive receiver of incoming data. It is now generally agreed that the mind is quite active in processing and labeling incoming data.

Each of us has certain biases that affect how we see the client's problem and how we evaluate possible solutions. Think back to the landlord/tenant case. What was the primary image you saw? A tenant in need of help or a landlord in need of punishment?

Psychologist Robert Redmount believes that there are three basic types of lawyers:

1. Those who seek to increase the client's *economic* position.

2. Those who seek to vindicate the client's *"rights."*

3. Those who seek to reduce the client's *conflict* position.

Sometimes, but not always, your concern should be with economics; sometimes, but not always, your concern should be with rights; sometimes, but not always, your concern should be with helping your client through a difficult situation.

Predispositions are like glasses: they bend the incoming data. As an intellectual matter, it is easy to recognize that we are all wearing glasses, or at least that others are. Assuming we too wear glasses, what is the actual distortion? Is it dark because it is dark or because we are wearing sunglasses?

While the rich world of philosophy may suggest that "reality" may forever elude us, Nutshell Writer must do better. First, be aware that what you see will be somewhat distorted by your "glasses." Second, in an attempt to determine how your glasses distort, discuss the case with others. What do they see? Finally, ask yourself if there is anything in the way you generally approach legal conflicts that caused you to label the problem as you did. Do you generally see your clients as folks whose "rights" have been violated? Or do you generally see them as folks who need help in getting out of a mess?

Playfulness

> *That's a stupid idea! Never work! Too expensive!*
>
> *Not our role! Go away!*

The primary obstacle to devising alternative solutions (and alternative ways of seeing the "problem") is *judgment*. Problem-solving involves two phases: first, coming up with possible solutions, and second, judging which is best. The first is a fluid, almost unwilled process: while thinking of a problem, solutions suddenly "pop" into your head. Ideas are the river, whereas judgment—this is a "stupid" idea; this one is "sound"—is the dam. Brainstorming and list making are dam breakers.

Brainstorming. Brainstorming suspends judgment until all possible alternatives are presented. When it is used in groups, the participants are encouraged to suggest the wildest solutions possible, and, until they have exhausted the possibilities, no evaluations of ideas are permitted. There is a lot of humor and a lot of people adding on to others' ideas. The basic point is to get the participants beyond, "Unless I can think of something smart to say, best to keep my mouth shut." Suspension of judgment is also the goal of list making.

List making: ideas beget ideas. Let us return to the "Build your client a house" solution. I'll admit that this alternative exceeds even my expansive definition of the lawyer's role. However, this does not mean that you should not have *considered* it. Ideas beget ideas and, as in the case of real life, even the absurd and the ridiculous have healthy children. If you can't build your client a house, perhaps your client can. There was, and perhaps still is, a federal program of "self-help" housing. Several families, under the guidance of a builder, would help each other build their houses. The point is this: by prematurely rejecting a silly idea—without turning it over in your head—you may never discover the sound idea that lies behind or underneath it.

Play!

At this point, you may object that it isn't the "lawyer's role" to suggest self-help housing to a client who has come about an Unlawful Detainer Complaint. However, to say something is outside the "role" is simply to assert a conclusion. Just why is it outside the role? Without a compelling case to the contrary, lawyers should help clients solve their problems even if the solutions were not embodied in a law-school course or even within the client's original characterization of the problem.

Making a list slows your mind down long enough to allow the generative process to occur. One thinks "Build the client a house" in a split second. In forcing yourself to write it out, you are allowing your mind to play with the idea long enough to give birth to another: "If I can't build him a house, maybe he can."

There is another reason for writing things down. It is one thing to "think" about a problem, something quite different to become actively engaged with it by writing about it. When you begin writing, you are apt to find yourself taking a much different route from the one you "thought" you would. Novelists occasionally speak of the book "writing itself"—that the characters and events assume an independent existence, that the writer does not consciously create them as much as he simply records them.

Mark Twain, in an afterword to his novel *Pudd'nhead Wilson*, wrote about writing it:

> *I have noticed another thing: that as the short tale grows into the long tale, the original intention is apt to get abolished and find itself superseded by a quite different one. This happened with* Pudd'nhead Wilson. *It changed itself from a farce to a tragedy while I was going along with it.*

Once the book was done, he had to go back and account for the characters who had been stranded when the course of the book shifted. He had the twin boys go out in the back yard, fall into the well, and drown.

> *I was going to drown some of the others but I gave up on the idea because it was not a large well and would not hold any more.*

Judgment and evaluation are means of *selection*, not *creation*; they are the tools of the editor. Writing and brainstorming create; they are tools of the author. Playfulness is key. Don't start writing knowing exactly where you are going. That's drudgery. Play around. Stephen King writes:

> *I believe plotting and the spontaneity of real creation aren't compatible.*

Write first, whatever comes. Then edit. As for your bad ideas, the well will be large enough.

Selection

So, which ideas are keepers? Which are destined for the well? Let's return to the top: we left you reaching for the phone, to call the landlord's lawyer. Good idea?

First, think through the various alternatives. If you are going to call, what are you going to say? What would be the best response you might hear? The worst? The most likely? How will you respond? Should you threaten to make a "federal case out of it?"

These are intellectual operations. It is far more beneficial to act through the solution rather than simply "think about" it. *Visualize the solution as it would be played out*. Play out the phone call with an internal dialogue—say what you will say, respond as the other lawyer might. Visualization, like list making, slows the mind. You are likely to see other approaches. It also forces you from the abstract to the concrete—it is one thing to think, "Then I will threaten a lawsuit," and it is quite another actually to threaten one. You can't say, "Now I'm going to threaten you with a lawsuit." And no matter what your actual words, what will you do if they laugh? Rehearsals help.

Competing solutions can also be evaluated in terms of "short-range good" versus "long-term" and in terms of "best outcome," "worst outcome," and "likely outcome." In many situations these criteria will be helpful. And, certainly where there is a wide variation in possible outcomes (big win/big loss solution versus little win/little loss), the decision is your client's to make. I will return to this topic in my chapter on Counseling.

The Paradox of Dogma

Maybe being dogmatic isn't the sin it is made out to be. "But it's not scientific!" We'll see.

The scientific method goes like this:

1.   Observe the data.

2.   Formulate a theory that explains the data.

3.   Create tests to prove or disprove the theory,

4.   If the facts don't fit, reject the theory and begin anew.

That is the high school version. But it ain't that simple. Every time theory hits the bumpy road of reality, funny things happen. Thomas Kuhn, in *The Structure of Scientific Revolutions*, begins with the proposition that there is never an exact fit between theory and nature. There are always bits and pieces, anomalies, that seem out of place. If you reject your theory every time it seems contradicted by a piece of data, you will never get anywhere.

Most scientists are dogmatic, and this is a good thing. In the early days of AIDS, there was controversy over the role of HIV in causing AIDS, a controversy that lingers in some quarters today. One anomaly with the causation theory was the observed fact that not everyone with AIDS tested positive for HIV. Should scientists, in light of this, simply give up their theory and go back to square one? No. They should work long and hard in figuring out just how HIV can cause AIDS when not everyone with AIDS tests positive for HIV. Dogged persistence will teach them much about AIDS and

much about HIV. The solution to this anomaly, by
the way, is that early tests for HIV were for the
antibodies to HIV and, in some cases, the immune
system was so impaired as to be unable to produce
antibodies; thus it appeared from the test that the
patient was free of HIV.

Dogma helps: if you give up after your first failure, you won't get very far.

Let's use a law example.

Police bring a case to a deputy district attorney.
He carefully reviews the evidence against the suspect and finally concludes that he is the culprit. The
DA now goes about gathering more evidence to
establish guilt. He thinks through how the crime
must have occurred and projects that the suspect
must have been at a certain location at a certain
time. In checking this out, however, he discovers
that the suspect was elsewhere. Does the DA now
change his mind and release the defendant? No, he
goes back to figure out how the defendant *could*
have been elsewhere and *still* be guilty. And, of
course, maybe he is guilty.

The joker is, maybe he *isn't*.

Dogmatism's dark side is that we may be *wrong*.
With hard work, however, we may "prove" ourselves right. Commitment to a particular theory will
shape the observed data, and error may never be
recognized. Anomalies may not be noticed, or may
be glibly explained away. Kuhn cites a study where
playing cards were shown, one at a time, to the
subject. In the deck there were a few anomalies, like

a red 3 of Clubs. When the deck was gone through quickly, these anomalies were *not* noticed, the card being identified as either a 3 of Clubs or as a 3 of Hearts.

Some lawyers, in the quick pursuit of their theory, overlook trifles, such as the word "not" in a statute reading "shall not." Always copy key statutes! Always slow down.

Even when anomalies are noticed, a facile mind can often explain them away without sacrificing the main theory: "Yes, the defendant *could* have been in Algiers and *still* have committed the robbery *if....*" A major portion of Kuhn's book deals with how anomalies seldom overthrow basic scientific theories. For example, the Ptolemaic system, which put the earth in the center of the universe, had the planets revolving around the earth in perfect circular orbits. Observations, however, showed that the planets weren't where the theory predicted they would be. Rather than giving up the theory, it was modified: the earth was still at the center and the planets revolved, not in their own circular orbits, but in orbits which moved around points which moved around the earth in perfect circles. With this modification, the observations fit!

Scientists, like the rest of us, seldom admit that they are wrong, and, like the rest of us, often fail to notice or simply explain away facts that seem inconsistent with their positions. Kuhn is a good read for lawyers.

But I have bigger fish to fry. That unpleasant data can be ignored or "explained" informs our understanding of *what we do*, whether we do science or law. It also informs our understanding of *who we are* and *what justice is*. I close with a disturbing excerpt from Tolstoy's *Resurrection*:

> *No man can play an active part in the world unless he believes that his activity is important and good. Therefore, whatever position a man may hold, he is certain to take that view of human life in general, which will make his own activity seem important and good. To maintain this idea, men instinctively mix only with those who accept their view of life and of their place in it. This surprises us when thieves boast of their adroitness, prostitutes flaunt their shame, murderers gloat over their cruelty. We are surprised, however, only because the circle, the sphere, of these men is limited, and principally because we are outside it; but does not the same state of things exist among the rich—who boast of their wealth, i.e., of robbery; the generals— who boast of their victories, i.e., of murder; the rulers—who boast of their power, i.e., of violence. We do not recognize their ideas of life and of good and evil as perverted, only because the circle of men holding these perverted ideas is wider and because we belong to it ourselves.*

Chew on it.

CHAPTER 2

TRUTH, LIES, AND MISTAKES

Have you ever wondered why you have never, not once, been able to convince anyone of your enlightened political views?

> *For such is the nature of men, that howsoever they may acknowledge many others to be more witty, or more eloquent, or more learned; yet they will hardly believe that there be many so wise as themselves: for they see their own wit at hand, and other men's at a distance.*
>
> Thomas Hobbes, *The Leviathan* (1651)

I'll tie the quote up later, but, even if I don't, it's worth it. I think it is one of the most insightful things ever written. Pause a moment, reread, and see if you agree.

Lawyers have to be smart about lies and mistakes. That's the truth. These are matters that cut across all of what we do. Interviewing a client, taking a deposition, conducting a cross-examination, or even negotiating a contract, we need to know, as best we can, who is telling us the truth, who is lying, and who is simply mistaken. This chapter will get you started.

Mistakes

We all know people lie, exaggerate, minimize, conveniently forget, and sometimes just play fast and loose with the truth. How do we know this? Because we have all been there, done that, on countless occasions, on playgrounds, in classrooms, and perhaps, even today, at breakfast. When we are doing this, we know what the truth is, but for a tangle of reasons, we ain't telling.

While we all know lies, it is harder to believe that we can be flat-out *wrong*. Sure, we have read about the errors of perception and recall, but they remain abstract. Seldom, if ever, have we *knowingly experienced* seeing something inaccurately or recalling it incorrectly. Hobbes would understand: "Sure, I understand how other witnesses can be wrong about who threw the first punch, but I *saw* it."

We know when we're lying but not when we are mistaken: that's the first principle: mistakes are harder to get to.

A background question: "Assuming this person isn't lying, could he or she be mistaken? Is there anything that could have distorted perception *or* recollection?" Be aware of the nagging problem of filler, of common errors concerning time, distance, and size, and of certain psychological biases that distort our judgment, perception and recall.

Filler

> *In one experiment, an older sibling told a youn-
> ger, "Do you remember when you were about
> four and we were at the Mall and a stranger
> almost walked off with you?" This never hap-
> pened. Nonetheless, once it is suggested, many
> children not only believe that it did happen, but
> fill in, obviously unconsciously, the missing de-
> tail: "Yes, that happened in front of a depart-
> ment store, near the escalator, and I think we
> just bought some chocolate ice cream."*

Depending on your childhood memories, this is
either good or bad news. Maybe a lot of what you
remember actually happened to other people or
were segments from long forgotten television shows.
Oh, well.

For our instrumental purposes, realize that the
child is wrong but believes he is telling the truth.
We would believe him. Not only by his affect, but
because he knows the details, even the flavor of the
ice cream. And appearances can be deceptive. Dan-
iel Schacter, in his marvelous book *The Seven Sins
of Memory*, tells us that witnesses who seem to be
highly confident are frequently no more accurate
that witnesses who express less confidence.

"Filler" applies to readers and listeners as well.
When you read the sentence, "Yes, that happened
in front of a department store, near the escalator,"
you saw a Mall, your Mall, not my Mall, the one I
saw when I wrote the sentence.

Another disturbing (or liberating) illustration of
filler comes from split brain research. One of the

ways once used to control epileptic seizures was to cut the corpus callosum that connects the right and left hemispheres of the brain; this prevented the seizure from moving from one lobe to the other. This had no effect on the individual's daily life, but did allow for some interesting experiments: whispering in one ear communicated with one side of the brain without the other side knowing. In one experiment, the subject was told to get up and walk across the room when a certain command was given. The command was given and the subject began to walk across the room.

"Where are you going?"

"To get a glass of water."

The psychologist William James once said that we don't run because we are scared, we are scared because we run. Maybe action precedes motivation, another perplexing thought. Maybe all you really know is that you became a lawyer; if asked why, your facile mind will come up with a believable explanation:

"To buy a Nutshell."

On a less cosmic level, filler plays a role. We don't see or hear "everything." From the bits we do see or hear, we conclude "the first punch," "Mozart" or "flying saucer." Unconsciously we fill in missing details (the surprised look on the victim's face). "How do I know the defendant threw the first punch? Well, I saw the surprised look on the victim's face, for one." Our minds are quite active in imposing order. For example:

wetalkinburstsourlistenersfillinthepauses

We/talk/in/bursts/our/listeners/fill/in/the/pauses.
That's why folks speaking foreign languages seem
to speak so quickly: we hear only the bursts.

Errors of time, distance, and size

In emergencies, time stands still. Recall when you
first heard your name called in Contracts. In emergencies, we likely over-estimate time as well as
snickering.

Distance is based mostly on size. We have a good
idea how far away a person is because we have a
pretty good idea of the size of people; conversely, it
is hard to estimate the distances of mountains. If
the identified object is larger or smaller than usual,
mistakes are more frequent: basketball players are
further away than they appear and small dinosaurs,
regrettably, closer.

Size is based on comparison. An average-height
person with a group of short people, will appear tall,
with a basketball team, short.

Hearsay

What we hear from others, or read in the paper,
may cause us to recall an event, truthfully, inaccurately. "Who have you talked with about this incident?" "Have you read anything about it?" "Did
your big sister ever say anything about the Mall?"

Two variations of hearsay distortion involve witness questioning. First, questioning can suggest answers. For example, assume a high speed hostage
chase, ending with police shooting the gunman. The
incident received a great deal of media attention.
After a few months, residents can be surveyed and

asked if they saw the television footage showing the shooting of the gunman. A large number will answer "Yes" even though there was no such film.

The other way questioning can distort recall is that, of necessity, it will highlight certain facts and events at the expense of others; the highlighted material is more likely to be recalled at a later date.

Misattribution

Sometimes we plan on doing something, like take out the garbage, visualize ourselves doing so, and then get distracted and just don't do it. Later, we may falsely recall that we did take out the garbage, indeed, we "see" ourselves doing it.

Another instance of misattribution involves eye-witness testimony. A witness sees a man at the grocery store and, a few minutes later, at the drug store, sees someone who looks like the man commit a robbery. At the line-up, the witness confuses the two events and falsely identifies the man at the grocery store as the man at the drug store. (Then Attorney General Janet Reno formed a group to work on the problem of eye-witness identification. Its report can be found at www.ojp.us-doj.gov/nij/pubs-sum/178240.htm—or so I have been told.)

Biases affecting perception and recall

In the emerging field of behavioral law and economics, scholars such as Professor Cass Sunstein have studied how people make decisions. Generally not by decision-trees nor economic analysis. No big surprise there. We use *rules of thumb*. Common biases, however, contribute to faulty decisions and no doubt contribute to inaccurate observations and recollections.

Extremism aversion

People usually don't like extremes, or "extremists," of whatever stripe. Seldom do we order the most expensive meal nor the cheapest. What is extreme depends on the alternatives: a car dealer offers the "*super* deluxe" package, not primarily to sell it, but to make the "deluxe" package a middle choice. We walk away, not thinking of the thousands we have spent, but the hundreds we have saved. Clever us! (Did I mention how much I saved buying the new beetle?)

Between alternatives, most people, most of the time, seek a compromise. This impacts negotiation and trial strategy: initial positions should tend toward exaggeration. Extremism aversion may impact recollection as well. For example, most of us like to think of ourselves as middle-of-the-road and middle class. After one law school party, *every* participant said: "Well, I may have been drunker than some but not as drunk as others." And when it comes to physical exercise, I am sure you will agree with me that those who do less than we do are slobs, those who do more, fanatics.

Hindsight bias

We tend to believe that what happened was inevitable. Indeed, the way we talk suggests inevitability: "The Civil War was *caused* by X and Y." It is difficult to recall options, choices, and roads not taken. As the English historian C. V. Wedgewood pointed out:

> *History is lived forward but it is written in retrospect. We know the end before we consider the beginning and we can never capture what it was to know the beginning only.*

Pause and consider here as well. How much of your recollection of events is influenced by your knowledge of the outcome? Knowing now that you are a lawyer, thinking back to your college and high school days, don't those events that lead to this decision tend to jump out, while others fade from view, such as your vow to move to Walden Pond?

Optimism bias

We are generally optimistic. Michael Jordan believed that almost all of his shots went in, even though only about 50% did. While optimism is generally a good thing, it can lead to big mistakes: we tend to believe we are less likely than others to be involved in an auto accident or come down with an illness; smokers tend to believe that they are less likely than other smokers to get heart disease and lung cancer. This bias might have caused a witness to discount, or just not perceive, certain risks.

Fairness bias

Good news! Most of us want to be fair, and this may even trump self-interest. In the Ultimatum Game, one of two players is given, provisionally, a sum of money, say $10. That player is instructed to give some of the money to the second player. If the second player accepts it, both keep what they have; if the second player rejects it, all of the money is returned. Bargaining is not permitted. Now, it would seems that Player Two should accept any amount offered by Player One, say $1. That would make Player Two better off. However, Player Two's sense of fairness will trump and the $1 spurned. Studies show that offers of less than 20% are routinely rejected, much to the chagrin of Richard Posner.

We are not just economic maximizers. If a witness is reluctant to talk to you, appeal to fairness. "I know that this will be something of a sacrifice on your part, but without your help, my client will lose her job."

Self-serving bias

Our judgments about fairness can be self-serving. No surprise there, but some insist on studies. Ask a couple "What percentage of the housework do you do?" and you will likely come up with a figure over 100%. (In my case, it is my wife who is overestimating.) Self-serving bias probably explains why fewer cases settle than should: both sides sincerely believe, based on the objective record, but filtered through self-serving lenses, that they deserve a bigger piece of the pie. One of your jobs, as a counselor, is to help your client overcome this bias.

Self-serving bias will cause witnesses to put themselves in a good light during the incident and, during a trial, to defend their testimony. As one trial lawyer remarked, "When it comes to their own testimony, there are no neutral witnesses."

Expectation

To the boss, pickets appear "threatening;" to the union organizer, "determined." Isn't it curious that so many people live up to our stereotypes?

By the way (a difficult thing to *really* believe), all of these biases and aversions affect not only what we are *told* by others, but also what we *hear* of what others tell us. Take expectation. Had Eeyore become a lawyer, it is doubtful he would have ever gotten a good case. Me, I never met one I didn't like.

Science

Well, at least these folks get it right. Right?

Mistakes abound in scientific papers. While very few scientific papers are the product of fraud, as *many as 30 percent* contain results or conclusions that are wrong or are not reproducible. This, according to Dr. Rosenberg whom we met in the Preface. He tells us that Einstein felt that his major talent was in deciding which conclusions were right and which were wrong. (Others might say that Einstein's other talents were more significant but, hey, that's relative.)

What goes wrong?

Too often investigators allow themselves to be fooled. Perhaps they haven't designed the experiment properly or perhaps they want a result so badly that it influences their judgment. Often a result depends on a subjective measurement, an unconscious bias can affect measurements of, say, the size of a tumor difficult to feel. Bias can also enter into the decision about which data to discard. A scientific article may involve work that covered many years and hundreds of experiments, and one cannot report all experimental results. But is the data in the article representative of all the experiments, or only the ones that seem to confirm the hypothesis? Investigators can easily rationalize. "The technician forgot to change the water in mouse cage number six for four days," they might say to themselves, "and that's why those mice died. So we shouldn't count them in the results."

> Steven A. Rosenberg,
> *The Transformed Cell*

We can take this to the bank: questions for pompous experts.

Q: Do you agree that not all scientific papers are correct?

Q: Have you ever read a scientific paper whose data or conclusions you have suspected?

Q: Have you ever murdered a mouse?

Lies

The devil can cite Scripture for his purpose.
An evil soul producing holy witness
Is like a villain with a smiling cheek,
A goodly apple rotten at the heart.
O what a goodly outside falsehood hath!

> Shakespeare, *The*
> *Merchant of Venice*

That pretty much sums it up. Figuring out who is lying is a central dilemma of literature, law, and whether Ben actually liked his pancakes. Our first choice is to find some-sure fire way that doesn't involve our making the hard call: throwing people in lakes, combat, oaths, and, in our own day, "lie detectors."

Occasionally you will know that someone will be tempted to lie to you and, if so, you can head them off at the pass. Realize that everything in life is social and that often people fear arrest, rejection, or simply ridicule if they tell the truth. You can advise your *client* of the attorney/client privilege. You can advise others that you will be circumspect with what they tell you and assure others that you are not judgmental and have heard it all before.

If you think someone has lied to you, here are some devices that might help you force the truth.

Confrontation

Confront the person with contradictions, prior inconsistent statements, and authoritative documents and other testimony.

Getting to bedrock

> *"The butler did it!"*

> *"Did not!"*

This exchange is rarely productive. Rather than taking a claim on directly, seek the data that supports it. "Why do you think the butler did it?" Once you get that information, you can then show that either it doesn't add up to the conclusion or that the information itself is false.

Slash and burn

The questioner quickly jumps from topic to topic, the theory being that the liar will have a harder and harder time remembering prior lies and how current answers are consistent with them.

Police manuals, detective stories and TV are replete with tricks to break the defendant: light in the face, good guy/bad guy approach, etc. (For a fascinating look at how police get around the Miranda warnings: D. Simon, *Homicide: A Year on the Killing Streets.*) Here are techniques that might work.

Mini-lie detector

Witness is asked ten or so questions to which he has no reason to lie. The interviewer watches him closely to sense his "truth-telling posture." Then the key question is asked. Does the witness now light a cigarette? Cross his legs? Blink? If he answers the question in the same manner as he has the others, he is probably telling the truth.

Bluff

Here the interviewer pretends to know the truth and that the witness is lying. Bluffs can run from simply implying that you know the truth to inventing witnesses who, the subject witness is told, all agree to a certain version of the facts.

Repeat back story

If a witness denies all knowledge of an incident, the interviewer tells him what happened, omitting a few essential details. A week later, the witness is asked to repeat back the incident: are the omitted details now included?

Sudden last question

Being interviewed, people keep their guard up. The technique is to finish the interview, engage in closing pleasantries, and then, as an after-thought, ask the key question. A related technique is to openly tape-record the interview. At the end, turn off the recorder and ask, "Now just between us, what really happened?"

The bottom line of all of this is a rather sad one: *trust no one.*

> *Since the world has still*
> *Much good, but much less good than ill,*
> *And while the sun and moon endure*
> *Luck's a chance, but trouble's sure,*

I'd face it as a wise man would,
And train for ill and not for good.

A. E. Housman

CHAPTER 3

TELLING STORIES

The good news is that trial work is easier than it looks. While it is a lot of work, basically you're telling stories. And you already know how to do that.

The bad news is that is it easy to get distracted and lose focus. There are a lot of details: laying proper foundations, making good objections, avoiding leading questions, and not arguing in opening statement. Add to this the formality of the courtroom, the brooding omnipresence of obscure evidence rules, and lengthy books on trial advocacy.

Every now and then, refocus. "Am I telling a story the jury will understand and believe?"

What constitutes a good story? What constitutes good story-telling? Before we get bogged down in the specifics of trial work, opening statement, direct examination, cross-examination and closing argument, let's look at stories and how to best tell them. These concerns will cut across everything you do in the courtroom.

Good Stories

"What makes for good writing?" Students would ask their English teacher in Robert Pirsig's *Zen and the Art of Motorcycle Maintenance*. He tried lecturing but that didn't work. He came up with a new approach. He would read two student papers and ask, "Which is better?" The class was almost always in agreement. His next question: "Why is it better?" His point:

> *You know good writing because you can recognize good writing. Once you recognize good writing, then you can ask yourself, "What is good writing?" and then come up with the criteria yourself.*

Don't forget this point. You know vastly more than you think you do.

Let's try the approach. In *Paul v. Davis*, the plaintiff brought a civil rights action against the Chief of Police for distributing to local businesses a flyer with the names and photographs of "active shoplifters". The plaintiff had been arrested for shoplifting but never convicted. There are several ways of telling this story; here are two, the first told by the United States Supreme Court.

> *Defendant Paul is the Chief of Police of Louisville, Kentucky. In an effort to alert local merchants to possible shoplifters who might be operating during the Christmas season, in early December he distributed to approximately 800 merchants in the Louisville metropolitan area a "flyer" of active shoplifters. The flyer consisted of five pages of photos, arranged alphabetically. In approximately the center of page 2 there*

*appeared photos and the name of the plaintiff,
Edward Davis.*

> *Paul v. Davis*, 424 U.S.
> 693.

Who has your sympathy, defendant Paul or plaintiff Davis? The case could have been introduced differently:

> *Plaintiff Edward Davis, a photographer for the
> Louisville Courier–Journal and Times, was ar-
> rested in Louisville, Kentucky on a charge of
> shoplifting. He pled not guilty and the charge
> was later dropped. With the onset of the
> Christmas season defendant Paul, the chief of
> Louisville Police, prepared a five-page flyer
> containing the names and mug shots of "Ac-
> tive Shoplifters." Copies of this bulletin were
> distributed to merchants warning them of pos-
> sible shoplifters. In fact, the flyer was com-
> posed not only of persons actually convicted of
> shoplifting, but included persons who had been
> merely arrested. Plaintiff's name and mug shot
> were included in the flyer.*

Who now has your sympathy?

How did these two stories create such different impressions? Reread them, and come up with your own criteria.

Basic Hallmarks

The first thing to note is that neither of the versions resort to flowery, adjective rich, language to achieve their effect. Neither appeal to justice or fairness, and neither fudge or stretch the facts. Both versions are "factual" and both discuss pretty much all the same facts.

They achieve such different impressions because they tell the story from different perspectives.

The Supreme Court tells the story from the viewpoint of the defendant Chief of Police. What would be one of the things he would immediately tell us? That he was engaged in a noble effort: alerting local merchants of possible shoplifters. It was, after all, Christmas. The protagonist in the law review version is the plaintiff, Mr. Davis. What would be one of the things he would immediately tell us? That he has a job, and that he was never convicted of shoplifting.

We tend to like the people whose viewpoint we best understand; their viewpoint is apt to become ours. It's not that others always lose; it's that they face an uphill battle in convincing us that the way we understood the story was wrong.

To tell your story so that the jury sees the events from the viewpoint of your client, your first task is to *know* your client's viewpoint. What would be one of the things your client would immediately tell the jury? Involve your client in planning your presentation and listen carefully to how your client views the various events that occurred. Tell the jury the story as the client lived it.

The legal question in *Paul v. Davis* was: does the state violate an individual's civil rights when it incorrectly publicizes the person as a criminal? In the cold world of logic, it doesn't matter who that person is or what the state's motivation. But in convincing juries, and, indeed, the United States Supreme Court, sympathy matters. Present your client in a sympathetic way. Remember that sympathy is won, not by adjectives, but by facts.

In addition to the critical importance of point of view, note the role of language. In the law review article, an innocent man's *"mug shot"* was being shown all over town; in the Supreme Court rendition, it's his *"photo."*

Never underestimate the power of language. Recall Contracts. A builder is hired by the County to build a bridge. He promises to do so. Half way through, the County repudiates the contract. The contractor continues to finish the job. Should he be allowed to recover for work done after the repudiation? It depends on how we characterize what he did.

If we see him "piling up damages," well, we're not going to stand for that! But if we see him "keeping his promise" then we may come to a different result. Is there a correct way to view what he did? *No.*

Representing Davis, in your opening, in your closing, and in the trial itself, refer to the "mug shot;" representing the Sheriff, refer to the "photo".

Time for another Socratic moment:

Example One

Ladies and gentlemen of the jury, the evidence will show that the decedent, a man well respected by the community and one who appeared to have everything, killed himself one night. I guess, when we are feeling sorry for ourselves, we should realize that we may not be as bad off as we think.

Example Two

> *Whenever Richard Cory went downtown,*
> *We people on the pavement looked at him:*
> *He was a gentleman from sole to crown,*
> *Clean favored, and imperially slim.*
>
> *And he was always quietly arrayed,*
> *And he was always human when he talked;*
> *But still he fluttered pulses when he said,*
> *"Good-morning," and he glittered when he walked.*
>
> *And he was rich—yes, richer than a king,*
> *And admirably schooled in every grace:*
> *In fine, we thought that he was everything*
> *To make us wish that we were in his place.*
>
> *So on we worked, and waited for the light,*
> *And went without the meat, and cursed the bread;*
> *And Richard Cory, one calm summer night,*
> *Went home and put a bullet through his head.*

Edwin Arlington
Robinson

Why is Robinson's so much more effective? Develop your own criteria. Reread them.

The poet deals with *specifics,* not summaries. Not only was Richard "well respected," he "fluttered pulses" when he said hello. Not only did he appear to have "everything," he was "imperially slim," "richer than a king," and "glittered when he walked." He didn't just kill himself "one night," he killed himself on a specific night, a "calm summer night," one we all have lived. And, of course, he didn't just kill himself, he "put a bullet through his head." These short hard words almost sound like a revolver shot.

Fluttered pulses deserves a paragraph. Understanding and belief are critical concerns for lawyers as story-tellers. Physical events are things we understand and believe. We all know what it is like when someone quite special greets us, we have all felt our pulse flutter.

Actors are taught that there is a physical attribute to every line, to every emotion.

Cement your conclusions with physical events. What did people *do*? What *happened*?

> "The lecture was boring; two people went to sleep, one walked out."

> "The movie was scary; I couldn't sleep for two nights."

> "The sound was quite loud; it woke the baby."

> "We feel sorry for ourselves; we go without the meat and curse the bread."

"The man was quite depressed; he put a bullet through his head."

Another distinction between the poem and the closing argument is explicitness.

I guess, when we are feeling sorry for ourselves, that we should realize that we may not be as bad off as we think.

Robinson doesn't have to tell us this, the bullet does.

Should lawyers tell the jurors what conclusions they should draw or should they allow them to come to their own? The issue of explicitness in trial work is one we will return to on many occasions. In an ideal world, jurors would come to their own conclusions, for then they would be wedded to them and would defend them with vigor in the jury room. *Provided* that they came to the conclusion you desired.

If you tell as many bad jokes as I do, you are familiar with the expression, "I don't get it." Well, probably a lot of jurors would not "get" Richard Cory, "What's this? The man goes home and shoots himself? I don't get it." And maybe some come to a different conclusion all together: the poem isn't about us being better off than we think, it's about how appearances can be deceiving.

Thus there are things to be said in defense of our lawyer.

Related to how explicit one should be about conclusions is how explicit one should be about the significance of facts. *Richard Cory* ends with a surprise: the suicide. While quite dramatic, this approach suffers from the fact that the reader does not know the significance of the facts until the end. "What does it matter that Richard Cory glittered when he walked?"

To make the significance of the facts jump out, Robinson could have begun with the suicide.

> *Richard Cory, one calm summer night,*
> *Went home and put a bullet through his head.*
> *This is despite the fact that he was imperially*
> *slim, etc.*

A good poet could make this flow. But a good poet could not now recreate the sense of drama and suspense.

What is the role of suspense in trying lawsuits?

If you are a mystery reader, you don't want to find out that the butler did it until the last page. Some trial lawyers (particularly those on TV) try cases as if they were mysteries, dropping clues and quickly changing the subject.

> *"So, you overheard the argument before the gun*
> *shot and it sounded like one of the people had*
> *an irritating upperclass British accent. What*
> *was for dinner?"*

Then, in their closing argument, they drop the bomb:

> *"The butler really did do it this time! We all*
> *know they have irritating upperclass British*
> *accents."*

The problem with this stealth approach, however, is that the jury will not pick up where the lawyer is going and hence may overlook (as I frequently do) the clues. The other approach is to tie things up *as you go along*:

> *Q: So, you overheard the argument before the gun shot and it sounded like one of the people had an irritating upperclass British accent?*
>
> *A: Yes.*
>
> *Q: And isn't it true that the butler has such an accent?*

The problem with this stealth approach is that it foreclosures the possibility that jurors will figure things out themselves, with silent shouts of "Eureka!" Another problem is that your opponent, knowing where you are going, will take defensive action, trying to show that the butler has more of an irritating low class cockney accent.

We'll return to this issue. One calm summer night, the Nutshell went home and returned to the issue.

Theme

Trial lawyers all agree that your story must have a simple theme, one you could tell a fifth grader in about 30 seconds.

> *"This case is about a hard working Sheriff who was doing his best to protect small business owners from shoplifting. Now he's being sued."*
>
> *"Mr. Davis, a photographer for our morning paper, awoke one morning to find himself false-*

> *ly accused of being a shoplifter. He found find his "mug shot" posted on the door of his grocery.*
>
> *"This case is about a contractor piling up damages."*
>
> *"My client did exactly what the County asked him to do and did exactly what he promised to do. He paid his workers. Now the County refuses to pay him."*

Once you have a theme, mention it in opening, refer to it in closing, and direct much of your evidence toward it during the trial. And keep things simple.

Simplicity: The Rule of Three

> *"I came, I saw, I conquered."*
>
> *"Life, Liberty, and the Pursuit of Happiness."*

What is wrong with that introduction? Think.

It seems unfinished. Something is missing. What?

The *third* example.

There seems something about the Number 3. It is marvelous, mysterious, and magical. Writing, we need three adjectives, two won't do. And how many times have you been sailing along and have been able to come up with only two examples? I freeze. The cursor blinks, and blinks, and, yes, blinks.

Realizing the Rule of Three could take us in different directions. We could ask, is this universal? If so, why is this grouping so appealing to the human mind?

But lawyers are pragmatists. How can we use it?

People remember better in blocks of three. Area codes are easier to recall than zip codes, and most car licenses use blocks of three. Some commentators recommend that you have three main themes. They point to the O.J. Simpson case where the defense set its theme in opening statement: "Contamination, Corruption, and Conspiracy." This changed during the course of the trial; focus groups were not buying "Conspiracy." Sure, maybe a couple of the investigating officers were up to no good but it seemed too much to believe that the entire L.A. Police Force was in on a conspiracy. In closing, the mantra became "Contamination, Corruption, and Cancer."

Alliteration is alluring; three is terrific; and liquor, quicker. But don't stay up all night sweating out a third example, or combining the third and forth into one. Two works and so does four, maybe even five. Just don't have too many main points. John W. Davis, the leading appellate lawyer of his day, argued that almost all appellate cases, including big ones like *Brown v. Board of Education*, come down to two or three main points. He advised lawyers not to get distracted by footnotes, but rather to "go for the jugular."

Focus

Edgar Allen Poe believed that a writer should always write with a goal in mind. He wrote:

> *In the whole composition there should be no word written, of which the tendency, direct or indirect, is not one of pre-established design.*

This discipline is not possible in the rough and tumble world of litigation. However, realize that pointless cross-examination (one that simply has the witness repeat what was said on direct), and meandering opening and closing arguments, are very bad story-telling. Engage in them, nevermore!

Delivery

Good story tellers are enthusiastic, know their goals, and aren't jerks.

Enthusiasm: Script v. Spontaneity

I tell students, "You can never prepare enough!" They write it down. The next day, I tell them, "Preparation is death!"

They are generally not amused. "Well, which is it? The best of times or the worst of times?"

My point is this. You must know exactly where you are going in a trial but you must be flexible because it will never go the way you expected. Stephen King takes a different approach to writing than Poe. In his book, *On Writing*, he tells us that he does not plot his books.

> *I believe plotting and the spontaneity of real creation aren't compatible.*

Lawyers plot. Going in, they know what they will want to argue at closing; they know what witnesses they will call and what they will ask; they know what exhibits they will introduce and when they will introduce them.

And yet trials never go as they were rehearsed. You must listen to the answers witnesses give, to the questions your opponent asks, and to the comments the judge makes. Be prepared to open new lines of attack and to dig new ditches of defense. Far too many lawyers simply plow ahead with what they planned.

How to capture the spontaneity of real creation? Consider, every now and then, getting away from the script. On direct, ask a question that wasn't rehearsed. On cross, consider making your *first* question one that jumped out at you listening to the direct. During closing argument, consider making your *first* argument a response to something your opponent said in hers.

Always prepare, but be prepared to jump into the moment.

Now a couple of points on delivery.

Silence

Falling silent is a very effective way of making and emphasizing a point. Listen to talk radio hosts. They usually speak slowly, and, more importantly, pause between thoughts.

Listening, the audience gets one shot at the material, it can't go back and reread.

After a key piece of testimony, stop. Let the jury think about it. Don't change the subject by asking the next question.

Unfortunately this is harder than it seems. We are all uncomfortable with silence and, when it is our turn to talk, we will blurt out just about anything ... (pause) ... just to break the tension.

Fear of silence hurts lawyers. During a trial, it compels us to blurt out our next question, thus blurring the importance of the last answer; during a legal argument, it compels us to answer a judge's question with the first thing that comes to our mind; during a negotiation, it compels us to make a counter offer without first evaluating the offer; and, during a client interview, fear of silence compels us to ask a question which will break the client's train of thought.

Silence, get used to it!

An exercise. Occasionally, when its your turn to talk, just pause and count slowly to five. It will seems like forever to you, but it will seem like a very short pause to your listener.

Talk to your witnesses about silence. It is not enough to tell them to pause and consider before answering questions on cross-examination. Why won't they? Because they fear silence, because they feel the glare of everyone looking at them. Explain that a pause feels much longer to the pauser than the pausee (yuk!). Practice with them: "I'm going to ask you some questions and I want you to count to five before answering them."

This raises a *fundamental* insight. It is never enough to *identify* good practice ("pause before answering"). You must always ask, *"Why doesn't good practice come naturally? What gets in the way?"* Once the obstacles are identified, and dealt with, good practice flows.

Intention: Lessons from Drama

Sure, an actor has to know the lines: "To be, or not to be, that is the question." But a lot more is involved. The great Russian director Stanislavsky spoke in terms of the need to know one's intention. "My intention here is to express despair." How can we do that? Few of us have been in Hamlet's situation; few of us have seen the abyss of suicide, never mind Denmark. But there have been times when we have suffered despair and hopelessness: as a child, at the death of a pet; as a teen, when "our only one" dumped us for our best friend. The actor's trick is to relive those moments and express their emotions in Shakespeare's lines.

Goal precedes *method*. If you are clear on your intention, your tone of voice, your movements, and your facial expressions will tend to line up to accomplish it. In our bones, we know how hopeless people act, once we are hopeless.

Lawyers can learn from this. In terms of intention, we are all over the lot. Often our intention, what there is of it, is rather pathetic: "appear brilliant" or "don't fall on my face." It shows. Before starting a task, be it a client interview, a counseling session or a negotiation, be clear on what you want to accomplish. State your intention as specifically as you can, and repeat it to yourself:

> *"My intention is to get my client to tell me about her problem, what she thinks caused it, and what she wants done about it."*

"My intention is to convince the other lawyer that I have a strong case and that fairness demands that it be settled as I suggest."

"My intention is to use my opening statement to tell my client's story so that the jury will view the situation as did my client."

"My intention is to have the jury realize that this witness is not to be trusted."

Intention is not constant. No one is woeful all of the time. We change, and even in moments of high drama, we experience flashes of the everyday. Emily Dickinson captured this for all time, "I heard a Fly buzz—when I died." To mirror life, the actor must have a *specific* intention as to each line. Sometimes Hamlet is angry, sometimes cynical, and sometimes amorous. Woe to the actor who utters "the play's the thing in which I'll catch the conscience of the King," in a tone suggesting that he just lost his puppy.

Scripting your closing argument, the time you will be center stage, consider your intention. It will not be constant; arguing the credibility of witness X, you will not be in the same emotional place as when you are discussing life in a wheelchair.

Intention can play a role even in witness examination. For each witness you will have your script, a prepared list of questions. Under the script lies intention. State it and look for a time in your life where you actually had it.

> *"In this part of the testimony, my intention is to get the jury to like (respect? trust?) my client."*

Think of a situation where you liked, or respected, or trusted someone. How did it feel?

> *"Here my intention is to get the jury to feel my client's pain."*

How did it feel when a loved one told you of his pain?

> *"Here my intention is to express disbelief as to the witness' testimony."*

When was the last time someone lied to you? How did you feel?

The way you stand at the podium, the way you look at the witness, the way you ask questions and respond to answers, all will line up to support your underlying intention.

But wait a minute! The jury will be looking at the witness. True, but *the witness is looking at you!* You are always center stage for the witness, and this audience of one will respond to your questions, *and* to your intentions.

Remember, of course, J. Alfred Prufrock. You are not Prince Hamlet nor are meant to be. The witness is Hamlet and your job is "to swell a progress, start a scene or two," in short, to facilitate the story, to be an easy tool, but not the fool. Don't express your intentions so much that the jury shifts its attention to you.

Don't be a jerk!

Juries, bless them, don't like lawyers who *needlessly* beat up on witnesses, who treat court personnel badly, and who walk with a stagger that suggests, in the words of Shakespeare:

> *"I am Sir Oracle. If I open my*
> *lips, let no dog bark."*

I generally refrain from being preachy but, please, never, not once, treat someone badly because they have less prestige than you.

> *William Bennett was on an airplane and the man sitting next to him was treating the flight attendant with disdain and contempt. Bennett struck up a conversation with him, asked for his business card, and then fell silent.*
>
> *"Why did you want my card?"*
>
> *"Well, I didn't introduce myself. I'm William Bennett and I am a high ranking member of President Reagan's administration. I wanted your card because when we land I'm going to phone the C.E.O. of your corporation and tell him what a jerk you are."*

Perfect!

. . .

This chapter, lawyer as story teller, took longer than I had expected. To review:

Job one is to tell your client's story to the jury.

This should be reassuring as you have been telling stories your whole life. Tell the story from your client's viewpoint, and make the client sympathetic. Sympathy flows from facts, not adjectives. Try to cement the story with physical acts: what people *did*, what happened in the universe. Consider the pros and cons of being explicit as to your conclusions and leading with them. Get a theme, one that you can tell to a fifth grader in 30 seconds. And don't clutter your story with extraneous details.

Job two is the actual telling of it.

Find the right balance between scripting and spontaneity. Make effective use of silence and realize the importance of knowing, and reciting, your intention.

Job three, don't be a jerk.

If you want to be one, fine. Just be *sure* to give your card to strangers.

CHAPTER 4

DIRECT EXAMINATION: CLARITY AND EXCITEMENT

Begin by drafting your closing argument. What do you want to say? What conclusions do you want the jury to reach? Once you know what you want to say in closing, turn to how you will get there. What evidence will you need to support your arguments? Which specific witnesses, and which specific questions will give you that evidence? You will probably want to have a trial notebook; under each witnesses name, the list of questions you want to ask. As you go along, you check off the evidence as it comes in.

When you have a draft of your case, consisting of your closing argument and lists of questions per witness, step back and ask:

1. How can I make my case more *understandable* and *interesting*?

2. How can I make it more *believable*?

This chapter focuses on how to make your direct examination clear and exciting; in the next, we take up the question of credibility.

Clarity

First, realize you start at a disadvantage. You know the testimony *too well* and could be, by now, *bored* with it.

A common teaching error is to assume that your students have the same background knowledge as do you. What was once hard and difficult for you, has become, after hard work, self-evident. One doesn't want to spend a lot of class time on the "self-evident."

You have worked hard on the case, you know how everything fits, and you know what is to come. The jury has never heard of the case until today.

Spend a lot of time on the self-evident.

When you first interviewed the witness, you were on the edge of your seat; the next couple of answers could make or break you case. What would they be?

Now you know. Your joy, relief, and concern have all been spent. Don't let your boredom or complacency show. The jurors are watching. If you're bored, they'll be bored. And what of your poor witness? Addressing a bored audience, you lose cabin pressure; enthusiasm and confidence vanish.

Recapture your excitement, your anticipation and, indeed, your fear.

Is clarity a concern? Go to a few trials. Facts suddenly appear and then fade away. Is Adams talking about the incident Jaffe talked about or the one Mason talked about? Or, were Jaffe and Mason talking about the same incident? Or, are there three different ones? And, what about Naomi?

You feel like raising your hand and asking a question. But, of course, you don't dare. It's like Contracts. Sitting in class, or in a jury box, you begin to think of dinner.

Of course, if you make the testimony understandable to the jury, you are also making it understandable to the opposition. Maybe that's not such a good idea. Maybe it would be better to wait until closing argument to show how everything fits. Once all the evidence is in, the opposition won't be able to effectively respond.

Making Chaos Theory our own

Criminal defense lawyers, to create reasonable doubt, may purposefully sow confusion. Another time chaos may be your choice is if you fear that the other side will perjure itself if it realizes where you are going. Other than these two situations, clarity seems preferable. This is because it is easier to convince someone as an initial matter than it is to change a person's mind. By the time of closing argument, most jurors will be leaning one way or another. If the jury is leaning against you, the sudden realization of the significance of a piece of evidence might come too late; while it may have convinced them earlier, now they are evaluating it as partisan.

As to *each* piece of evidence, ask yourself:

"Given the fact that the jury doesn't know this case as well as I do, does the jury realize how this evidence fits into the case? If not, what is the case for not making it clear?"

As we will see in our discussion of cross-examination, it may be necessary to conceal from *witnesses* where you are going with your examination. Otherwise they may tailor their testimony so you won't get there. However, once you get where you want to go, it should be clear to the jury why you took the trip.

The tools and techniques to help the jury understand the testimony include:

— making clear opening statements

— using exhibits and demonstrations

— using introductions and transitions during the questioning

— proceeding by topic rather than by chronology

— drawing out and repeating important testimony

— telling your experts to talk English

— editing out extraneous matters.

I'll expand upon these and then warn you of one danger: the problem of *filler*. The details you don't supply, the jurors will. I'll end this section with a brief look at some exciting judicial reforms aimed at improving juror understanding.

Opening statement

In addition to establishing a theme, use your opening statement to identify your witnesses and preview what they will say. Consider visuals such as charts and PowerPoint presentations.

You don't want to rob your case of a sense of drama so you will want to hold back on some details. Teasers work: "Then we will call Officer Knowles who was the first one on the scene. He will tell you what he saw and what the defendant told him. You might be surprised."

A later chapter focuses on Opening Statements and *might* disclose what the defendant said.

Books without pictures: demonstrative evidence

I once read *Alice in Wonderland*. I *believe* she asked, "What's the use of a book without pictures." Had there been a *picture*, a cartoon of her asking that question, then I probably would have remembered.

There are numerous "studies," and academic careers, devoted to establishing the self-evident: that seeing is believing and that most people understand information better, and retain it longer, if it is presented visually rather than orally.

Reviewing your case, ask "Would a demonstration, an exhibit, or computer generated display help the jury understand this point? What about an analogy?"

Introductions and transitions

Asking "what happened next" is always safe. No one can object to that. However, the answers you get will most likely be hard to understand. "So X happened next?" a juror might think. "So what? Why is X important? What's for dinner?"

Take the following case. Involving Hansel and Gretel, it is destined to become the *Hadley v. Baxendale* of child abandonment law.

The children have testified that, after dinner on September 1, they overheard their stepmother and father planning to take them into the Black Forest to abandon them. Representing the stepmother, you call her to the stand and ask:

> "Directing your attention to the evening of September 1, tell the jury what you did after dinner."

For those jurors who do not recall that the alleged conspiracy occurred on the first, what follows will not make sense. One solution, with a flare of drama, is to proceed in this fashion:

> Q: Did you hear your Hansel and Gretel testify in this matter?
>
> A: Yes.
>
> Q: Did you hear them swear that on the evening of September 1, they overheard you and Weak Male Figure planning to abandon them in the Black Forest?
>
> A: Yes, I heard that.
>
> Q: Did that happen?
>
> A: No, it didn't. The first was a Thursday and on Thursdays I spend the entire evening,

> *from 6 to midnight, as a volunteer at the*
> *local hospital.* (You never bothered to hear
> her side, did you?)

You can accomplish the same goal by just telling
everyone what you are up to:

> *Q: Ms. Stepmother, the first area I would like*
> *to explore with you is whether you and your*
> *husband conspired to abandon the chil-*
> *dren. There has been an allegation made*
> *that you did so on September 1. Did you?*

After you have finished with this testimony, you
can introduce the next topic with a transition:

> *Q: Now, Ms. Stepmother, I would like to spend*
> *some time finding out about your relations*
> *with Hansel and Gretel. When did you first*
> *meet them?*

Loop back is another device.

> *Q: So, Ms. Stepmother, you deny the conspira-*
> *cy. Now I would like you to tell about your*
> *relations with Hansel and Gretel. When did*
> *you first meet them?*

It is okay to incorporate a portion of the witness'
last answer into your next question. However, what
is not okay is to simply repeat, time and time again,
what the witness answered.

In addition to aiding the jury's understanding,
transitions can prune irrelevant testimony. Suppose
you have two pieces of evidence you wish to bring
out with the witness:

1. That she saw the Chevy run the red light; and

2. That, when the ambulance arrived (20 minutes later), she heard the driver of the Chevy admit fault.

After establishing the running of the red light, ever fearful of the infamous leading question, one might ask, "What, if anything, happened next?" With this question, it will take about ten minutes of irrelevant testimony (a crowd gathered, flares were put out, traffic was rerouted) to get to the point of the ambulance arriving. Instead, why not:

> *"Now, sometime after the crash*
> *did an ambulance arrive?"*

This is not a leading question as it does not suggest the answer. A leading question would be:

> *"After the crash, isn't it true*
> *an ambulance arrived?"*

Even this question, although leading, would probably be allowed. Most judges will allow you to lead a witness in preliminary, non-controversial matters.

Another approach to avoid the march through the irrelevancies is to advise the witness before trial that when you ask, "What happened after the crash?" she should relate the arrival of the ambulance and skip the intervening events. The problem is that the witness will come off coached and partisan, jumping for the jugular without prompting. Use transitions, not rehearsals.

Order: Proceed by Topic

The order of your questions is extremely important. The concepts of *primacy* and *recency* reminds
us that people remember best the first thing they
hear and the last thing they hear. So, with each
witness, what point do you want to lead with? What
do you want to close with? (Use the same concept in
determining the order of your witnesses: open and
close with strong ones, put the plumber in the
middle.)

Often it is easier to understand a story if it is told
chronologically. If so, do so. But you don't *have* to.
Clarity and drama often can be improved if you
proceed by topic. All you have to do is give up the
safety of "What happened next?"

In the above example, the witness first saw the
accident and then later heard the defendant's statement. "What happened next?" will eventually get
you to the statement. (The statement, by the way, is
admissible even though, as an out of court statement, it looks like hearsay. It isn't. Everything the
defendant has said can be introduced *against* the
defendant as a party admission.)

Say that you want to end with the accident, not
the conversation. Child's play.

> *Q: You were at the scene of the accident?*
>
> *Q: Were you there when the ambulance ar-
> rived?*
>
> *Q: Did you hear anything the defendant said?*

> Q: *Returning to the time of the accident. What did you see?*

These are not leading questions as they do not suggest the answer; even if they were, as preliminary and introductory questions they are proper. You are safe.

Draw Out and Repeat Important Testimony

Climatic scenes are often shown up close and in slow motion: the murder knife descending, the basketball bouncing on the rim, the car careening toward the guard rail. For key testimony, slow it down so the jury can *see* it. A prosecutor gives this example. You can do better than the quick, blurred, knock out punch:

> Q: *What did you find when you searched the defendant's house?*
>
> A: *Some cocaine, measuring equipment, and some marijuana.*

Slow it down, involve the jury.

> Q: *When you first entered the house, what did you do?*
>
> A: *We called out to see if anyone was there. Then, with our weapons drawn, we checked the house to see if anyone was there. Once we had more or less secured the house, we began our search.*
>
> Q: *What was the first room you searched?*
>
> A: *Well, a room in the back. A spare bedroom. It wasn't being used as a bedroom. More of*

> *a work room. The shades were drawn so the*
> *room was dark. When we opened the blinds,*
> *light flooded in.*

Q: *What did you then see?*

Go slowly. Involve the jury. Let them see the scene. Let them hold their breath. Will the knife find its mark? Will the ball go in?

Repetitions are fine. Remember, the jury has not heard this tale before. You cannot ask the *same* question, time and time again, or you will face an *"Asked and Answered"* objection. So ask different questions getting at the same fact.

> **Q:** *You say you found cocaine? How do you*
> *know it was cocaine?*
>
> **Q:** *Where exactly did you find the cocaine?*
>
> **Q:** *What was it wrapped in?*

Omit Unnecessary Details

In the classic book for authors, *Elements of Style*, Strunk and While advise "Omit unnecessary words." The shorter, the less cluttered, the more understandable the message. Their advice was not to write outlines or bare bones; it was to make each word *count*.

As to *each* piece of evidence, ask, "Do I need it?" If you don't, drop it. Never clutter your case with "You never can tell."

Simplify, simplify, simplify. So advises an experienced litigator. If you can, use three witnesses, not eight; if you can, make three cross-examination points; not ten, and, if you can, have the witness testify in twenty minutes, not thirty.

The Problem of Filler

> *"I am a checkout clerk at the supermarket. The defendant walked in and pulled a gun."*

That seems clear enough. But it is clear *only* because we have filled in the missing details. We see the defendant come into the store where we shop. The question the jury will have to ask is whether the clerk was in a position to see the defendant well enough to identify him. Perhaps our store is laid out differently. Perhaps the distance between the door and checkout counter is further or closer; perhaps there are more or less objects in between; perhaps there is more or less activity.

Be aware of the concept of *filler*: what the witness doesn't supply by way of detail, the jury will.

So how do you supply the details? Many try to do it with oral testimony:

> *"Well, there are six registers and off to the left is where they keep the tomatoes."*

Better to use a diagram of the store.

Courtroom demonstrations can also increase the jury's understanding. Again, oral testimony alone might not make it:

> *"The defendant and I were facing each other, about three feet apart. He angrily lifted his sword above his head. I was terrified. Then he said, 'Come to think of it, it's not Assize time'."*

A demonstration would help.

Judicial Innovations that Help

A recent book, *Jury Trial Innovations,* published by the National Center for State Courts and the ABA's Litigation Section, has many good suggestions which will allow better understanding of the testimony:

— encouraging judges to give more instructions at the beginning of the trial to frame the issue

— allowing the jurors to ask questions

— allowing for "interim commentary:" "I am now going to call Professor Atwood to tell you about. . . ."

Most of the recommendations would not require rule changes.

Excitement

At a pretrial hearing, a criminal defendant asked for a new lawyer. "How come?" asked the judge. "This one never pays any attention to me." "What do you say to that, Counselor?" "I'm sorry, your honor. I wasn't paying attention."

No one understands if they are about to go to sleep. Make your case exciting. Probably the surest way to make testimony interesting is to be interested in it. I've already said that: try to capture your emotions when you first interviewed the witness and did not know the answers.

Related to this, realize *the dangers of rehearsals* and *the value of spontaneity*. The traditional advice is to rehearse the direct, and no doubt that is good advice. But don't rehearse so much that the direct becomes a play.

Recently, I have produced several educational videos. Off camera the answers were vibrant and enthused. On camera I would ask the same questions again and the answers were yawners. Why? I think because the interviewees, rather than answering the questions, were trying to remember their prior answers.

Your witnesses should know basically what you are going to ask and you should know basically what they are going to answer. At trial consider changing the order or the wording of the questions to create spontaneity.

We've covered some other devices to make the testimony come alive. Draw out key testimony so that the jury sees the event in slow motion, the ball bouncing on the rim. Begin some testimony not with a whimper, but with a bang:

Q: *Did you kill your wife?*

Use *silence* for emphasis. Just don't ask the next question for a while, let the answer float. Silence is also an effective way to get the attention of a jury that seems to be drifting.

The order of your examination is important. Recall the concepts of *primacy* and *recency*: lead and close strongly. Note that your strongest point may not be the last one in time. The long stay in the hospital came after the terror of the accident. If you want to end with the terror, you can easily do so with the effective use of *transitions* and *introductions*.

Another way to enliven the testimony is with *confrontations*.

> *Q: Hansel, is that your stepmother over there?*
>
> *A: Yes.*
>
> *Q: Did she try to kill you?*

The possibilities for drama are countless. Melvin Belli, the personal injury lawyer who first popularized demonstrative evidence, once represented a man whose leg had been amputated due to the accident. He called the man, who used crutches to get to the witness stand. During his direct, Belli walked around the courtroom and, at one point, took the crutches back to his table. After redirect, looking a his papers, he told the witness, "You can step down now." After a few minutes he looked up,

"I said you could step down now."

CHAPTER 5

DIRECT: BELIEVABILITY

Trials often come down to a very simple question: *Who do you believe?*

Well, who do *you* believe and *why*? These questions are now your job. Think back to someone you believed and to someone you didn't. Compare and contrast. Watching trials, ask yourself "Do I believe this witness and why?" Discuss this with others.

Usually it comes down to intuitions "Well, I just feel I can trust that person and what they said had a ring of truth." Can we tease this out and make a checklist?

General Matters

During direct:

— Deal with the problem of the unduly partisan or defensive witness as both undermine credibility; do this *before* trial.

— Introduce witnesses in a way that triggers bonds with the jurors.

— Consider the best use of experts.

— Consider how to best deal with attacks on your witnesses alleging bias and the inability to perceive and recall. Should you draw the sting?

— Show the jury that the witness knows: lay good *foundations*, have the witness testify as to *details*, and, if possible, as to some *action* taken that validates the truth of the testimony.

— Consider whether there are any holes in the story that need to be filled.

— Step back and let the witnesses testify, so the jury can take their measure.

— Avoid *leading* and *vague* questions and practice asking questions that *set parameters*.

Dealing with the Unduly Partisan and Defensive Witness

We have all seen witnesses who take every opportunity to take nasty jabs at the opposition:

Q: *Did you see the collision?*

A: *Yes I did, and right afterwards, the defendant walked over and kicked a cute little puppy!*

We have all seen witnesses during cross examination who will never admit to anything without a fight or an explanation:

Q: *Isn't it a fact you spanked them all soundly and sent them to bed?*

A: *Look, I'm an old woman who lives in a shoe and I don't know what to do!*

Few things undermine a witness's credibility as much as the appearance of undue partisanship or evasive and defensive answers which suggest something to hide.

Why do witnesses do this? Because they want to *help*. Because they think it's up to them. Before trial, tell them that they will *hurt*. Tell them that your case does not turn only on their testimony. Tell them to answer your questions on direct and that, if you want the cruelty to puppies thing, you will ask for it. Tell them, on cross, simply to admit to the inconvenient points the opposition brings out. Explain that you have redirect to correct for any false impressions that the admissions might create.

Personalize the witness

We are suspicious of people who aren't like us. That's why experts have a hard time: most jurors didn't go to Harvard, don't dress up in white lab coats, and don't clone sheep.

You'll have an easier time of it if your witness is *like* most of the jurors in terms of race, gender, socio-economic class, and age. Sad, but true. But even if the witnesses don't match up in broad terms, they might in interests and activities.

> Q: *Well, doctor, that is a long list of credentials. Do you have any time for anything else?*
>
> A: *I coach my daughter's softball team and we always watch, as a family, "The Simpsons."*

Somewhere during direct, personalize the witness: here's someone like you, someone you can trust.

> *Q: Where do you live, and for how long?*

> *Q: Do you have a family?*

> *Q: What do you do for a living?*

Usually these are the first questions asked; they are easy, non-controversial, and will allow the witness to get comfortable. (Another way is to take the witness to the courtroom before the trial and have the witness sit in the witness chair.)

Although you probably can, *don't* lead the witness across these preliminary questions:

> *Q: Now you have lived here for the last 12 years?*

> *A: Yes.*

Your goal is to get the witness to talk; set up the expectation early:

> *Q: Where do you live, and for how long?*

You shouldn't *always* start with the biographical data. It is something of a yawner. Consider, occasionally something more dramatic, then return to the introductory stuff.

> *Q: Do you spank the children soundly and send them to bed?*

> *A: Yes I do.*

> *Q: Before you get into that, tell the jury something about yourself. Where do you live?*

How much personal data you elicit will depend on the witness. With a criminal defendant or a parent fighting for child custody, character is of manifest importance. But even with the least important witness, some introduction is appropriate.

There is a technical problem with all of this: it is *not* relevant. Except where character is at issue, such as in a criminal case where the defendant chooses to put it at issue, evidence of good character is not relevant. While it is relevant to "making the witness believable," that is *not* an issue. The law assumes all witnesses are truthful until their truthfulness has been attacked; hence, the general rule is that *you cannot credit your witness unless her credibility has been attacked.* But lawyers often violate this rule and, as in the case of a wide strike zone, as long as it applies equally, who cares?

Personalize the witness but don't go on too long. You will draw: "Your Honor, this is irrelevant. Counsel is attempting to credit the witness." If you feel that the objection is premature, respond with something like, "Your Honor, the jury will be asked to make important decisions on this person's testimony. They are entitled to know some background."

Experts

In the movie *Sleeper* Woody Allen awoke 200 years in the future. Asked by hospital doctors what he ate, he self righteously replied, "Vegetables and goat cheese."

"What! Didn't you know about health food? Chocolate, whipped cream and deep fried fats?"

Jurors are suspicious of experts. We have all heard too many conflicting claims. So, what is it about fiber?

Jury studies indicate that, while jurors may joke about the experts, they often adopt their suggestions as to how to evaluate the evidence. Credentials don't seem to matter a great deal. Experts should give the jury a way to think about the evidence. Clinical evidence is more persuasive than statistics. "I treat several teens who still wet their beds" versus "Statistics show that 8% of teens wet their beds."

Preparing your expert: "Use understandable language, give examples and, please, no pomposity."

Before experts can give their "expert" opinions, they must be qualified as "experts."

This involves a long, and frankly mostly boring, showing of how much better the expert is than the rest of us. It has always struck me that this is backwards: the opinion should come first and then the question of just how the person is qualified to make it become vibrant. A way of dealing with this would be to first develop the general expertise in order to qualify the witness as an expert, then get the opinion and then return to those aspects of the experts training and experiences that particularly allow him or her to come to that conclusion.

This is a variation of the "cart before the horse" problem, an organizational problem that cuts across a lot of trial work. In fact, it was there in your legal education. From day one, in your briefs, you were to put the "facts" first, then the issue. But how is one to know what facts are important before one knows what the issue is? This is the same issue we discussed in a previous chapter when we discussed the poem *Richard Cory*. Ending with the suicide was quite dramatic. However, had the poet lead with it, the significance of the poem's details would have been more pronounced.

Draw the Sting?

Although I am not a great believer in the old adage, "Take the sting out!" it seems wise to acknowledge *clear* cases of potential biases during direct, before the opposition can make a big deal of it on cross.

Q: *Are you related to the plaintiff?*

A: *I'm his sister.*

Q: *Does that mean you would lie for him?*

A: *No. I wouldn't want him to lie for me and I'm sure he wouldn't want me to lie for him.*

But let's assume that the potential source of bias is not so clear. Say the witness went to high school with the plaintiff? Should you bring that out?

I'm not so sure. The more sting you take out, the more cluttered and unsure your case becomes. It begins to sound like an apology. Further, if you bring up the "sting," you are acknowledging that it is a problem. Finally, by mentioning it first, you allow your opponent to do so *without* cost. Jurors are almost always sympathetic to the witness; they can see themselves up there testifying. Jurors almost never like to see a witness beat up. Now, if you do *not* bring up the high school connection, then, on cross, the opposition, *if* it chooses to do so, runs the risk of alienating the jury.

"That lawyer was a bully. Trying to get us to believe the person would lie because they went to high school together 20 years ago. Pulling at straws."

If you don't bring the matter up on direct, and your opponent does on cross, remember that you will always have redirect to allow the witness to answer the implied accusation.

An additional consideration. That you have taken the sting out does not mean that that is the end of the matter. Your opponent can still make a big deal of it on cross. "So you went to high school with the plaintiff, did you?" (The "asked and answered" objection goes only to one's own questions.)

The same general analysis goes to sources of potential *mistake*. Some will be so clear that the jury will think you are trying to pull a fast one if you do not bring it up during direct. For example, if the witness is testifying to an overheard conversation, the jury should learn, from *you*, that the witness wasn't wearing her hearing aid. However, unless the potential problem is clear, hesitate. The more tenuous, the higher the cost to your opponent by opening the topic. As many of the sources of mistake are disabilities (hearing, sight, recollection), to attack a witness on those grounds is doubly dangerous; many of the jurors, or their friends, might have similar disabilities. If you are going to shoot the King, you better not miss.

Showing How the Witness Knows

Foundations

Non-expert witnesses can testify only to what they saw, heard, felt, tasted or smelt but, *before* they can, it must be shown that they were in a position to see, hear, feel, taste or smell. That is known as *foundation*.

Let's say, in an intersection case, you represent the plaintiff and call a witness, put her at the scene at the time of the accident, and then ask:

> Q: *What was the color of the light when the defendant entered the intersection?*

The defense lawyer can object "lack of foundation." The mere fact that she was at the scene of the accident does not mean that she was in a position to see the color of the light.

Defense lawyer: Object. Lack of foundation.

Judge: Sustained.

> Q: *Let me back up. Do you know what color the light was?*
>
> A: *Yes*

Q: What was the color of the light when defendant's car entered the intersection?

Defense lawyer: Objection. Lack of foundation. There is no showing how this witness knows.

Q: Okay, let me back up. How do you know what color the light was.

A: My husband told me.

Here the "lack of foundation" objection smoked out testimony relying on inadmissible hearsay. But what should the defense lawyer do if she knows the witness saw the light herself?

Nothing! And this gets us back into the issue of making testimony believable.

Assume you get away with your foundationless question ("What was the color of the light") and the witness answers "Red." The problem is, during deliberations, a juror might ask, "Just how did she know it was red?"

Lay *good foundations*, even if your opponent doesn't insist on it.

Q: Before the accident, could you see the intersection?

Q: How far from the intersection were you?

Q: From your position, could you see both the defendant's car and the color of the light?

Q: Did anything call your attention to the intersection right before the accident?

Q: Did you see the color of the light as the defendant's car entered the intersection?

> *Q: What color was it?*

In addition to strong foundations, *details* smack of truthfulness. Let's assume, to make your case an easy one, that there is evidence that the defendant, not only ran the light, but was drunk. One way to present the evidence:

> *Q: Did you observe the defendant get out of his vehicle just after the accident?*
>
> *A: Yes, I did.*
>
> *Q: Were you able to form an opinion as to his sobriety?*
>
> *A: Yes.*
>
> *Q: And what is that opinion?*
>
> *A: He was drunk.*

Here is another way of presenting it:

> *Q: Did you observe the defendant get out of his vehicle just after the accident?*
>
> *A: Yes, I did.*
>
> *Q: Where were you in relation to him?*
>
> *A: I was standing on the curb, about five feet from the driver's door. He got out of that door.*
>
> *Q: Was there anything interfering with your perception?*
>
> *A: No.*
>
> *Q: What were the lighting conditions?*

A: *It was a clear day. Just after 2 in the afternoon.*

Q: *How long did you observe the defendant?*

A: *Well, he looked at me when he got out of the car. He stood there facing me 10 to 15 seconds and then he staggered off.*

Q: *How was he attired?*

A: *He had a T-shirt on with a picture of a tiger. Under the tiger, it said "I never met a man I didn't like."*

Q: *What was the defendant's condition?*

A: *His eyes were bloodshot, his clothes were messed up. I noticed a strong smell of alcohol and when he asked, "Is this the way to Pismo Beach?" his speech was slurred. He could barely stand up.*

Q: *How do you know he could barely stand up?*

A: *Well, when he got out of the car, he leaned on the door. When he walked off, I saw him almost fall twice.*

Q: *Do you have an opinion as to his sobriety?*

A: *Yes. He was drunk.*

The message of both versions is the same: the defendant was drunk. Legally, both are proper: a lay witness can form an opinion as to sobriety. Both are *understandable*. But when the time comes for the jury to sort out all the bits of testimony it has heard, the longer version is much more likely to be

recalled. No one can pay total attention and the
shorter version may have been crowded out of consciousness by the jury's thoughts of existential
angst. Information theory applauds redundancy.

The longer version is more *dramatic* as the exam-
iner did not go directly to the conclusion, but rather
slowly built toward it.

The longer version is more *believable*. Implicit in
the testimony, "He was drunk," are two conclusions: first, that the witness could adequately perceive the defendant; second, that what he saw and
smelled led him to the correct conclusion. And what
makes conclusions believable?

Details and actions

People talk in conclusions: "This is the man who
robbed me," "I clearly overheard the plaintiff," "I
knew from his behavior that the defendant was
apologetic." Break down these conclusions into the
factual details upon which they rest. *Do this before
trial*. Ask the witness: "How do you know he is the
man who robbed you?" Get the details in conference and then bring them out on direct at trial.

During this pretrial conference, the witness may
not be able to articulate the factual basis on which
his conclusion rests. Draw it out. Ask yourself, "If
the witness' conclusion is true, what else would be
true?" If it is true that the witness "got a good look
at the robber," it is probably also true that the
lighting was good, that the witness was close to the
robber, that he had sufficient time to observe him,
that he can describe his clothing and so forth. Now

you simply ask the witness about these possible factual supports.

Finally, in addition to strong foundations and adequate details, credibility can be enhanced by showing that the defendant took some *action* that validates the testimony.

    Q: How did it taste?

    A: Rotten.

    Q: What happened after you ate it?

    A: I threw up on my date.

As you know, the hearsay rule is riddled with exceptions. One involves medical records. What the doctor writes in the file can come in even though it is hearsay, an out of court statement introduced for its truth. The reason is that, given the serious nature of medical records, one can be assured that both what the doctor wrote and what the patient said is accurate. The point I'm making in this section is similar: one good way to check to see if something is true is to see if people took action on it. My previous example, while probably not as funny as I hoped, also misses the mark. A better example would involve voluntary action.

    Q: Once you concluded the man was drunk, what did you do?

    A: I told the police officer that he should arrest him for drunk driving.

Preparing for an examination, ask "Did you take any *action* based on what you saw, heard, felt, tasted or smelt?"

Fill obvious holes

Step back from the testimony and ask if there are any obvious holes. Discuss the matter with others as you are likely to be too close. For example, in the case of Hansel and Gretel, why did the kids go with their stepmother into the woods, knowing her intention? And, if the cottage was made of candy, why not ants?

Don't count on your opponent to raise these problems on cross. Realizing that you have redirect to fill the holes, your opponent may simply wait until closing to point out the problems. Or maybe your opponent just doesn't see the holes. Dollars to donuts, a juror will. "Where were the ants?"

Fill only obvious holes, not every potential hole. Sure, maybe Hansel and Gretel are making it all up because Step Mom won't let them play with Jack and Jill, but, unless this has been raised, don't bother to negate it. In a short story, a murder takes place in the living room and the murderer wipes his glass and the table for fingerprints. "Maybe I touched the piano. Maybe I went into the kitchen." The next morning police find the murderer in the attic, wiping clean old trunks. Trying to close all possible holes, you'll end up in the attic.

The Jury is Watching

We use our eyes, as well as our ears, to assess credibility. Pretrial, tell your witnesses to turn to the jurors and direct their answers to them. If the judge allows, position yourself at the end of the jury

box so the jury can see the witness's face. Tell your
witnesses not to look at you before answering questions on cross. Reassure them that they will do fine
and that you have redirect to repair any damage.

During the trial, jurors will be looking at *you* and
your *client*, for reactions, for slips, for clues. During
breaks, act as if you like and respect your client;
don't move away. During the trial, when you are
sitting there, maintain a poker face. As to your
clients, what advice? Stay alert and interested. Taking notes will also help them focus attention. How
should they react when bad things are said about
them? Obviously they shouldn't shake their heads
vigorously or moan loudly. On the other hand, I
don't think a disinterested yawn is appropriate either. React honestly but don't play to the jury:
jurors are good at spotting hams.

Let the Witness Testify

The Problem of Leading and Vague Questions

Finally, the testimony itself. You always want the
key words to come from the witnesses, not from
you.

Even if your opponents don't object (and often
they shouldn't) avoid *leading questions* on key matters.

> Q: *After the accident, you saw the defendant
> throw a bottle into the bush, isn't that
> right?*

> A: *Yes.*

The question is leading as it suggests the answer. Even if your opponent does not object, likely the jurors will realize, at some level, that you are testifying and the witness is a puppet. It is much stronger if the witness says the key words.

Further, the answer 'yes' doesn't give the jury much of a feel for the witness.

To avoid the problem of leading, some lawyers resort to vague questions. Even if your opponents don't object (and often they shouldn't) avoid *vague questions* on key matters.

> *Q: Did anything after the accident surprise you?*
>
> *A: Yes. The defendant threw a bottle into the bush.*

This is somewhat vague. It is objectionable in that it gives the witness a wide choice of responses, some of which might be objectionable, such as the hearsay statement, "Well the cop said it was the defendant's fault." Even if there is no objection, a focused and damning response to a vague question, like the one above, suggests the witness is a partisan.

To avoid both the problem of leading and the problem of vagueness, learn to ask questions which set *parameters*.

> *Q: Between the time of the accident, and the arrival of the police, did you see the defendant do anything strange?*
>
> *A: Yes*

Q: And what was that?

You want the witnesses to give the key testimony and you also want them to have enough lines and enough space to allow the jury to get a sense of them.

Set the parameters somewhat broadly in order to allow your witness to strut. Questions that are too broad, "Tell us what happened that day" are objectionable as they "call for a narrative." Even if you don't get that objection, broad questions triggering lengthy and focused responses, suggest rehearsals.

One of the dangers with even brief narrations is that the witness will get into impermissible matters before the opposition can object. One way to avoid this problem is to instruct your witnesses to testify only to matters that they observed and to offer conclusion only if asked. If the judge gets the sense that the witness will not get into impermissible hearsay or improper conclusions, the more likely the witness will be able to narrate and the more likely the jury will get a sense of the witness as a person.

Focus groups, and jury consultants

Your case is *always* worse than you think. In Moot Court or Trial Advocacy courses, we have all been assigned the "clear loser," only to find, after our hard work, that we were lucky because we drew the clear winner. The adversary stance distorts.

How do you know your witnesses will be believed? That the jury will understand the point? That your order makes sense? Talk to friends, family and strangers. One lawyer in Chicago has a paralegal go out on the street and round up ten people with the promise of lunch and $100 for two hours of their time.

Tell them to be candid; otherwise you will hear what you want to hear. "I don't think the other party will be believed once the jury finds out X. Tell me if I'm wrong."

Talk to non-lawyers. Lawyers overvalue our craft, our ploys, our feints, and our rhetoric. We believe we matter the most. In an in incredible book, *Jury: The People v. Juan Corona*, Victor Villasenor interviewed each member of a jury that returned a "Guilty" verdict after 13 days of deliberations. He takes the reader through each day, hour by hour, who said what and who responded.

What strikes one is how seriously the jury took its job: they had actually voted to convict on Day Twelve but decided to spend the night thinking if they had overlooked anything. What is also striking is how the jurors viewed the lawyers. The first day they talked about the lawyers; they appreciated and applauded their art, their ploys, their feints, and their rhetoric. After a couple of hours, someone said, "Enough! Now let's look at the evidence."

Talking to friends and neighbors is the cheap advocate's focus group and jury consultant. Sure, you may not get a representative sample, but you get one a lot more representative than you and other lawyers. In major litigation, big bucks are spent on jury consultants who run focus groups to evaluate the case, to consider how to best present it, and to decide what kind of jurors would be ideal. They can make a major contribution. If you are involved in big ticket litigation, hire them. However, if you are involved in big ticket litigation, why are your reading a Nutshell?

CHAPTER 6

MAD DOGS AND ENGLISHMEN

There are the familiar proscriptions on cross: ask only leading questions, never ask "why," never ask a question unless you know the answer, and stop when you're ahead. To show the wisdom of such advice, war stories are offered:

A lawyer is defending a rather atrocious assault. The prosecution's first witness testifies, "I was on the scene and the defendant bit off the victim's nose." On cross, the defendant's lawyer attacks the witness's ability to perceive the event.

Q: *The fight was at night, was it not?*

A: *Yes.*

Q: *And there was no moon?*

A: *Yes, that's right.*

Q: *Now, you were standing about 100 feet away from the fight; isn't that right?*

A: *At least.*

Q: *And your back was turned until you heard the victim scream; isn't that right?*

A: *Yes.*

Q: *And the victim screamed only after his nose was bitten off; right?*

A: Yes.

At this point, the storyteller tells the audience, the lawyer should have sat down. Don't forget you have closing argument to destroy the witness. But lawyers always ask one question too many!

> *Q: How can you testify that the defendant bit off the nose?*
>
> *A: Because I saw him spit it out.*

Raucous laughter.

Interesting teaching technique: lessons by laughter. I've been accused. But the laughter masks a troubling issue: if the last question is *not* asked, hasn't the lawyer painted a false picture? How can we justify using gambits that distort truth?

Maybe there is an invisible hand that will make things right. But the adversary system will not always right itself. *The gambit only works if the system fails.* If, on redirect, the prosecutor asks, "How do you know?" the gambit not only fails but makes it look like the defense counsel was trying to pull a fast one. But will the prosecutor ask? In less obvious cases, the prosecutor may not realize that damage has been done. (Lawyers are advised to conceal the damage until closing argument, when their opponent will be unable to repair it.) Even realizing the damage, the prosecutor may not dare to ask the question because the prosecutor may not know the answer. Unless the witness has a good explanation, asking for one just enhances the damage.

This does not mean, however, that lawyer craft exists *only* in making the worse cause appear the better. We need to consider the hot fire of litigation.

An Aside: The Nature of Reality

Lawyer gambits, although they can be used to distort truth, are designed to protect it. Witnesses are cheerleaders, and facts are not what they are cracked up to be.

Assume that the witness who claimed knowledge of the nose incident hadn't actually seen anything. He was at the scene and heard a commotion, but he actually saw nothing. After the incident, someone told him "What happened" and, later, when interviewed by police, the witness, either to make himself interesting or simply because he got confused, told the story as his own. At trial, as the cross-examiner slowly attacks the possible supports for his testimony, the witness will grow desperate to support it. Given the chance to escape, "How do you know?" the witness will probably take it: "Well, er, I saw him spit it out."

Francis Wellman, in his classic, *The Art of Cross Examination*, gives a striking illustration of witness partisanship. In admiralty cases, "almost invariably all the crew on one ship will testify in unison against the opposing crew, and, what is more significant, such passengers as happen to be on either ship will almost invariably be found corroborating the stories of their respective crews."

Whatever the reason—even if only the flattery of being called as a witness by one side—very few witnesses are nonpartisan. This gets in the way of finding the truth.

Partiality would be less of a difficulty if facts stayed in one place. If the witness accurately *saw* the event, *perceived* it without bias, and if he accurately *remembered* what he saw, then, short of perjury, close questioning would eventually bring out the "facts." Unfortunately, perception and recollection are affected by motivation and desire. When depressed, one can review one's life and find nothing but gloom; when joyous, nothing but light. In a sense, the conclusion "I am happy" precedes the supporting data. Out of the numerous events in life—some happy, some sad, some indifferent—the happy ones line up behind the smiling face. For an elaborate presentation of the thesis that theory precedes fact even in scientific thought, see Kuhn, *The Structure of Scientific Revolutions*. I'll give one brief illustration I discussed previously.

According to Ptolemy, the earth was the center of the universe, with the sun and planets circling it. An early problem with this system was that, when astronomers looked, the planets were not where the theory said they should be. Well, for those of us who learned science in high school, that would be the end of the matter. "Ptolemy's wrong: those data prove it." But scientists, like the rest of us, have an investment in what we believe; we do not go gently into that good night.

In fact, the theory was not abandoned. The data were explained away by slightly modifying the theory. The earth was still the center of the universe. The planets and sun, rather than going around the earth in perfect circular paths, now rotated around points that went around the earth in perfect circular paths. Presto, the data fit. Theory saved.

But, before one gets too upset with this rigidity, realize the virtue of dogmatism. Without it, we would be leaves on the wind, changing our minds every time something didn't seem to fit. We would never extend our understanding of our universe: maybe the planets *do* rotate around points, maybe invisible bugs do cause disease.

The lawyer's ploys ("Never ask 'why' on cross," "Don't let the witness explain," "Don't ask a question unless you know the answer") are needed in a world where witnesses are often cheerleaders and where facts can be manufactured, fudged, or explained away.

These same ploys, however, can be used to distort the truth. This gets us into difficult issues of professional and personal ethics. I promise to take no more than a page.

> *An advocate knows but one person in all the world. To save that client by all means and expedients, and at all hazards and cost to other persons, and, amongst them, to himself, is his first and only duty; and in performing this duty he must not regard the alarm, the torments, the destruction which he may bring upon others. He*

> must go on reckless of consequences, though it
> should be his unhappy fate to involve his coun-
> try in confusion.
>
> > Lord Brougham, House
> > of Lords, 1821

* * *

> "Wow, that cross was terrific. Turned the state's
> star witness, the girl friend, into a drugged-out
> slut."
>
> > Student, Trial Advocacy
> > Workshop, Yesterday

The trouble with trial advocacy courses is that
there are no real people. The arrows bloody no one:
no real girl friend staggers from the stand. And the
critique is generally tactical:

> "Maybe you went too far. The jury would like
> the stuff about the drugs, but maybe the wom-
> en would resent the attacks on her sexual af-
> fairs."

In practice, there are *only* real people.

Professor Richard Wasserstrom introduced the
notion of "role-differentiated" behavior. In some
contexts, it is quite defensible. For example, it is
proper for parents to prefer, in terms of their time
and money, the interests of their children over
those of others.

When it comes to the legal profession, role-differentiated behavior can turn ugly.

"If it were up to me, I would never try to help myself by sacrificing someone, by destroying that person on the stand, by bringing up drug abuse and a checkered sexual history. I don't think that would be moral. But it's not up to me. My job is to represent my client."

That's one view of the professional ethic. But does the lawyer know that the client is willing to sacrifice his girl friend? In all probability, the lawyer *didn't* ask.

"Look, it will help your case if I attack your girl friend who the state has subpoenaed. I have enough on her to turn her into a drug-crazed slut. Do you want me to?"

The lawyer *assumed* that "Do everything, no matter how much it hurts others" was among the marching orders, orders that the lawyer, as lawyer, must obey. But maybe, just maybe, a client, when forced to choose, would decide to forgo the attack. If the lawyer doesn't ask, then no one has to take moral responsibility.

If the client says, "Fry her," our ethics are that you must. You can reject the order on strategic grounds ("It will backfire"), but not on moral grounds. If we were starting all over again, would you adopt such a rule? As Holmes once wrote: "It is revolting to have no better reason for a rule of law than that it was so laid down in the time of Henry

IV." (Holmes was, I believe, using Henry IV as a metaphor for all mad Englishmen.)

What are its costs and benefits of "role-differentiated behavior?" Professor Wasserstrom would put the burden of persuasion on those arguing for moral free zones.

Consider the effect on both society and practitioner. Over time, what are the costs to lawyers living in such a universe as Lord Brougham described? What will be the costs to you?

I want to leave you with the words of Professor David Mellenkoff from his book, *The Conscience of a Lawyer*, not because I always agree with them (sometimes I do), but because they are so powerful. Never let it be said lawyers can't write.

> *The lawyer, as a lawyer, is not a sweet kind of loving moralizer. He assumes he is needed, and that no one comes to see him to pass the time of day. He is a prober, an analyzer, a planner, a decision maker, a compromiser, eventually a scrapper, a man with a strange devotion to his client. Beautifully strange, or so it seems to the-man-in-trouble; ugly strange to the untroubled onlooker.*

> *This man-in-trouble is you, and I, and our neighbor, at the right moment. The lawyer, some lawyer, is there for each of us, with a lack of discrimination among clients and causes so disgusting to authoritarians of every stripe and stature.*

The lawyer does not exist to spread the word of truth and goodness to the ends of the earth. Somewhat more limited, the lawyer's mission is the nonetheless awesome task of trying to make a reality of equality before the law. If your 'truth' or mine gets dented some in the process, it is only because we deal here with something less than the Kingdom of God, and something more than one Truth.

CHAPTER 7

FRIENDLY CROSS–EXAMINATION

Q: Let's see now. Oh, yes. Are you really, really, sure that it was my client you saw and not somebody else?

A: Yes.

Q: Positive?

Cross and Burning Houses

Pointless cross-examination allows the opposing witness, the one that killed you, to testify, *twice*. Once is enough! The longer you cross-examine without scoring, the more believable the witness. The witness has hurt you on direct, that's a given. The question is, "Can I do anything about it?"

Cross has been compared to rescuing a puppy from a burning house. Have a clear goal before you go in, once you are in, stay focused, and then get out quickly, before the roof falls in. The longer your cross, the more likely you will lose ground.

You don't have to cross at all. If there are no puppies, shrug. "I have no questions of *this* witness, Your Honor." Practice the shrug; eventually you will be able to do it in such as way as to suggest that, not only has the witness not hurt you, but that the witness is beneath the contempt of civilized folk.

Shadow cross is another option. No cross at all might suggest to the jury that you accept all of the witness's testimony. Ask a few collateral questions, score some minor points and sit down. This will be illustrated momentarily when we look at limiting the direct. If you are going to cross, know why.

Goals

There are five basic things you can do on cross:

1. *Help* your case by having the witness collaborate some of your contentions;

2. *Limit* the adverse testimony by showing what was not testified to;

3. *Confront* the witness with your theory of the case;

4. *Undermine* the adverse testimony by discrediting the *witness*;

5. *Undermine* the adverse testimony by discrediting the *testimony*.

These are not mutually exclusive and, indeed, it is possible to accomplish all five in one examination, particularly in your dreams.

In this chapter we will look at the first two goals, using the witness to help your case (risking asking questions you don't know the answer to), and limiting the adverse testimony (by highlighting what it didn't include). Your tone will generally be friendly as you are not attacking the witness. Always remember that, if you use a hostile tone, the witness will immediately become defensive and may not go where you wish to lead. In the next chapter we will look at hostile cross, when you are attacking the witness and/or the accuracy of the testimony.

Helping Your Case

Ladies and Gentlemen of the Jury, even my opponents' witnesses agree with our contention that it was a cold and windy night.

This is a very effective argument. Planning your case, the first question to ask yourself, as to each witness your adversary will call:

1. What facts *must* the witness admit which will support my case?

2. What facts *might* the witness admit which will support my case?

Safe ground

The facts the witness *must* admit are those testified to on direct.

Q: *On direct, you testified that it was a cold and windy night, isn't that right?*

By highlighting, you have the witness testify twice and in the order you wish. Using cross to highlight favorable pieces from direct is fine. "Asked and Answered" is an objection that only goes to questions asked by the same party, as in:

Q: *Tell me again, what kind of night was it?*

Of course, there are no guarantees in trial work (and that's why writing about it, as opposed to doing it, is so much fun). When I was a public defender, a colleague was defending a burglary and the victim, an elderly woman, had testified that no one was in her apartment when she returned to find it torn apart.

> Q: *So, you can't say that my client was the one that did it.*
>
> A: *Yes I can. I lied on direct. He was in my apartment, along with his hoodlum friend sitting there in the first row. They threatened to kill me.*

My colleague lost that one; the good news is that he picked up another client.

You are generally on safe ground asking the witness to confirm what they testified to on direct. The alternative is to say nothing now and save the point until closing argument. This raises the issue I discussed on the chapter on direct: should you wait until closing to tie it all up or should you make things clear as you go along, hoping to convince the jury before you get to closing? As you recall, I generally favor clarity.

You are on relatively safe ground asking opposing experts to confirm the qualifications of yours:

> Q: *You are familiar with the work of Doctor Bronnimann?*
>
> A: *Yes.*

> Q: *And you would agree that he is one of the*
>   *best pulmonary doctors in town?*

What about those matters which are more problematic?

Asking questions without knowing answers

Suppose, in a car accident case, you want to prove that your client braked before entering the intersection. On direct, the opposing witness has testified as to seeing the collision but did not mention whether or not she saw your client's brake lights go on. Given her other testimony, she *might* have seen them. Dare you ask?

If an opposing witness collaborates your theory, it is a gigantic plus. But the risks are huge. Because the witness has not committed to the favorable testimony on direct, you may get stabbed in the back.

> A: *Yes, I saw the brake lights. They did not go*
>   *on.*

The traditional advice is *"Never ask a question on direct unless you know the answer."* Tradition is wise. Let's question Tradition. On a mountaintop in Tibet, Novice asks:

> *"Oh, Master, tell me, what is life?"*

> *"Life is a river."*

> *"A river?"*

> *"What? Have you traveled all this way to learn or have you come to argue?"*

In thinking about whether to risk asking the question, consider:

1. If the opposing lawyer is competent, the less likely you will be burned. If she knew the witness would testify that the brake lights didn't go on, she would have asked on direct.

2. The less partisan the witness, the less likely you will get burned. Assuming she saw your client brake, will her partisanship cause her to lie or to unconsciously block or misinterpret what she saw? Before risking these kinds of questions, have a good feel for the witness. Examine as to other areas first to get a sense of her bias and possible hostility.

3. If the witness thinks a lie, or exaggeration, will be exposed, the less likely you will be burned. That's why you visit the scene; to bluff.

Q: There is a traffic control device at that intersection, isn't that right?

Q: There is a bus stop on the southeast corner, correct?

Q: And, on the northwest, a Quickie Mart?

These questions alert the witness: "I've been there; watch out."

4. If you can effectively deal with an unfavorable response, the less damage it will do, thus tilting the balance for going for broke.

You are on relatively safe ground if the witness has previously answered the way you wish, perhaps in a deposition or in a statement to police. If the witness answers differently, you can impeach with her prior statement. As Professor Bergman points out, the risk in asking questions of this nature varies with the kind and strength of the evidence you have with which to rebut the possible unfavorable answer. He points this out in his wonderful book, *Trial Advocacy in a Nutshell*. Now that you have bought mine, I can praise his.

"Beyond the scope of direct"

There may be matters that the witness knows that were not touched upon during the direct testimony. Say that the eye-witness, who testified only to the accident itself, overheard, two days later, the defendant making a damaging admission. Can you bring this out on cross? That testimony would go "beyond the scope of direct" and in some jurisdictions that's taboo. Usually this is not much of a problem because you can call the witness as part of your case. The only downside is that as the witness will now be yours on direct, you cannot ask leading questions *except* if the witness is hostile and you get the court's permission to treat her as such.

As to which are the taboo jurisdictions, that's beyond my scope. However, I do know life; actually it's more of a stream.

Limiting the direct: What the Witness Didn't Say

Your goal here is to turn mountains into mole-hills. Who could be more evil than the Evil Step-mother?

> *Q: Now Hansel, in your direct testimony, you didn't say your stepmother ever hit you, isn't that right.*

> *Q: Nor, on direct, did you say she let you go hungry.*

> *Q: Nor, on direct, that she sent you to school badly dressed.*

> *Q: Nor, on direct, that she never helped you with your homework.*

> *Q: Nor, on direct, that she never cheered for you at your little league games.*

Note that these questions are all framed in reference to what Hansel did not say in his *direct* testimony. This is safer than a non-restricted question. This is because:

> *Q: Your stepmother never hit you, isn't that right.*

> *A: No, she does hit me.*

Your response, "You didn't say that on direct," seems a little lame. See how it is stronger the other way:

> *Q: Now Hansel, in your direct testimony, you didn't say your stepmother ever hit you, isn't that right.*

    A.   *No, she does hit me.*

    Q: *Hansel, that wasn't my question. My question was what you said on direct. Would you please answer that question.*

Here Hansel, not you, is on the run.

Opening doors

One danger lurks in this approach. You may *open the door* to otherwise inadmissible evidence. If the stepmother was being criminally prosecuted for abandoning the children in the forest, likely the state could not bring in other bad acts such as hitting or refusing to feed them. If you, as her lawyer, ask about these matters, they can now come in.

Let me try another example of limiting the direct without opening the doors.

The witness has testified it is his opinion that your client was drunk. As there are degrees of drunkenness, who knows what factual configurations the jury conjures up hearing the testimony? Without directly attacking the core of the testimony—that your client was drunk—you can limit its negative impact:

    Q: *Now, on direct you testified that you did not talk with my client. So whatever your opinion as to his sobriety, you are not, I take it, telling the jury that his speech was slurred?*

    Q: *And, because you didn't speak with him you are not testifying that he could not carry on an intelligent conversation?*

> Q: So far as you know, he could carry on a coherent and intelligent conversation.

> Q: On direct you testified that you observed my client for about 15 minutes. During that time he was standing, isn't that right?

> Q: So in testifying that it was your opinion that he was intoxicated, you were not suggesting to the jury that he couldn't stand, am I right?

Stress what the witness did not see to bring into sharp relief just how little he did see. Otherwise the jury may exaggerate the importance of the testimony.

This method of cross-examination, developing the negative, can be effective with experts.

Experts and roads not taken

With that condescending pomposity of professionals, the expert testifies, "I did test 'X' and my scientific conclusion is 'Y'." The jury will hate her but probably will believe her. And she will probably destroy you if you attack the core of her testimony by attempting to show test 'X' is invalid or that she performed test 'X' improperly. Her very pomposity attests to her competence. A better strategy is to develop the negatives. Before trial, find out what other kinds of tests can be used to reach the conclusion 'Y'. Your cross will look something like this:

> Q: To find 'Y', one could also conduct test 'A', isn't that a fact?

> Q: And test 'A' is as reliable as test 'X'?

Q: *Test 'B' is also recognized in the scientific community as a valid and reliable test to find 'Y', isn't that right?*

Q: *And so with test 'C'?*

Q: *Now, from a scientific point of view, the more tests you run which give you the same result, the more sure you are of your conclusion, isn't that correct?* (Let her deny that if she dares.)

Q: *In reaching your conclusion of "Y," did you conduct test "A?"*

The ideal, of course, is a long string of "No" answers.

If successful, this method of cross-examination turns mountains into molehills. It limits but does not destroy unfavorable testimony. But what if the molehill is enough to kill you?

CHAPTER 8

HOSTILE CROSS

In the last chapter we looked at using cross-examination to develop material favorable to your case and, failing that, using it to limit the thrust of the adverse testimony. I called that "friendly cross" in that probably your tone will be matter-of-fact rather than hostile. Indeed, the witness will not necessarily be defensive as you are not attacking him, by suggesting he is lying or mistaken, nor are you attacking the core of his testimony, by suggesting it is wrong.

This chapter looks at the situation where your goals are hostile to the witness, where you are trying to undermine either the witness or his testimony. The tone of your questions, friendly or hostile, is a question of tactics.

As to *hostile questioning*, there are two immediate costs. First, it will put the witness on the defensive and this may prevent you from leading him to where you want to take him. Second, unless the jury feels the witness deserves hostile treatment, it will resent the approach and begin rooting for the witness.

The case *for* hostile questioning is that it may intimidate a witness so that he more readily admits to unfavorable information. Further, if your theory is that the witness is a perjurer, there is something incongruous if you treat him with great respect. The jury will be looking for clues from your demeanor.

Because the line between attacking the witness and attacking the story is a blurry one, and because often you want to do both, your cross-examination may come off as a series of random shots, one suggesting the witness is mistaken, another suggesting that the witness is lying, and a third suggesting that the story defies common sense. I think it is critical, before you begin cross, to know what you are going to say about the witness in your closing argument.

> *Is your theory that the witness is lying or mistaken?*

> *Is your theory that the story doesn't hold together? If so, why?*

> *Finally, if there have been prior inconsistent statements, so what? Does that mean that witness is now lying? Or is now confused? Or that the story fails to hold?*

In an ideal world, you would be able to show that the witness is lying or mistaken, *and* that the story doesn't make sense. Probably, in most cases, you will try to do a little of each. However, sometimes you will be stuck with only one. In any event, for analytical purposes, I will treat the attacks separately.

Note, again, with many witnesses, probably with *most* witnesses, an attack on either them or their testimony will get you *nowhere!* It will simply allow the witnesses to repeat, and repeat, their harmful testimony. Don't forget you have your own witnesses to call and most cases are won on their own strength, not on the weaknesses exposed in the opposition. That said, one choice you have is simply to confront the witness with your theory and sit down.

Confronting the Witness With Your Theory

Q: *Hansel, isn't it a fact that there were no bread crumbs, no witch, no chicken bone, and that you made all of this up because your stepmother won't let you play with Jack and Jill?*

Of course, unless you're Perry Mason, you'll get a denial. But so what? Such questions signal the jury that you do not accept the testimony, and it reminds them of your theory of the case. Fair play and good drama require that, before you attempt to prove the accusation as part of your case, you should make it, face to face.

In this regard, it is *ethically improper* to ask an accusatory question ("When did you stop kicking your puppy?") unless you have a good faith basis to do so.

Let's now turn to meeting the unfavorable testimony. There are three basic ways. The first, discussed in the last chapter, is to *limit* it ("What the witness said on direct is not as bad as it sounds"). Second, you can *discredit the witness* ("So the story sounds bad but don't believe it because the witness is mistaken or lying"). Third, you can *discredit the testimony* ("The story sounds bad and for the life of me I can't think why the witness would be mistaken or lying, but no one should believe a tale like that").

Discrediting the Witness

Bias and Glasses

> Q: *On direct you testified that you and the defendant spent the entire evening of the robbery listening to Mozart. Now you are the defendant's mother, are you not?*

The fact that someone got up, took an oath, and swore to a certain state of affairs is something to be reckoned with. Even if the story is shaky, still jurors may hesitate to reject it unless they believe the witness was lying or mistaken.

It may be the witness is *lying*. Is there sufficient motive? Just because a witness has a motive to lie, doesn't mean the witness is lying. Often, to take the sting out of your attack, your opponent will bring up the motives and have the witness discount them. On cross, you can revisit the issue.

Consider doing more than merely pointing to the motive to lie. Can you flesh it out? Why would a mother lie for her son?

> Q: *Now you love your son, isn't that right?*

Q: *And you are worried that he might go to jail?*

Q: *If he goes to jail, you will have a hard time visiting him?*

Perjury is a hard sell. *Mistakes* are easier.

Did the physical setting, such as shadows and movement, cause a mistake in perception? Did the witness' mental state, such as confusion, distraction, fear? Was the event distinct enough to be recalled uniquely or is there a probability that the details of similar or routine events are spilling over? Then there's the matter of filler, unconsciously filling in missing details to make sense of our perceptions or to make what we recall consistent with what others have told us. ("Who have you talked to about this? What have you seen on T.V.?")

People tend to see and recall what they want to. Hence the relevance of bias, interest and prejudice: not only can they suggest *perjury*, but also they can suggest *mistake*. As I will indicate in my chapter on Closing Argument, I think it is very important for you to be clear in your own mind whether you believe the witness is lying or is merely mistaken. Clearly your demeanor in examining the witness will differ in these situations.

Prior Inconsistent Statements

Another way to impeach a witness is with *prior inconsistent statements*. It makes sense to discuss them between discrediting the witness and discrediting the story as they can be used in both endeavors, to show that the witness should not be believed or that the story does not make sense. Again, before you try to impeach with such statements, know what use you are going to make of them in your closing argument.

Preparing for trial, read all of the prior statements the adverse witnesses have given, in depositions or prior hearings. Your ear will be ready for inconsistencies.

Some trials, unfortunately, are conducted as if the *only* thing the lawyers learned in three long years was the doctrine of prior inconsistent statements.

> *Q: Hansel, isn't it a fact that in a prior hearing you said you kept the bread crumbs in your right pocket and now you say it was your left!*

Jurors know, even if lawyers don't, that we are all inconsistent some of the time. Indeed, some can argue that a witness' inconsistency, or that between witnesses, *proves* truthfulness: "If Hansel and his sister were making this up, you could be sure they would have got it straight and told exactly the same story."

Important prior inconsistent statements are very useful. Note now that in many jurisdictions, prior inconsistent statements come in, not only for impeachment, but also as substantive evidence. This deals with the Al Capone problem.

A: *I know Al Capone and Al Capone's no gangster.*

Q: *Didn't you previously tell police that he was?*

A: *Yes, but I was lying. They promised me cigarettes.*

If the prior statement merely comes in to impeach the witness, the jury could *only* reject the witness' testimony that Al was a stand up guy; if it comes in as substantive evidence, the jury can believe what the witness told police and can convict Al on that basis.

I will review the mechanics of impeaching with a prior statement in Chapter 16.

Discrediting the Testimony

T.V. to the contrary, it is *never* easy to get prosecution's star witness to confess to murder.

There are three basic ways to go after the story itself:

1.   Examine for inconsistent collateral detail;

2.   Seek bedrock detail which may not hold; and, everyone's favorite,

3.   Slash and burn.

Examine for inconsistent collateral detail

Rather than attacking the core, explore to see if there are collateral details that undermine it. Ask yourself:

— *If the witness saw the accident well enough to testify as she did, what else would she have seen?*

— *If my client made the promise as the witness claims, what would have the witness done?*

— *If I had been in the situation of the witness, what else would I have seen, heard, felt, and done?*

The basic notion is to figure out what specific details would *likely* be present *if* the witness' testimony is correct. On cross, you show that they were not present. Voila! You win!

Not so fast.

1.   Will the witness *admit* to the inconvenient detail?

2.   If so, can the witness *explain* it away?

These questions trigger a lot of chess playing. Let's start with an easy example, one where the witness must admit to the inconvenient fact.

You represent a criminal defendant and you know that the arresting officer will testify to incriminating statements your client made at the time of the arrest.

"*If* the defendant made incriminating statements, *then* what would have the officer done? For one thing, note them in the police report."

Once you discover no such reference in the report, you have a choice on cross: *confront* the officer immediately, or sneak up on the officer by *closing doors* on possible explanations she might give to minimize the harm. Let's look at the direct approach first.

> Q: *On direct, Officer, you testified my client admitted to you to throwing the first blow. But there is nothing in your report to that effect, is there?*
>
> A: *Not everything goes in the reports. Besides, after the arrest, I was called to a major incident and, frankly, when I got back to the station, I didn't have time to fill out the report in detail.*

What is one to make of this?

First, note that the officer did not answer the question. Don't let witnesses do this to you.

> Q: *Officer, I didn't ask you about what goes into the reports, and I didn't ask you what you did after you arrested my client. I asked you a very specific question, one which can be answered "yes" or "no." Is there any reference to what the defendant told you in your report?*

This calls the jury's attention to her wiggling. But what of her explanation?

Witnesses who try to explain away inconvenient facts usually mess up. First, by trying, they admit the fact hurts. Second, they often trip up. Here you can pursue this "major incident" explanation and, if it is fiction, you will probably be able to expose it. As we all know, it's hard to write convincing fiction even in the calm of one's home. If the officer had been prepared properly, the prosecutor would have told her, just admit to the facts; if there is an explanation, I'll come back to it on redirect:

> A: *No. There is nothing in my report as to that.*

On redirect:

> Q: *Officer, on cross examination, you admitted that there was nothing in your report about the defendant telling you he threw the first blow. Why is that?*

Now the officer can explain to a friendly, not hostile, audience.

The other approach to take is to close the door on possible explanations before popping the question. Here the question you ask yourself in preparing the examination is "How can the witness explain the inconvenient fact away?"

> Q: *You did a good job investigating this event, isn't that right?*

> Q: *You weren't distracted or too tired, or too busy, to do a good job.*

> Q: *In fact you gave it your full attention.*

> Q: *Officer, at police academy, you are trained in writing reports, correct?*

> Q: *And you know that they are very important, fellow police officers, prosecutors and even judges may rely on them, correct?*

Q: *And, like everything you do, you try your best to do the best job you can.*

Q: *And while you can't put everything in a report, you will put the important things in the report.*

Q: *And if a defendant admits to starting a fight, you would agree with me that that is important.*

This approach, closing doors before popping the question, can work in other areas of life as well.

Q: *Now, the fact is that you're not already married, isn't that right?*

Q: *And you're not in love with anyone else, isn't that a fact?*

Q: *And we're not first cousins, correct?*

Thus far, we have assumed that the witnesses *must* admit to the inconvenient fact. You can either confront them immediately, and hope they fall down running away, or you can close the doors by getting them to negate possible explanations. But what if the witness *need not* admit to the fact?

Here your choices are basically the same: you can confront the witnesses with the inconvenient facts (and hope they admit them) or you can sneak up (and hope that they will be placed in a position where they must admit them).

Let's say the witness will testify that your client offered a huge signing bonus.

"*If* the witness was offered a huge signing bonus, *then* what would the witness have done? Well, for one thing, tell friends."

Q: *On direct you testified how happy you were when my client offered you a huge signing bonus. Yet, isn't it a fact, that you never told any of your friends you got the bonus?*

Assuming no friends were told, the witness has a difficult choice. One will be to try to deflect the question:

A: *I can't remember.*

Q: *You get a huge signing offer and you can't remember if you told friends?*

A: *That's right.*

Q: *Then you cannot tell this jury that you did tell any friends, isn't that right?*

Or the witness can risk perjury.

A: *Yes, I told them.*

Q: *Tell me, who?*

Here the witness will be writing fiction in front of hostile critics.

Rather than directly confront, you might want to sneak up on the witness and get the witness to admit that friends were not told without realizing how that fact undermines the claim that a signing bonus was offered. How not to tip your hand? Start far away from the confrontation and develop the facts in a friendly, non-accusatory fashion. Jump around some so that the witness doesn't realize where you are going.

Once the witness *does* admit to the inconvenient fact, you still have to worry that it might be explained away. Again, you might want to directly confront the witness and hope the witness stumbles with weak explanations. Your other choice is to close the doors.

> "Why wouldn't someone getting a signing bonus tell their friends? Lawyers, if they get a job, you don't hear the end of it."

The problem is that your questions will not seem relevant.

> *Q: During the two weeks after you got the offer, who did you have lunch with?*
>
> *Q: You're a pretty open person. Do you like to share good news?*

Your opponent, smelling a rat, will object:

> *"Your Honor, this is not relevant."*

Remember that the main problem with irrelevant evidence is that it wastes court time.

> *"Your Honor, I'll tie it up in a minute or so."*

But your opponent has broken your flow and signaled the witness that something might be afoot.

Rather the sneaking up of the testimony by looking for inconsistent collateral detail, one can always mount a frontal attack: does the testimony rest on strong supports?

Going after bedrock

A world-famous astronomer finishes his address and, in the back of the room, a hand is raised.

"That is a very elegant theory, Professor, but you got it all wrong. Actually the world moves through the universe on the back of a gigantic turtle."

Playing along, the astronomer, with just a hint of condescension, replies, "Well, if that is so, how does this gigantic turtle of yours get around?"

"On the back of a still larger turtle. And don't bother with any more questions, Professor, it's turtles all the way down."

I tell that story to my Contracts students to illustrate the problem of infinite regress. I don't know if they get it, but it is the *only* thing they remember.

It is comforting to think that there are *facts* and *conclusions*, but, like turtles, it's *conclusions all the way down*. "This is the guy who robbed me," *seems* like a fact but it is really a *conclusion*, riding upon the backs of other conclusions:

1. I saw him well enough at the time.

2. I can remember what I saw.

These conclusions ride on others:

1. I saw him well enough at the time.

   a) I had time to see him.

   b) The lighting was fine.

   c) He has distinctive enough features that I can recognize.

You get my drift: always downward. Finally we get to atoms, neutrons, and eventually quarks. Quarks? Bedrock at last? No, they are only some physicist's conclusion.

Much of traditional cross can be thought of as an attack on *lower-level turtles*. The closing argument will be that the main conclusion ("This is the guy who robbed me") is not adequately supported: the lighting wasn't that good or the witness doesn't clearly remember the incident. In essence, the argument is that *the witness jumped to conclusions*. Here again, as the witness will be interested in defending his primary conclusion, you need to sneak up or, as we like to say in polite company, "close the doors."

Another way of getting at bedrock is by taking on the testimony directly and, doggedly, asking why or how.

> Q: *Why did you think it was a serious offer?*

> Q: *How are you sure it was my client?*

You hope you will find that the witness's conclusion is supported by flimsy evidence. The danger is you might unearth granite.

> A: *I'm not likely to mistake a man who had a gun pointed at my head.*

This danger may be overrated. If your opponent is a good lawyer, the witness would have testified as to the gun on direct, unless, of course, your opponent is not only good but crafty and is laying a trap for you.

Slash and burn

Here the lawyer jumps around from topic to topic, hoping to force the witness into a contradiction or into asserting a fact that is either clearly wrong or easily shown to be. The basic technique is to ask, rapid-fire, a series of questions which force a series of "yes" or "no" answers, keeping the witness off balance. Your questions must be very focused and should contain only one fact. Unfocused and compound questions call for longer answers.

There is no need to snarl. This technique works due to disorder and speed, not tone. Ask a question with accusation in your voice, dollars to donuts you'll get a "No."

The theory is that liars have a hard time keeping their stories straight. But so too do elderly folks, young folks, and pretty much all of us. Don't misuse the technique.

Your opponent will have probably warned the witness of the technique and advised her to take some time before answering the question. During trial, your opponent will break you flow with:

> *"I object, your Honor, the examining lawyer is not allowing the witness time to answer or to think."*

Some of you may learn better by tight logical prose, others by stories. Cartoons work for me.

In the courtroom, a dog is being cross-examined. The dog's lawyer has jumped up:

I object, your Honor, the examining lawyer is purposefully confusing Shadow by going back and forth between people years and dog years.

* * *

We have covered a lot of ground. Remember:

1. Never cross-examine needlessly, only when you must, and only when you can accomplish something.

2. The shorter, the fewer points, the better. The roof is burning!

3. Don't get carried away. Jurors don't like to see men and women in black suits beat up witnesses who look and talk a lot like them. Unless you have enough to show that the witness is really Darth Vader, perjuring himself simply to do evil, there is no reason to ask the questions with accusation dripping from your voice. It is not a sin to be someone's mother, to wear glasses or even to change your mind. Go gently.

CHAPTER 9

ASKING QUESTIONS

*"You're having a hard time figuring out
why this is a separate chapter, aren't you?"*

Asking good questions is not something lawyers *know*; asking good questions is something lawyers *do*. Good questions are our musical scales, our backhands, our jump shots; things we practice and practice so that they become routine, there for us when we need them.

At the end of this chapter, I'll give you some exercises to help hone your questioning techniques. Before that, I will discuss the various forms of questions, leading versus non-leading, and when to use them. But let's begin with the most important skill of all: listening.

Listening

When you are talking, what is most distracting? The other person, bored. Confidence and enthusiasm crash. What is the most encouraging? The other person, excited, listening to what you are saying, nodding and occasionally smiling, leaning forward to catch you next word. You soar.

Some lawyers conduct direct as if they were going through a pre-flight checklist. If you're bored, the jury will be bored. If you're bored, your witness will realize *no one* cares.

Recapture the excitement, the fear, of the first time you asked the question, when a bad answer would destroy your case, when a good answer would send you around the room in a victory lap.

On *cross* the danger is not boredom, it is anticipation.

> **Q:** *It is a fact, is it not, that you ran the stop sign?*
>
> **A:** *Well, yes, I did overshoot the stop sign a little. You see, my brakes have been out for some time. I was meaning to have them repaired but you know how things are.*
>
> **Q:** (cutting witness off) *Now, in fact, your car stopped about ten feet into the intersection, isn't that right?*

When you ask a question, *look* at the witness and *listen* to the answer. Don't look down at your pad and think about your next question. Be prepared to go off on new directions. Digest the answer before moving on; count to three.

Listening creates spontaneity, movement and interest. It has an additional advantage: it reduces nervousness. If you focus on your questions, you are really focusing on your performance and on yourself. Without getting personal, obviously this is going to make you quite nervous. If, on the other hand, you focus on the answer, your attention is turned outward.

Kinds of Questions

One *question,* one *fact.*

> Q: *So you were badly mistreated by relatives but somehow got to the Ball anyway where you had a pretty good time and hung out with the dashing prince and then you lost one of your shoes?*

What's the problem with this question? What does "no" mean? That her relatives really weren't that bad or that she found the prince boring? That's part of the problem; more importantly, it condenses a great story into a blur. It takes time to process information; jurors simply won't be able to catch up. They will still be with the bad relatives when the clock strikes twelve.

Compound questions, those containing more than one fact, are *objectionable.* But cagey opponents don't *always* object. Here a cagey opponent will welcome this compound question because a cagey opponent sometimes doesn't want the jury to understand the testimony.

One *question,* one *fact.*

The other general thing about questions are their classifications: *open* and *closed, leading* and *non-leading,*

Open questions *cannot* be answered "yes" or "no." They force witnesses to respond in their own words.

> Q: *Where would you rather be?*

Closed questions *can* be answered "yes" or "no."

Q: *Would you rather be in Philadelphia?*

Leading questions *suggest* the answer.

Q: *You'd rather be in Philadelphia; wouldn't you?*

A question can be *leading, even if* it does not explicitly suggest the answer, if it supplies the witness with important details.

Q: *Does W.C. Fields tombstone read, "I'd rather be Philadelphia?"*

A: *Oh yes, that's what it says. Not, as in the case of Mel Blanc, the man who did the voices for Looney Tunes, "That's All, Folks!"*

Everyone knows: ask *leading* questions on *cross* and *non-leading* questions on *direct*. We learned that at our mother's knee, and yet often we do just the opposite. Why? On *direct,* we *know* the answer and want to get to it: "Then you went to the grocery store, right?" On *cross,* we *do not know* the answer and have to ask non-leading questions: "What did you do next?" Let's work on correcting this.

Questions on Direct

Q: *You love your kids, correct?*

A: *Yes.*

Q: *In fact, they are the most important things in your life.*

A: *Yes.*

> *Q: And you would never inflict unnecessary pain on them.*
>
> *A: No.*

These are all leading questions and are objection-able on direct. But only an idiot would object. Why? Direct is where witnesses get the chance to tell their stories, in their words, with their emotions, and with their inflections. Jurors must be allowed to get a sense of them as people. Are they to be believed? Do they really know what they are saying? Do they love their children?

> *Q: You love your kids, correct?*
>
> *A: Yes.*

Back off.

> *Q: Tell me about your relations with your chil-dren.*

Leading questions are *objectionable* on direct. The witness is to *testify*, not merely nod agreement to the lawyer's assertions. There are a few times lead-ing questions are permissible in direct: going over preliminary and non-contested matters, questioning children and when a good witness goes bad and becomes hostile.

A cagey lawyer realizes that usually an objection to leading is pointless. It simply allows the question to be rephrased and, this time, answered by the witness.

> *Q: Tell me about your relations with your chil-dren.*

A: *They're the focus of my life. I love them deeply.*

Substantively the only time you will want to object to leading is where the witness is shaky and may *not* be able to give the answer the lawyer is looking for. *Tactically* you might want to object to call the juror's attention to the fact your opponent is leading or to rattle your opponent who has not purchased this book.

On direct, generally ask *open* questions, questions which cannot be answered with a simple "yes" or "no", questions which *force* your witnesses to give the key testimony in a way that the jury can evaluate their candor, recall and love of their children.

There is one problem. To avoid leading questions, one might jump into the fire of vague questions: "What, if anything, happened in your life?"

Open-ended versus vague questions

Q: *Where would you rather be?*

This question, while open, defines the topic. This allows for appropriate objections:

Q: *Where would you rather be?*

Q: *Objection, your Honor, where the witness would rather be is not relevant.*

Some open-ended questions can be extremely broad, vague and offer little guidance:

Q: *What happened on November 17th of last year?*

Questions like these are objectionable because they are *"vague"* or *"call for a narrative."* The problem with narratives is that the opposing lawyer will not know what roads the witness might take, roads that might involve *hearsay*, *speculation*, or matters previously determined to be *inadmissible*. Except for these reasons, a cagey adversary will not object. Why?

Vague questions followed by focused and damning responses seemed rehearsed.

> Q: *What happened on November 17th of last year?*
>
> A: *The defendant came by about two. Over tea, he admitted to treason.*

Your witnesses should seem non-partisan, not overly anxious to stick the knife. "Force" your witness to give up the bad news:

> Q: *On November 17th did you see the defendant?*
>
> A: *Yes. He came by for tea.*
>
> Q: *Did you have a conversation with him?*
>
> A: *Yes, I did.*
>
> Q: *Did the defendant say anything during that conversation that was out of the ordinary?*
>
> A: *Yes, he did.*
>
> Q: *And what was that?*
>
> A: *He admitted to treason.*

Not only does this make the witness less partisan, it also draws out the point to make it more memorable.

The ideal question on direct is a *limited*, *open-ended* question, one that is focused, either by *topic* or by *time*.

> *Q:* *After the accident, before the police arrived, what happened?*

> *Q:* *Tell the jury about the walk you took with your Stepmother last September.*

Questions on Cross

On cross, ask leading questions.

Leading questions are not really questions at all; *they are statements of fact followed by a question mark*. Reread the last sentence: it is the root of the whole enterprise.

Like Smoos in *Little Abner*, leading questions are marvelous. While mostly praised for helping control the evasive witness, their main value is that they allow you to tell *your* story with no distracting clutter offered by the witness.

Leading questions allow you to edit unnecessary and confusing material. In a negligence case, assume that an adverse witness has testified that your client, the defendant, ran a red light. On cross you wish to develop some favorable testimony: that the road was wet and that the defendant applied the brakes before entering the intersection. On cross there is simply no need, as there is on direct, to lay a foundation for the testimony by putting the witness on the scene and so forth. You simply go for it:

Q: *The road was wet, wasn't it?*

Q. *Isn't it true that the defendant applied his brakes before he entered the intersection?*

Cross *doesn't* mean angry. Leading questions are *not necessarily hostile.* Reread that last sentence; it too is the root of the enterprise. Leading questions can be friendly. Basically you are making a statement and merely asking the witness to confirm or deny it. You can do so in an accusatory tone of voice, implying that the factual statement is harmful to the witness, or in a friendly tone of voice, suggesting that the fact helps the witness.

Whatever your tone (accepting or rejecting), *your voice should not go up at the end of your question/statement.* Reread the last sentence. When we ask real questions, our voices go up at the end, thus inviting a response. In declaratory sentences, our voice drops at the end, thus inviting nothing. On cross, you are not inviting responses, you are making statements. Learn to ask leading questions, not as questions, but as statements: keep your voice flat at the end.

Scales to practice, grounders to field

Here are three exercises designed to help you ask questions containing only one fact, to help you avoid big words, to give you some practice emphasizing the importance of emphasis, and, finally, to give you practice asking leading and non-leading questions.

Exercise One: One Question, *One* Fact

Recall Cinderella, short version.

> *Q: So you were badly mistreated by relatives but somehow got to the Ball anyway where you had a pretty good time and hung out with the dashing prince and then you lost one of your shoes?*

Break this question into a series of one-fact questions. How many can you get?

Exercise Two: Graduate Student Vocabulary

Tell law students to stop talking legalese and they talk like graduate students. Not everyone has our vocabulary and using big words not only offends, it confuses. In an example I used previously, I was guilty. Underline the offending words. Ask the same question as a high school graduate.

> *Q: Did you observe the defendant get out of his vehicle just after the accident?*
>
> *A: Yes, I did.*
>
> *Q: Where were you in relation to him?*
>
> *A: I was standing on the curb, about five feet from the driver's door. He got out of that door.*
>
> *Q: Was there anything interfering with your perception?*
>
> *A: No.*

Q: *What were the lighting conditions?*

A: *It was a clear day. Just after 2 in the afternoon.*

Q: *How long did you observe the defendant?*

A: *Well, he looked at me when he got out of the car. He stood there facing me 10 to 15 seconds and then he staggered off.*

Q: *How was he attired?*

A: *He had a T-shirt on with a picture of a tiger. Under the tiger, it said "I never met a man I didn't like."*

Q: *What was the defendant's condition?*

A: *His eyes were bloodshot, his clothes were messed up. I noticed a strong smell of alcohol and when he asked, "Is this the way to Pismo Beach?" his speech was slurred. He could barely stand up.*

Q: *How do you know he could barely stand up?*

A: *Well, when he got out of the car, he leaned on the door. When he walked off, I saw him almost fall twice.*

Q: *Do you have an opinion as to his sobriety?*

A: *Yes. He was drunk.*

Exercise Three: Importance of emphasis

Take the following question:

Q: *Didn't you have a hard time sleeping because of the storm?*

By emphasizing different words in the question, it can be essentially five different questions.

— Ask the question emphasizing "you."

— Ask the question emphasizing "hard time."

— Ask the question emphasizing "sleeping."

— Ask the question emphasizing "because."

— Ask the question emphasizing the "storm."

I know it sounds silly. Just do it!

Exercise four: Leading and Non-leading

Get a good, operational feel for leading and non-leading questions. You should be able to ask them without stopping to think what they are.

Ask a friend for half an hour. Ask what the person did yesterday afternoon, trying to get as much detail as possible. Because you don't know what the person did, your questions will be non-leading (you can't suggest what you don't know): "What did you do after lunch?" "Did you enjoy the movie?" "Have you been to that theater before?"

Do a direct

Once you have a sufficient number of details, at least six or seven, take your friend on *direct*. Now that you know what happened, it will be more difficult to ask non-leading questions. "What happened next" is safe but without educational value. Ask open-ended questions which are somewhat focused, either by topic or time:

Q: *Tell me what you liked about the movie.*

> *Q: After you left the theater, but before you got home, what did you do?*

Knowing the answers, you may get sloppy and ask leading questions. Further, you may be a tad bored (unless your friends are more interesting than mine). Ask your questions with a sense of urgency and curiosity. Through your reactions to the answers, convince your friend that you find the events of that afternoon fascinating. At the end of the exercise, ask your friend if you were able to accomplish this.

Do a cross, twice

Then take your friend on cross. Go over the same material, this time telling your friend what happened, one fact at a time. Pause to allow for a "yes" or "no." These are leading questions. "Then you went to the movies." "You thought that the movie was horrible, isn't that right."

Go through the leading exercise twice. First time through, ask the questions (make the statements) as if there was nothing wrong with how your friend spent the afternoon (cross need not be cross). Second time though, make the same statements in a tone of voice that suggests your shock, disbelief and moral outrage at what was done.

If your friend is answering the questions with anything but yes or no, it is probably because your questions end with a rising intonation, thus inviting response. Practice questions as statements.

As a variation of this exercise, tell your friend to assume the role of someone who will not willingly admit to the things that were done that afternoon, that they somehow constitute a crime. This will force you to recognize, and deal with, evasive answers.

Now probably all of this sounds silly. "Sure, I can do that. Why bother?"

Because it has been my experience that it is one thing to understand something intellectually and quite something else to actually *do* it. Knowing *what* is different than knowing *how*.

"Really, Coach, all you have to do is pick up the ball and throw to First."

CHAPTER 10

CLOSING ARGUMENT:
BASIC CHOICES

*At a trial advocacy workshop the student was
about to give her closing argument. The instruc-
tor walked over and took her notes. As he
walked away, she shot a look of hatred and then
turned to the jury, smiled, and soared.*

Spontaneity is *always* better than script. Looking
at the jurors, gauging their reactions, editing on the
fly, it doesn't get much better.

Spontaneity is *always* better than script, but *only
if* you have prepared. Work hard on what you will
say. Write a detailed outline. Or a script. Edit for
style and substance. Practice, out loud, not just in
your mind. Corner friends; do riffs in the shower.
You need to hear the cadence. The night before,
reduce it all to a short list of major points, just in
case.

You won't forget anything. But if you do, that's
okay. While there is debate as to the significance of
closing argument, few would argue that cases turn
on one or two omitted arguments, arguments that
jurors probably thought of themselves, two days
ago. Most cases will turn on two, possibly three,
main matters; these you won't forget.

Critical Moments: Taking Off and Landing

In the trial advocacy literature, *primacy* and *recency* are stressed: what people hear first and last are the most memorable and have the most impact. Some lawyers begin:

> *"Ladies and Gentlemen of the Jury, I would first like to thank you for your attention during the trial."*

People have to settle in before they begin to listen. This opening, like the stale dinner joke, focuses attention without losing ground.

Silence is a much better alternative. Approach the podium, look at the jury, and say nothing. After 30 seconds, the audience is yours. Whispers work too. Bellow and everyone sits back and gets a tad lazy; speak softly and everyone leans forward and concentrates.

The only problem with the "thank you for your attention" opening is that it totally lacks pizzaz.

> *"It was the best of times, it was the worst of times."*

> *"It is a truth universally acknowledged, that a single man in possession of a good fortune must be in want of a wife."*

> *"As Gregor Samsa awoke one morning from a troubled dream, he found himself changed in his bed to some monstrous kind of vermin."*

Novelists die for the opportunity to write a good first line. Don't throw yours away with an ingratiating, insincere apology. What is the most important thing you want to tell the jurors?

Trial lawyers speak of the importance of theme, a simple organizing statement around which turns the entire enterprise. One introduces the theme in opening, works it in during the case, and often refers to it opening, and closing, the final argument.

Symmetry is always nice. Consider using your first lines to link your closing argument to your opening statement:

> "At the beginning of this trial I told you we would prove X, Y, and Z. We have."

Or something dramatic: looking directly at the jurors, after 30 seconds:

> "My client is not a murderer."

The last thing you tell the jurors is probably the most important of all. Think long and hard of your close. It is probably well to memorize it. Leave the jury with a haunting sentence, or question, or image.

Cujo is a the story of a dog gone mad with rabies. He cannot control himself and ends by killing his BOY. Near the end of his novel, Stephen King tells us:

> "It would perhaps not be amiss to point out that Cujo had always tried to be a good dog."

Joseph Ellis, in his marvelous book, *Founding Brothers*, ends with the death of John Adams. Adams always knew that his long time ene-my/friend, Thomas Jefferson, would become history's darling and that he, Adams, would be assigned a lesser role in the founding of our country. Adams is on his death bed; unbeknownst to him, Jefferson had died a matter of hours earlier; Adams' last words: "Thomas Jefferson still lives." Ellis' ends his book:

> *"He was wrong for the moment but right for the ages."*

A final, third, example. While it may not have been the last line, I have recently come across one that shrieked: "Work me into your book!" In the 1940's, Fred Allen and Jack Benny had extremely popular radio shows. Occasionally they would come on each other's program to trade insults. After one particularly good shot by Allen, Benny responded:

> *"You wouldn't dare talk to me like that if my writers were here."*

Email if you can work that into a closing argument.

Critical Choices

Who knows whether closing arguments matter? Some argue that is it all over after jury selection, others after opening statement. In all likelihood, by the time of closing argument, the jurors are probably leaning one way or the other. You'll have several strategic choices to make:

> — *Should you marshal the evidence or focus on one or two main points?*

— *Should you talk to all the jurors or focus on a few?*

— *Should you be candid or contentious?*

— *Should you anticipate attacks on your position?*

— *Should you argue "Where's Mama?"*

Let's run through some considerations.

Marshaling v. Focus

The traditional advice is to *marshal* the evidence: you bring the various bits of evidence together to support the *factual* conclusions that lead to the *legal* conclusion you want the jury to reach. Take the simple negligence action. The outline for liability might look something like this:

Defendant was negligent (Legal Conclusion)

   A.   *He was driving too fast* (Factual Conclusion)

      (1) fact (testimony of eye witness)

      (2) fact (skid marks)

   B.   *He was chatting on his cell phone*

   (1) fact

   (2) fact

   (3) fact

Marshaling the evidence is filling in the blanks, showing how each piece of evidence fits. It is a great approach if you are ahead. Much advertising is designed to maintain market share, rather than to enlarge it. It reassures current customers "You're no fool." If you are ahead going in, your closing argument may be calmer, more of a "tying down loose ends" affair.

But what if you are behind? You must give the jury a *new* way to think about the evidence, perhaps by dwelling on one or two fatal flaws. Poking holes, however, is not enough. It is *never* enough simply to show why your opponent should *lose*; you must show why you should *win*.

Defending a criminal case, if the prosecution fails to prove guilt beyond a reasonable doubt, this means you *win*, not that the prosecution *loses*. People don't like to make decisions on technicalities, they want to be on the side of angels. If you are arguing reasonable doubt, tell the jury why the standard is the way it is and what important rights are at stake; tell them why the angels will rejoice with an acquittal.

This insight cuts across legal practice. It is not enough to show people *why* they should come out on your side, you must also *motivate* them to do so. Say you are making a motion to dismiss an action on an oral contract, arguing that enforcement would violate the Statute of Frauds. Don't simply point to the statute and take a victory lap. Tell the judge why it is important *not* to enforce oral contracts; as we all know, there are exceptions within exceptions to all legal rules, and, what we might not all know, judges don't like technicalities any better than the rest of us.

Audience: all or few?

After argument, the jurors don't go *vote*; they go *deliberate*. Two points immediately flow from this:

1. Your argument must have staying power. Emotional appeals, smoke and mirrors, last, what, five, ten minutes?

2. It might be better to think of closing, not as *your* opportunity to convince *everyone*, but as your opportunity to help your *allies* convince *everyone* during deliberations.

Focusing argument on a few jurors is often the choice of criminal defense lawyers who hope for a hung jury. Even civil lawyers can do this, focusing their argument, and their eye contact, on the one or two jurors who most likely will become the foreperson of the jury. This leads nicely into your next choice point: candor versus contentiousness.

Candor or contentiousness?

The case for *candor* starts with the realization that jurors have a difficult decision to make. According to John W. Davis, probably the most successful appellate lawyer of his time, he approached appellate argument with *"a sincere and single desire to be helpful to the Court."*

If you are sincerely trying to help a group of people reach an important decision, your demeanor will change and you will probably address different issues. You will be less shrill and you will back away from arguments you don't believe. Sensing your goal, jurors are likely to drop their guard, stop looking for weaknesses, and listen to what you have to say.

Rapport and trust can be critical. If the jury trusts you, you are almost home. The more reasonable you are, the more you see both sides, the more you will seem like a friend, and the more people will trust you.

> *"I know what you're thinking. How can a major corporation put a product on the market having given it only one test? That is a very good question. But remember the three experts we called to testify as to the accuracy of the test? How others have relied on the test, all without incident?"*

No doubt you *believe* your client should win. Consider your role as simply helping the jurors see how you came to that belief.

The case for *contentiousness* starts with "You never can tell!" Deny everything. It is folly to acknowledge any of the opposition's points because you never know. Perhaps there were a couple of jurors who didn't see any problem at all with conducting only one test: now they will be unable to argue that position during deliberations. Worse than that, now they feel betrayed by 'their' lawyer.

Should you argue only points you believe in? Same question. The case for honesty is that people usually pick up insincerity and friends don't ask friends to come to stupid conclusions. On the other hand, you never can tell.

Contentiousness also rests on the notion that you are basically supplying ammunition for your allies on the jury. They will need cover, and overstatement on your part will give it to them. Some personal injury lawyers don't give the jury a specific figure, hoping, I guess, that the jury will run amuck. However, if you don't name a large figure, most jurors will be reluctant to do so. Similarly, most people are reluctant to call people liars. If you believe opposition witnesses lied, call them liars; if you are reluctant, so too your allies.

Consider the role of *extremism*. People don't like extreme positions and tend to *compromise*. "Extreme" is defined by initial demands. In a personal injury case, a judgment of $490,000 looks extreme if the demand was $500,000; if the original demand was $1 million, $490,000 looks meager.

To review what was happening in the world while you were trying to get a date, O.J. Simpson, a famous football player and actor, was charged with killing his wife and one of her friends. The theory of the defense was that one of the investigating police officers, Mark Fuhrman, planted evidence. The defense offered evidence that he used racial slurs. Now, during his closing argument, Johnny Cochran could have said:

> *"The evidence suggests that Fuhrman was lying."*

Instead, Cochran compared Fuhrman to "Hitler," and said he was the "personification of evil."

> *"Fuhrman is a lying, perjuring, genocidal racist."*

Probably Cochran convinced few jurors that Fuhrman was a Hitler. What he did do was to make it very easy for his allies to say, "Maybe not Hitler, but Fuhrman is surely a run of the mill racist and perjurer." Had Cochran called Fuhrman a "run of the mill racist and perjurer," his allies on the jury would have less room to appear reasonable.

Malcolm X convinced white America that Martin Luther King was a reasonable sort of guy.

Is there a middle road between candor and contentious? No doubt. Probably you will vary between the two in different parts of your argument. Realize the danger of extremes. If you are too contentious, you lose credibility. If you ask for a million dollars in a slip and fall case, the jury will not split the difference and come in at $500,000. The jury will think you are nuts. There was evidence supporting Cochran's characterization of Fuhrman.

There is also danger in being too candid, too reasonable. Jurors *expect* some puffing and grow suspicious if there's none. Learned Hand made a similar point about the used car dealer's "You're gonna love this car!"

> *"Such statements, like the claims of campaign managers before election, are rather designed to allay the suspicion which would attend their absence than to be understood as having any relation to objective truth."*

Sometimes it is better to be candid, sometimes better to be contentious. Sometimes a diamond, sometimes a stone. If you are always making the *same* choice, then you are probably not making the *best* choice.

Rule of practice: Whatever style you adopt, you should be able to articulate why it is the best style given the particular case.

Should you anticipate attacks on your position?

This is akin to the question of whether you should "take the sting out" on direct examination. You don't want to anticipate to the point where your argument becomes one long apology. On the other hand, you don't want the jury to suspect you were trying to pull a fast one when they first hear the telling rejoinder from your opponent.

My advice would be *not* to anticipate unless the jury will think you were trying to mislead it by not mentioning the problem.

As plaintiff, there is less need to anticipate attacks as you argue first and last. If your opponent attacks your position after you have made your first argument, you can respond to it in your closing argument. The problem is more acute when you are defending; after you close, that's it. You don't have a chance to get back up and respond to the attacks your opponent has made on your position. Given that, it is probably wise to make the attacks yourself and then answer them.

Should you argue "Where's Mama?

Finally, an easy one. Yes!

A traditional attack on your opponent on the evidence that *wasn't* produced. As to each contention, assuming that it is correct, what additional evidence *could* have been introduced to support it? My first case involved a young man accused of stealing a car. My defense was alibi: he was a home with his mother. *I forgot to call his mother!* The prosecutor's argument was short:

"Where's Mama?"

There are two variations of arguing the gaps. One is arguing promises not kept. Make a list of what your opponent promises during opening statement. Then, in closing, "My opponent promised the three witches. Where were they?"

The second involves baiting.

"My opponent will get up here after I sit down. What I am waiting to hear, and what you will be waiting to hear, is an answer to the following question."

Of course, if your opponent can answer the question, then you are in trouble. And the ploy may not work for other reasons; your opponent may simply ignore it or respond:

"I was asked to answer a question. I don't have a clear answer to that question. Reality never comes in perfect packages; there will always be questions, bits that don't seem to fit. As Hamlet said, 'There are more things in heaven and earth, Horatio, than are dreamt of in your phi-

losophy.' As to questions not answered, let's look at the ten not answered by my opponent."

If I can work in Hamlet, you can work in Benny.

Trial practice is a lot like war. A new stock argument, like a new weapon, is good for only one or two encounters.

CHAPTER 11

CLOSING ARGUMENT: STRUCTURE, DELIVERY, MISTAKES

In this chapter we'll look at organization issues, delivery, and common errors. In the next, I'll give you an illustration.

Organization and IRS Transitions

There is no rule that you go chronologically. In a personal injury case, just because the jury must first find the defendant liable before assessing damages, there is no rule that you can't first argue damages and then liability. Organize your argument in terms of clarity and dramatic impact.

Rule of thumb

Put your strongest points at the beginning and at the end. Bury the plumber. *Rule of practice:* Whatever order you choose, be able to say *why* it is better than the alternatives. Never, not once, adopt an organizational structure without thinking long and hard.

In a typical case, you will have some good things to say about your case, and some nasty things about your opponent's. This raises organizational issues. Say there are three issues, surprisingly enough, A,

B, and C. One approach, relying on strong/weak/ strong, would be to start with arguing your position on all three issues, then discuss why your opponent is weak on all three, and then conclude arguing your side again. (Repetition, to repeat, is just fine.)

An alternative structure would be based on the issues. Discuss *Issue A* first, your case concerning it, dissing the opposition, concluding on your strengths. Then move to *Issue B*. The advantage of this approach is that it is more focused and easier to follow.

Leading with conclusions or facts?

One interesting organizational problem concerns conclusions and facts: which should come first? Say that you want the jury to conclude that a person was drunk and you have slurred speech, the smell of alcohol, and stumbling as evidence. You have a choice: first, you can state your conclusion and then support it by reciting the evidence or, second, you can begin with the evidence and work toward the conclusion.

There are certain advantages with going with the evidence first.

1. It is always best if jurors come to the conclusion on their own. After the smell of alcohol, some jurors might conclude, "Drunk!" and, if they do, they will go to their graves believing it.

2. You avoid the "nay-sayer" problem. Start with your conclusion, some jurors will auto-

matically assume the role of Devil's Advocate and look for weaknesses.

Improving Clarity: Explicitness and IRS Transitions

Clarity is improved by *explicitness* and *hard-working transitions*. To illustrate, I'll use a previous example:

Defendant was negligent (Legal Conclusion)

A. *He was driving too fast* (Factual Conclusion)

   (1) *fact* (testimony of eye witness)

   (2) *fact* (skid marks)

B. *He was chatting on his cell phone*

   (1) *fact*

   (2) *fact*

   (3) *fact*

Don't just mosey around reminding the jury that one of the witnesses thought the defendant was speeding, that the skid marks were long, and, although he denied speeding, he admitted being late for dinner. By explicitness I mean showing how these specific facts impact on your case. Explicitness is the answer to the question, "So what?"

So what, these three facts?

   They mean the defendant was speeding.

So what, he was speeding?

   It means he was negligent.

Fine, well and good. But what is the *relationship* between the eye witness testimony and the skid marks? It can be either "and" or "or." To conclude that the defendant was speeding, must the jurors believe both the eye witness *and* the skid mark evidence. Or is one enough?

What is the relationship between "speeding" and "chatting?" Again, the relationship can be either "and" or "or." To conclude the defendant was negligent, is it enough for the jury to believe that he was speeding *or* that, even if he wasn't speeding, he was negligent by driving while chatting? Or must they believe both?

Hard-working transitions will make all of this clear. I have come up with a nemonic, although not much of one: I call these transactions IRS transitions.

> They *introduce* the topic: I
>
> They *relate* the topic to the last topic ("and" or "or"):   R
>
> They tell its *significance*:   S

For example, to introduce the discussion of speeding:

> *Ladies and Gentlemen of the Jury, let's look at the evidence of speeding* (I), *because, if he was, that means he was negligent* (S).

This is much more helpful than simply "Let's look at the evidence of speeding" because it tells the jury the *significance* of that evidence.

After speeding, you want to discuss chatting.

> *The evidence also shows he was chatting on his cell phone* (I). *While we believe that the evidence*

proves he was speeding, even if you believe he was going the speed limit, (R), if you find he was talking on the phone, then you must find he was negligent. (S). Now let's look at the evidence.

This is more helpful than "Next, he was chatting." It tells the jury the *significance* of that conclusion. It is more helpful than "Next, he was chatting and if he was, he was negligent." It tells the jury the *relationship* between chatting and speeding. It need find only one, not both.

It's IRS transitions all the way down. For example, you'll need a transition between the eyewitness testimony and the skid marks:

Even if you do not believe the witness (R), if you believe the skid mark evidence (I), you will conclude he was speeding (S), and thus that he was negligent (S).

Delivery

A very experienced trial judge, and a longtime student of trial practice, was asked what is the most important thing about closing argument.

"Don't talk down to the jury. Talk to them as you would a group of friends, when you have something important to tell them."

This makes a lot of sense. Your guiding image should not be "Acceptance Speech" but rather "Hallway Conversation."

While you don't want to talk down to the jury, "talking down" is a matter of attitude. *Respect* the jurors. No doubt every one of them has accomplished grand things, things that you are incapable of. *Respect* the difficult decision the jurors will have to make. Treating the jury with respect, you won't talk down.

Recall what we said about good story telling. Tell the story your client lived. Avoid abstractions; focus on acts and actions.

In his essay, *Politics and the English Language*, George Orwell argued that our society is troubled because our language is troubled: We don't bother to see what we are saying, we just talk. To illustrate, he rewrote a passage from the Bible as it would probably be written today:

> *Objective considerations of contemporary phenomena compels the conclusion that success or failure in competitive activities exhibits no tendency to be commensurate with innate capacity.*

This replaces:

> *I returned and saw under the sun, that the race is not to the swift, nor battle to the strong, neither yet bread to the wise, nor yet riches to men of understanding, nor yet favor to men of skill.*

If you are going to use metaphors, make sure they are good ones. Returning to Orwell:

> *"Prose consists less and less of words chosen for the sake of their meaning, and more and more of phrases tacked together like sections of a prefabricated hen-house."*

Metaphors enliven discourse by creating images. "It looked like something the cat drug in" once was a terrific metaphor because people would see a bloody and mangled corpse of some poor rodent. Metaphor dies; no one sees anything. Even though I have never built a "prefabricated hen-house," it works for me: I can see someone tacking things together to build a shoddy building.

A good analogy throws light upon the current dilemma. Do your analogies help the jury understand your argument? Can your opponent "distinguish" them or, still worse, turn them on you.

As to stock arguments, ask how you would respond to them. Most have already been neutralized.

Then there is the matter of intention. Recall the lessons from drama: before you walk on stage, recite what you intend to accomplish:

"I intend to convince those twelve people that my client, M. Baxendale, should not be liable for the broken crankshafts."

One final problem deserves discussion, the problem caused by the one-way nature of closing argument. Even though your tone might be conversational, closing arguments aren't conversations. Conversations are a two-way street, with your listeners asking for clarifications and telling you if they agree. Not so with argument. Say you are arguing Point X. What are the possibilities?

1. The jurors already agree with Point X and, if you argue it further, you are wasting your time.

2. The jurors don't buy Point X and never will; if you argue it further, you are wasting your time and probably undercutting your credibility.

3. The jurors aren't convinced of Point X but may be with further argument.

Some lawyers believe that they can read the jury, others claim they generally don't have a clue. You will hear a lot of tales concerning how to read the jury, look to body language (with crossed arms indicating rejection) and to facial expression. I'm generally not convinced: crossed arms might indicate "I agree with Point X but I hate to."

My best advise is to maintain eye contact with the jurors, to be open to the possibility that you aren't as clear as you think, that you are wasting your time pursuing Point X, because no one will buy it or everyone already has, and be willing to edit on the fly.

Mistakes

Most of the mistakes concern style. Some lawyers just get up there and repeat the facts. A waste and an insult: the jury was paying attention. *Organize* the facts. Other lawyers don't know when to shut up. State your theme, focus on the two or three key points, and sit down. As is true in all of trial work, less is better.

Some mistakes concern substance. Usually opponents give you wide berth hoping for a reciprocal leeway. However, be aware that there are objectionable things that you should avoid.

Arguing Evidence not in Record

Freud called it the Graduate Student Nightmare and I am sure we have all had it. You are about to take a final for a class you forgot to take. And assorted variations on that theme. Here it's "Oh no, I forgot to introduce that evidence!"

This is a common mistake. As a prophylactic, some lawyers say:

"I'll be discussing the evidence you heard during trial. Maybe what I say is not exactly how you remember it. If so, go with your memory, not mine. I'm not trying to confuse you or mislead you. But sometimes, like everyone, I make mistakes."

Putting Yourself at Issue

Before the Civil War, there was a lawyer who would call his kids to the stand. "What would happen if Daddy died?" They would cry and wail.

His closing was short. "Ladies and Gentlemen of the Jury, unless you find for my client, I will kill myself."

This is no longer considered good form. Don't put your own credibility at issue. Avoid: "In law school I vowed never to represent a child molester and thus my client isn't!" You can get tripped up in discussing the evidence. Rather than saying, "I think the defendant is lying" simply say, with as much personal conviction as you can muster, "The evidence shows the defendant is lying."

Emotional appeals and predicting doom

Jurors are to decide based on the facts, without reference to their emotions and without reference to where the chips may land.

Right.

Of course your argument will be emotional but not expressly so. Remember that effective story telling comes from facts, not adjectives.

Gross appeals to emotions are improper. A defendant should not be convicted simply because the victim suffered greatly. Nor should a defendant be acquitted because he will be sent to prison and face dire consequences. Corporations should not be found liable to "send a message" to other corporations. Nor should victims be denied relief because insurance rates will go up.

The parties to a lawsuit should be judged on their own merits. I was once sitting in on a high school class that was discussing a video of a juvenile court sentencing hearing. The judge talked a lot about the need to send a message to other high school students doing drugs. A boy in the last row raised his hand.

"That's not fair to the guy. They should do what's right to him and not worry about what will happen to other kids."

I turned and whispered to his teacher.

"That's a very sophisticated argument."

"Oh, he's being sentenced next week. He's just practicing."

CHAPTER 12

CLOSING: AN ILLUSTRATION

To illustrate closing, and to introduce you to a great passage, I begin with Professor Grant Gilmore in *The Ages of American Law.*

> *Law reflects but in no sense determines the moral worth of a society. The values of a reasonably just society will reflect themselves in a reasonably just law. The better the society, the less law there will be. In Heaven there will be no law and the lion will lie down with the lamb. The values of an unjust society will reflect themselves in an unjust law. The worse the society, the more law there will be. In Hell there will be nothing but law, and due process will be meticulously observed.*

Gilmore, for our purposes, is the state's star witness in *The Case of the Nervous Shepherd.* N. Shepherd is charged with cruelty to animals for shooting a lion. His defense is that the lion was threatening one of his flock. Gilmore is called by the prosecution to deny that claim.

> *Q: Professor Gilmore, did you observe the shooting?*
>
> *A: Yes.*

Q: Prior to the shooting, was the lion in any
way threatening any of the sheep?

A: No. In fact, they were lying down together.

Like many academics, Grant Gilmore is about to
be hoisted upon his own academic writing. On cross
N. Shepherd's lawyer asks the clerk to mark the
above writing and asks the judge for permission to
approach the witness. With a touch of the hostility
all lawyers hold for all law professors:

"Professor, do you recognize this?"

"I believe it is early Gilmore."

"Professor, would you mind reading the sen-
tence concerning the lions and the lambs?"

The closing argument becomes:

Ladies and Gentlemen of the Jury, don't believe
Gilmore when he says the sheep and lion were
lying together. Why the man admits to Utopian
visions!"

The lawyer has misread Gilmore; lawyers *always*
misread academics and then claim it is our fault (we
too have our resentments). But that's not what I
want to comment on.

The closing argument is what I call an *implicit*
argument. The link between his Utopian vision and
his lack of credibility is not spelled out. Why does
one having Utopian vision lack credibility?

There are two problems with implicit argument,
one which must be corrected, the other which may
or may not be.

First, the link between Utopian vision and credibility may not be clear to the *lawyer*. This is not acceptable. Brain research suggests that the two sides of our brain fulfill somewhat different functions, with the left side being more analytical, the right side being more creative and better at seeing relationships. What happens is this. The left side is thinking about Gilmore's credibility and, suddenly, the right side grunts "Utopian vision!" At some level, the right side sees the relationship; it is now the job of the left side to articulate it. If you think hard about the possible relationship between Utopian vision and credibility, you will not only understand your argument better but will see additional relationships as well. If you don't take the time, your argument becomes a series of grunts.

This is a central insight into good lawyering. Never simply rely on your insights; force yourself to articulate why they are good. This way you'll know best how to express your grunt.

The second problem with an implicit argument is that, even when the lawyer knows the link between Utopian vision and credibility, the jurors might not get it. One has a choice as to whether to solve this problem. In an ideal world, the jurors, or at least some of them, would see the link themselves and would present it, and defend it, as their own work during deliberations. If the lawyer is explicit about the link, then this possibility is foreclosed. On the other hand, if the link is subtle, perhaps no one will see and the argument will be lost.

Let's now redo the Gilmore closing and, for illustration, make it quite explicit even though we realize its costs.

> *Ladies and Gentlemen of the Jury, I now wish to turn to the prosecution's case. My client, Mr. Shepherd, says that he shot the lion because it was threatening his flock. The State acknowledges that this is a good defense because it tried hard to disprove it. If you believe that Shepherd shot the lion to save his sheep, then you must acquit him.*

Here the link between factual finding and verdict is explicit.

> *The State called Grant Gilmore, who claimed that he saw the incident and that the lion was not threatening the flock; that they were, in fact lying down together.*

> *This story is not believable and I'll tell you why.*

Here the conclusion is stated before the supporting details. This will make what follows easier to understand but raises the same issue I just discussed: it forecloses jurors' "Eureka!" and runs into the nay-sayer problem, jurors who will not take the position that the conclusion is *not* supported by the reasoning. The alternative is to put the reasoning first and the conclusion last. Continuing:

> *One way we test a story is by our common sense. Does it make sense from what we know of the world?*

Here the reasoning process is explicit.

*For example, if someone returns from Tucson in
July and claims it was too cold, we tend not to
believe him; he is making it up or is badly
mistaken.*

Most of us, most of the time, base our decisions
on analogies. This probably goes back a long ways:
"Does this Valley look *like* the one where I hunted
the Woolly Mammoth?"

The problem with analogies is that they may not
fit. Is not believing someone about the ski trip
sufficiently like not believing the lion story so that
we should look to it as guidance? Maybe there are
sufficient differences in the two so that the analogy
does not hold.

Note that your opponent will have the opportunity to point out that your analogies don't stand up,
prove too much, or, worst of all, prove the converse.
Moral: don't get sloppy and don't take your opponent's analogies sitting down; think about them.

*In the world we know, lions eat lambs, they do
not lie down with them.*

While there was no evidence introduced about
what "we all know," arguing common sense doesn't
violate the rule against arguing matters not in the
record. It would violate the rule to argue the results
of a survey that was not introduced in evidence: "A
recent study indicated that 93% of those surveyed
agreed that, more likely than not, things would go
rather badly for the lamb, with an error rate of plus
or minus 2%."

> *Because Gilmore's tale does not square with the*
> *world as we know it, don't believe it.*

Again an express link between argument and
result.

> *Further, we test a story by who tells it to us. The*
> *story may make perfect sense, but if the source is*
> *suspicious then we are suspicious. Does the*
> *storyteller have a motive to lie to us? If so, then*
> *we can reject the story on that basis alone.*

Here the reasoning process is made clear. What is
not clear is the relationship between the two points:
unbelievable story and untrustworthy storyteller.
The are two possibilities: dependent and independent. They are dependent *if* the jury must conclude
both are correct in order to reject the testimony;
they are independent *if* the jury can reject the
testimony even if it concludes only one is correct.

When you're arguing several points in support of
one conclusion, you should make these relationships
clear. "Even if you don't find Gilmore's story incredible, you still should reject it because he has a
motive to lie."

> *The prosecutor has argued that the defendant,*
> *N. Shepherd, has a motive to lie when he testi-*
> *fies. Obviously he has a motive to lie, we are*
> *told, because he has been charged with a crime.*
> *This is a stock argument. Prosecutors always*
> *make it. Think about it. The police arrest the*
> *wrong person. "I didn't do it!" he screams.*
> *"Don't believe him," the prosecutor will tell you,*
> *"he has a motive to lie."*

Stock arguments beget stock replies. "The Plaintiff's three witnesses told different stories; don't believe them!" "The fact that they told different stories shows that they didn't get together to make things up; believe them!" Like new weapons, stock arguments generally last for only one war.

> *The State next tells you that Mr. Gilmore has no motive to lie, that he is a neutral witness. Is he? He testified that he saw the incident well enough to say that the animals were sitting. He has a motive to protect that testimony; he is not neutral as to whether or not you believe him.*

This is absolutely right. Witnesses want to be believed.

> *You recall that I asked him a series of questions about how far away he was, how the lighting was, how long he had observed the scene before the shooting. In all of his answers, he gave you the impression that his view was very good and his attention very focused. Don't you find this a little unbelievable? That he had a perfect view of the scene, no question about it. That he his attention was focused on that particular event, no question about it. That today he recalls perfectly just what happened, no question about it.*

A witness who comes off as too perfect is suspicious. Preparing witnesses for trial, tell them to readily admit to things that might hurt your case. The less partisan they look, the more believable they are.

About half an hour ago, a man who was sitting in the front row got up and left. I saw that all of you looked at him. How many of you would be willing to testify you had a perfect look at him. That your attention was focused on him. That you remember all the details perfectly? If you are that sure, take a few minutes during deliberations to see if you all recall the incident in the same way. What was the color of his tie? Did he have a newspaper? Was there someone sitting next to him?

This is risky. So too when jurors are urged to conduct test or experiments in the jury room, such as field sobriety tests. If the jurors don't fall on their face, the lawyer will.

Note too that this may be a faulty analogy. If you were on the other side, you would have to argue that failing to recall all of the details of a man leaving a courtroom is essentially different than recalling all the details of a lion and lamb lying together.

I am not suggesting that Mr. Gilmore is lying. No doubt, he thinks he saw the lion and lamb lying down together. We are suspicious of a story not only if the teller has a motive to lie to us but also if we think that the person may be mistaken.

Should the lawyer waive off the perjury argument? If she does, she will insult those jurors, if any, who think he was lying and will take this argument out of deliberations: "Come on, even the other lawyer admitted Gilmore wasn't lying." On the other hand, if Gilmore is sympathetic and loveable, as law professors are, she runs the risk of alienating the jury by calling him a liar.

> *We all know that people tend to see what they want to see. From Gilmore's writing, we all know he wants to see lions lying down with lambs.*

This could be improved by an analogy. Can you think of an example of people seeing what they want to see. Can you draw upon an instance from our shared culture, such as from popular movies, a classic novel, or recent current events? If one of the jurors is a tennis player, consider "If you play tennis, when you get passed at the net, you tend to see the ball fall a little long." (In my case, it *was* long.)

> *This is what happened. Gilmore did see the lion lying down but that was after it was shot. Despite what he claims, he must have turned when he heard the shot; then he saw what he wanted to see.*

Bravo! This gives the jury a new way of thinking about the evidence and it gives everyone a way out. They can now disregard Gilmore's testimony without disregarding him.

> *There is more than enough reason to reject Gilmore's testimony. If you do not believe Gilmore, you must acquit my client.*

Here an explicit link between analysis and verdict. And note that there is nothing more, no stock closing, no thanking or groveling, just a statement of what the lawyer wants the jury to hear.

That Gilmore wrote of lions and lambs is a choice morsel. Some lawyers would intuit that but would not expend the mental energy it takes to tie it up. They would throw the matter to the jury.

> *"Ladies and Gentlemen of the Jury, don't believe Gilmore when he says the sheep and lion were lying together. Why the man admits to Utopian visions!"*

Do the work. With each point you make in closing argument you should be able to articulate just how it fits in your overall theory of the case.

> *Witness bias means you cannot believe the testimony; not believing the testimony means you must acquit the defendant.*

Again, once you can articulate it, you need not do so during the argument, counting on jurors to make their own discoveries.

But if you can't articulate to yourself how your points fit, your closing will be a stew of unrelated choice morsels, which may, in fact, not be all that choice after all. But don't realize the weaknesses with your argument while making it. If the shadow of doubt passes over your face, you will lose direction, confidence and, perhaps, your lunch.

CHAPTER 13

OPENING STATEMENT

Opening statements are like introductions to books; they go first but they are written last. Reading the Prologue, one gets the sense that the author sat down one fine winter morning and decided to write a book covering certain topics, all of which thereafter flowed logically and elegantly. More likely, what really happened, late one summer night, out of desperation, the author sat and began hacking away at some little point that had been troublesome. This led further and further afield, with random wanderings, blind alleys and curses. Eventually, home again, the bloody battles completed, and now comes the calm introduction, and all is light, logical sequence and well-executed plan.

Road maps and story telling

Opening statements are often referred to as "road maps." They tell the jury where you are going, what evidence you will produce, and how it all "fits."

> *In this trial we will prove that my client, Mary Worth, was badly injured by the defendant, Miniver Cheevy. The evidence will show he had been drinking heavily and then drove his car at*

184

a high rate of speed and hit Mary Worth's car in an intersection.

We will first call Mr. Hey Buddy, a bartender at Miniver's neighborhood bar. On the night in question, he will tell you Miniver Cheevy cursed his fate and kept on drinking.

To prove that the defendant was speeding, we will call Ms. Smith, an accident reconstructionist, who will testify that the skid marks left by the defendant showed he was going at least 50 miles per hour.

We will then call two eyewitnesses, Rebecca Jones and Sigmund Freud; they will testify as to the defendant's speed.

We will then call Dr. Kildare. He will testify as to the plaintiff's injuries. He is not a real doctor, but plays one on TV.

The road map analogy is helpful. Having spent months preparing a case, you know where everything fits; the jury hasn't a clue. Your first job, like other famous first jobs, is to create *order* out of *chaos*. Without a good road map, the jury may get lost somewhere near Santa Fe.

But you can do more. John W. Davis, the lawyer we met previously, wrote that, in appellate argument:

> *"The statement of facts is not merely part of the argument, it is more often than not the argument itself. A case well stated is far more than half argued."*

Many cases are won, and probably some lost, during Opening Statement.

Trials are *not* about the witnesses, exhibits, or jury instructions. Trials are about *real people* and *real events*; they are the stuff of drama: explosions, murders, betrayal, and, in the case of commercial litigation, *repeated* late deliveries!

Recall what we said about good story telling. Tell the story your client lived. Things that *are* happening are always more engrossing than things that *have* happened. Go for the present tense.

> *Mary Worth is on her way home from work. She approaches the intersection of Elm and Main. The light is green. Suddenly, off to her left, headlights. They're coming fast. Will she be hit? Will she be killed? The sound of squealing brakes, then the deafening clash of metal smashing metal, then the trees and sky and pavement all spin upside down as her car flips, and the sound of breaking glass, building and building and then, silence. And blackness.*

> *The next thing Mary is aware of is pain. Pain in her back. Pain in her legs. She is alone in a hospital room. She tries to move her leg to get comfortable. Her leg won't move.*

Good storytelling does *not* consist of flowery phrases, emotional outbursts, and vile maledictions. Good storytelling is simple and straightforward and uses nouns and verbs much more than adjectives and adverbs. Instead of lamenting the "great pain" your client has suffered, talk of the specifics: how often she must take painkillers, how often she must leave movies early, how often she wakes at night. Stress particulars: instead of saying only that the pain wakes her three to four nights in a week, describe one particular night and what she does, alone, in pain, at four o'clock in the morning.

Road maps alone may get us to Sante Fe; good storytelling helps us see those cute little buildings.

Caveat on storytelling

Don't include everything. The opening statement that tells all robs the trial itself of drama and surprise. Consider teases, as in, "Next week on Survivor."

> *Officer Knowles was the first police officer on the scene. He talked to the defendant Miniver. He will tell you that Miniver was hostile.*

> *But then Miniver told Officer Knowles something very surprising. Let's wait until Knowles is on the stand.*

There are competing considerations. Details make a good road map and a compelling story. The better the road map, however, the less surprising, the less interesting, the eventual journey.

Personalize your client

Never "the plaintiff," seldom "my client," most often "Mary Worth." Personalization is more than proper names. Give the jury some feel for who your client is. With thought, you can avoid the resume approach—"Let me tell you something about my client"—by weaving biographical information into the fabric of the story.

"Ms. Worth knew the road well, as she had driven it for the last eight years taking her children to school."

Some try to depersonalize their opponents so that the jurors sees them as "defendants" rather than as people they can identify with. There are limits.

"I object, your Honor. My opponent knows the name of my client, Miniver Cheevy. I object to these continual references to, 'The defendant, child of scorn'."

Defendants' Opening Statements

Defendants, both criminal and civil, curse their fate and keep on drinking. "Not fair! They get to go first. Psychologists tell us of the importance of primacy; it is almost impossible to overcome first impressions. Oh, woe is us!"

The "Greatest" boxer of them all, Mohammed Ali, liked to go *second*. He spoke of "rope-a-dope." He would rest on the ropes while his opponent came at him, both fists flying. Soon the opponent was exhausted, and the time had come for a few well-chosen counterpunches.

Typically, a plaintiff has the burden of proof as to several elements. She must sustain each one or she loses. Hers is a complicated matter; she needs clarity. For the defense, *chaos may help*. Politicians know that the more voters are confused, the more unsure they becomes and the more likely they will vote no.

If it is possible that the plaintiff's case will not come in as planned, it is *not* a good idea to commit yourself to a theory of defense. *What is said in opening is a party admission.* If, in opening statement, the defense asserts, "Sure, my client did him in, but the evidence will show that he deserved it," it will be difficult to later argue that the prosecution failed to put the defendant at the scene of the crime.

A *shadow opening* is one that does not commit you to anything. Simply talk about burden of proof, the fact that all stories have two sides and the need to keep an open mind. It may be possible to *reserve* your opening statement until after the plaintiff has rested and it is time for your case. Most lawyers advise against this as they feel it is important for you to get up and say *something* early on.

Another possible defense opening is to focus attention on the key elements.

> *My client, Miniver Cheevy, admits that the accident was his fault. He admitted that to Officer Knowles. He admits, and very much regrets, that he caused Mary Worth harm. He is a man who, after all, loves his Shakespeare. The only thing this trial is about is the extent of damages Mary Worth suffered. She spent time in the hospital and we are willing to make compensation. She had medical bills and we will pay for them. She lost some work and we will make compensation. She suffered pain and suffering and we are willing to pay a reasonable amount for that. Yet she wants more. A lot more. She*

> *wants an award covering "permanent" disabili-*
> *ty. This is the only issue that divides us. In*
> *listening to the plaintiff's evidence, listen closely*
> *for testimony that the injuries are permanent.*
> *Everyone wants to be a millionaire, but this is a*
> *court of law, not a lottery.*

Note what you have done. Mary Worth, no doubt, would like to spend most of her time on the strongest part of her case, trashing Miniver. After this opening, if she does, it will seem that she is beating a dead horse. A good opening by the defense can shift focus from an opponent's strengths to her weaknesses.

Delivery

Remember the importance of *intention*.

> *"My intention is to have the jury relive the*
> *terror of Mary's accident."*

> *"My intention is to show the jury that Mary is*
> *greedy."*

This will not only help your focus but will help with physical problems, such as where to put your hands. If you are focusing on what you are saying, and why, your hands and gestures will take care of themselves.

Second, try addressing your remarks to one juror sitting in the back row. This assures proper voice level and eye contact with at least one juror.

Third, as in the case of closing argument, your tone and general demeanor should be conversational, talking with a friend about an important matter.

Fourth, realize the importance of silence. A pause underlines a point and allows the jury to consider it.

Finally, while you should have a prepared a script, realize the importance of jumping into the moment and don't worry that you will forget the key points.

Mistakes

Discussing the law and inadmissible evidence; overstatement, opening doors, arguing, and not knowing how to get off stage.

Discussing the law

Some judges get testy if you start instructing the jury as to the controlling law. That's their job. Some reference to the law is fine:

> *"The law says someone is negligent if that person does not act as would a reasonably prudent person. The evidence will show that the defendant did not."*

However, if you feel you need to discuss the law in any detail, check with the judge first.

Discussing evidence that might be ruled inadmissible

If you are unsure about whether some evidence will get in, ask for a pretrial hearing. *Bring cases* and *authorities*. If the judge reserves ruling until trial, don't mention the evidence in opening.

What if the ruling is adverse? A few words on the *intimidation of judges*.

Judges don't like to be reversed. While this may not be the sole guiding light of their existence, be aware of its importance. Assume a close question of law. One lawyer has a reputation for taking appeals, the other for accepting anything from the bench with a pathetic smile and a "Thank you, Your Honor." To establish credibility with the bench, take some appeals.

Overstatement

Don't promise what you cannot deliver. Your opponent will be writing down what you say the evidence will show and, at closing, will gleefully point out what it didn't.

Opening the doors

If you have successfully suppressed your client's confession, don't open the door to its introduction by stating, in your opening, "There will be no evidence that my client confessed." Don't open the door to evidence your opponent could otherwise not introduce by making an assertion that can only be met with that evidence.

Argument

Everyone knows that *you cannot argue during opening*. Few, however, know what argument actually is.

Clear cases are clear: emotional appeals for justice, discussions of the need to "send messages," and operatic curses. But what about close cases:

> "We will prove X, Y, and Z and, from those facts, you will conclude that the defendant was negligent."

Technically, "argument" is the drawing of inferences and conclusions from "fact." It is "argument" because differing inferences and conclusions are, no doubt, possible. Professor James Jeans, in his fine book *Trial Advocacy*, tells us that we can recognize argument by asking: "Can a witness testify in such a fashion?" As the opinion rule will prevent a witness from testifying that the defendant was "negligent," the above statement seems inappropriate.

In theory, during opening statement, you tell the jury what facts you will present and, during closing argument, you argue what conclusions the jury should draw from the facts.

Opening statement: *We will prove facts X, Y, and Z.*

Closing argument: *We have proved facts X, Y, and Z. Because of X, Y, and Z, you should conclude that the defendant was lying.*

This scheme self-destructs because it rests on two false assumptions: first, that there is a clear line between facts and conclusions and, more immediately significant here, that "facts" can be understood standing by themselves. They cannot. That the light was green has meaning only in relation to whether someone was or wasn't negligent. A statement of "only" facts would be a series of unconnected dots; a road map which doesn't show connectors, *i.e.*, the roads, is simply a list of place names.

Some argument is inevitable. Note that it can be somewhat disguised by putting the conclusion *first* rather than stating the facts and then arguing to the conclusion. Compare:

> Opening: *We will call three witnesses who will testify X, Y, and Z and from that testimony you will conclude that the defendant was negligent.*
>
> Opponent: *Objection: Argument.*

with:

> Opening: *To prove our allegation of negligence, we will call three witness who will testify to X, Y, and Z.*

There is an unspoken convention that *it's not nice to object* during *opening* or *closing* unless things are terrible. You can rely on this convention, plus confusion as to what argument is, to get away with some argument during opening. However, even if your opponent does not object, you will alienate the judge if you get too carried away.

Appeals to justice, appeals as to the need to send messages, and operatic curses are all clearly argument.

Never-ending stories

Work hard on your opening statement. When people go on and on, it usually means that they don't know what they want to say, things just keep popping into their minds and the rest of us must pay. If you have focused on what you want to say, clarity and brevity are typical byproducts.

It is well to *memorize* your closing riff so that you can go to it when the time is right. Otherwise they might need one of those Vaudeville hooks.

CHAPTER 14

JURY SELECTION

Centuries ago, two Chinese philosophers strolled the endless gardens of the Summer Palace. They paused beside one of the quiet ponds.

"Look," one remarked, "The goldfish are swimming happily."

"You cannot know how they feel. You are not a goldfish."

"You cannot know what I know. You are not me."

I love that story. It is more than clever contentiousness; it is Wisdom.

This *seems* to have something to do with jury selection; the problem with Wisdom is that it is hard to apply. We'll see.

Whom Do You Want?

In courthouse corridors, you'll hear: "As a personal injury plaintiff, you want emotional, sympathetic types: Catholics, Southern Europeans, Irish, people who work with their hands. As a civil defendant, you want stern, hardheaded people: Germans, Norwegians, Presbyterians, bankers. Prosecutors want the same type. And of course, criminal defendants want people who have been oppressed: Blacks, Jews."

My rule of thumb, "As a prosecutor try for 12 infuriated Prussians; for the defense, 12 drunken buffoons." But what to do with drunken Prussians and infuriated buffoons?

Besides being racist and sexist, the category approach to jury selection rests on two assumptions: that the jury make-up is critical and second, assuming it is, that we can predict human behavior. A new industry has arisen, that of "Jury Consultants," and it is very much committed to the view jury composition matters and that, with effort, and for a fee, it is possible to rig a jury in your favor. Before running out and spending big bucks, let's pause and think.

How important is jury make-up?

No one denies that drunken buffoons and infuriated Prussians will *initially* view the same set of facts differently. The question is whether, after deliberation, different juries would come to different verdicts. In jury deliberations, we burn a hot fire.

> *Juror One: I just don't believe her.*
>
> *Juror Two: Why not?*
>
> *Juror One: Well, you know, she's an immigrant.*
>
> *Juror Two: What!?*

Jurors take their jobs seriously. In law school we all laughed when we read of a judge instructing a jurors to "disregard the previous answer." Well, they do.

Juror One: You remember what the cop said.

Juror Two: Yes, but the judge said we shouldn't consider that. Do you have any other reasons for your position?

Most judges I have talked with are drum majors for juries, particularly when it comes to deciding who is telling the truth, who is liable, and who is guilty. Juries are less good at assessing damages as such assessments are not part of the jurors collective common sense and life experience. Indeed, one commentator has proposed bifurcating damage cases into liability, to be decided by jurors, and damages, to be assessed by a panel of judges.

While there are no doubt some exceptions at the extremes, it would be shocking if different juries would come to different verdicts in terms of liability or guilt. However, it would be almost equally as surprising if, in major cases, different juries would come to identical verdicts in terms of the amount of damages or the degree of guilt. And, as they say, God is in the details. Can we predict which group of jurors will break the bank? Will give the defendant a break with a second degree verdict?

Can we predict human behavior?

Decades ago, President Dwight Eisenhower was walking by the Reflecting Pond on the Washington Mall.

"Look, over there, the Governor of California, Earl Warren. He is swimming, swimming conservatively."

It used to be said that the Devil Himself couldn't see into a person's heart. Now we have experts.

"Watch the body language. If people fold their arms, that means they are rejecting you." Perhaps. But I am doubtful. I have had just too many experiences misreading my students' expressions.

Extreme forms of body language I can read. A cartoon shows the judge asking, "Members of the Jury, have you reached a verdict?" and the foreman holding his tie above and behind his head.

But do the best you can. Ask yourself what kind of a juror you want on your case: Young? Smart? Someone who will likely fall asleep? ("Ladies and Gentlemen of the Jury, you didn't hear the prosecution offer one word of testimony concerning motive.")

One issue to consider is whether you want jurors "like" your client. At first blush it would seem that you obviously would: "like" jurors would empathize. Further, they would see the evidence somewhat differently than would jurors of dissimilar backgrounds.

Susan Glaspell's classic story, *Jury of her Peers*, illustrates both points. Set in rural farm country near the turn of the century, two women, the wives of the Sheriff and the County Prosecutor, sit in the kitchen while the men folk investigate a murder.

The men suspect that the victim's wife is the murderer but cannot think of a motive. Unlike their husbands, the women were able to understand the significance of an empty birdcage: the husband killed the woman's pet bird, her only companion on the lonely prairie, and this was her motive. Not only were the women able to see the evidence from the different perspective, but they also empathized with the wife: they hid the birdcage.

But don't overlearn the lesson. Sometimes women are harder on, and less sympathetic to women and minorities are sometimes much less understanding of minorities.

Some lawyers try to avoid strong personality types. It would be great if they were on your side, but horrible if they are against you. You do not want a one-person jury.

You might pay particular attention to potential jurors who might become the foreperson and this is an important role. Jury studies show that juries are likely to pick, as the foreperson, someone who has previous jury duty.

In exercising your peremptory challenges, the best advice I have heard is to rely upon your *and* your client's gut reactions. Do you like the juror? Feel that the juror will listen to your side?

You should be aware of the constitutional issues lurking in jury selection. For example, *Batson v. Kentucky,* 476 U.S. 79 (1986), held that a black defendant was denied equal protection when the prosecutor used peremptory challenges to remove all blacks from the jury. Other cases have ruled gender discrimination impermissible.

What Do You Want to Ask?

It obviously will not do to ask:

> *"Juror number three. Are you now, or have you ever been, a buffoon?"*

Preparing for jury selection, you will prepare a list of questions to be used, either by you or the judge, during *voir dire*, the questioning of jurors. There are form books on specific questions for specific kinds of cases. Ask yourself, "What might go wrong in deliberations?" and then design questions to head off the difficulties. Prejudice and juror expertise can go wrong.

Prejudice (racial, sexual, ageist, or even occupational) may kill you. You cannot inquire directly, as very few believe themselves prejudiced. Like smog, it can't be seen up close, only far away. You can, however, construct questions that will give you some idea as to the individual's feelings and here your client's reactions to each juror is important: "Do you get a sense that this juror will give you a fair shake?"

Juror expertise may kill you. You want your case decided on the evidence you present, not on a tidbit some juror may come up with.

Recall your first week in law school. Whom did you believe? At Orientation the Dean, and assorted dancing bears (professors), told you what to expect. You didn't believe a word. Then they paraded out some practitioners. You began to listen. Finally, the student representatives. "Well," you said, "maybe there's some truth in what they say." The only person you *really* believed was another first year whom you met in the bathroom who told you about a cousin whose good friend went to law school. I call it, with apologies to half of the class, "the guy at the next urinal" phenomenon.

Realize that, in "we/they," we're the "they." Your case involves forgery by typewriter. A hundred and one experts testify that the two documents were typed on the same machine. In the jury room, the clerk typist looks at the two and slowly shakes his head—"No way."

In preparing for voir dire, anticipate things *you don't want discussed* in the jury room:

> Juror: *Look, the defendant is a big corporation and the plaintiff needs the money.*

> Juror: *Yes, that's what the defendant says. But that nice young policeman was there and he says different, and I always believe what policemen say.*

> Juror: *I just don't think people should be compensated for pain and suffering.*

> Juror: *It's enough for me to convict because he had one drink before getting in the car.*

> Juror: *Why "beyond a reasonable doubt?" Why not "a real strong hunch?"*

You can draft voir dire questions to flag these problems:

> *"The law allows for awards for pain and suffer-ing. Do you have any objection to that?"*

> *"To be found guilty of driving under the influ-ence, the law requires that the driver's ability be impaired by alcohol. It is not enough that the defendant had been drinking. Do you have any quarrel with that law?"*

One of the best voir dire questions I have ever heard was asked by a criminal defense lawyer who prefaced it with a good three minutes talking about the importance of reasonable doubt finishing with:

> *"Juror Number Three, does that about sum up your view?"*

Some lawyers use voir dire, not so much as a way to select the jury, but as the first chance they get to try their case.

> *"If the evidence showed that the defendant hurt my client's arm in pulling him from the burn-ing car, you would not let the fact that he saved his life get in the way of returning a substantial damage award, would you?"*

Mechanics

The mechanics vary greatly, not only by jurisdic-tions but often by courtrooms. In some, the judges do all the voir dire; role of counsel is restricted to presenting written questions. In others, the judge has counsel present their opening arguments to the entire jury panel, before voir dire begins, on the theory that then jurors can more adequately re-spond to the central inquiry: Is there anything about this case or about the participants that would make it difficult for you to be impartial? In some courtrooms you must announce before the jury your strikes, in others, that is done outside of the prospective jury.

I can't figure a good way to get out of this chapter. It is always nice to come around and end where you began, here with something about either Chinese philosophers or goldfish. But I draw a blank. Perhaps something can be made of "jury of peers." Let's see. Maybe, I could have a tomato, about to go on trial, complaining. "I won't get a fair trial. It's a jury of pears."

A drunken buffoon would love it.

CHAPTER 15

PREPARING YOUR WITNESSES

Recall the first time you were called on in law school. You were sitting there quietly enough, minding your own business, thinking about all the fun your high school friends were having, *right then*. Suddenly, you heard your name, followed by "Blah, blah, blah, blah?" A hundred faces turned toward you.

That's what it's like to be a witness.

Only worse. From T.V., people learn that, under clever cross-examination, the traffic accident witness cracks and confesses to murder.

A week or so before the trial, get together with your client and with each of your witnesses to prepare their testimony. You will want to deal with witness anxiety, the appearance of partisanship, and then go over the direct and possible cross.

In General

Don't meet with witnesses together. If you do, it will come out on cross and look like you were up to no good. Witnesses, consciously or unconsciously, will try to make their testimony consistent with that of others: that's when they get in trouble on cross. Further, it hurts, rather than helps, if all the witnesses tell the same identical story. It comes off as rehearsed, or worse.

Anxiety

Reassure your witnesses that everyone gets nervous. Consider taking them to a trial, to observe, or to the courtroom where they will testify. Have them sit in the chair.

Go over the basics: what to wear; when to arrive; and how long they should plan on being there. If it is likely "the rule" will be invoked, tell them that they cannot watch the trial before they testify and, as they sit waiting in the corridor, they cannot discuss what happened in the courtroom with witnesses who have already testified.

Cheerleading

Your witnesses will be rooting for you. However, cheerleaders are suspect. Advise your witnesses to avoid the *appearance of partiality*.

1. Don't *volunteer* information damaging to the other side without being specifically asked:

   Q: *Did you see the collision?*

   A: *Yes I did, and right after the wreck, the defendant jumped out of his car and ran over and kicked a puppy.*

2. Don't *fudge* by making things look a little worse for the enemy, a little better for you.

3. Don't *explain* away information that undermines your testimony.

4. Be *honest*. Juries are very good at spotting phonies.

Tell your witnesses that, if you want the puppy, you'll ask for the puppy. Explain that your case rests on more than their testimony and that it is fine for them to admit to facts even if they think they hurt your case. Underscore that, on cross, they should not conceal nor attempt to explain away information unfavorable to you. If explanations are needed, you will ask for them on redirect.

Attorney/Client privilege

What you tell your *client* concerning testifying is protected by the attorney/client privilege. The *fact* that you discussed the testimony is not. Your discussions with *witnesses* are not protected by attorney/client. If your opponent asks them, "Did you go over this testimony with the lawyer?" they should answer yes. Tell your witnesses it is okay for them to have talked with you concerning their testimony. The traditional advice is, if the other lawyer asks, "What were you told?" your witness should be instructed to say, "I was told to tell the truth."

Preparing for Direct

Discuss the key points of the testimony.

What are the major points you want to cover with the witness? As you are basically telling your client's story, ask your client, what do you want the jury to know? A similar question can be asked of your witnesses. Likely they will bring up matters you overlooked.

Develop sufficient detail to back up those points.

Why it is that the witness is sure the light was green? Recalling the importance of action, did the witness *do* anything that collaborates the testimony?

Discuss the importance of narration and eye contact.

> "The jury will be trying to figure out if you really know what you are saying and if they can trust you. It is better for you to answer my questions in sentences and paragraphs, not just in grunts and nods. Talk to the jury; pick one out in the back and you will talk loud enough. Talk slowly."

Discuss hearsay, speculation and inadmissible evidence.

Lay witnesses can only testify to what they saw, heard, felt, tasted or smelled. They cannot base their testimony on what others have told them nor can they base it on speculation. Explain this to your witnesses. When they testify without getting into objectionable material, likely the judge will allow them more room to narrate.

Be sure to caution them against testifying as to inadmissible evidence. Some witnesses, thinking they are doing you a favor, will blurt it out. If so, the judge might blurt out: "Mistrial!"

Depositions and documents.

Witnesses should read their prior testimony and be familiar with any documents that might come into play.

Note: What you *show* your client and your witnesses to refresh their recollections *may be subject to disclosure*. Many states have rules similar to Federal Rule 612, which provides:

> *[I]f a witness uses a writing to refresh his memory * * * before testifying, if the court in its discretion determines it is necessary in the interests of justice, an adverse party is entitled to have the writing produced at the hearing, to inspect it, to cross-examine the witness thereon, and to introduce those portions which relate to the testimony of the witness.*

A routine question on cross-examination: "In preparing for your testimony today, did you read over any writings?" (Disclosure of the writing, however, may conflict with work product or attorney-client privilege. If the matter looms large, do some research first.)

Roleplaying direct.

Roleplay at least some questions, if simply to allow the witness to get a feel for the format and to allow you to get a sense of how the witness answers questions. Does the witness speak too quickly? Too softly?

If you are going to have the witness conduct a demonstration, or use a chart, then rehearsals are mandatory.

Rehearse, but not too much.

Witnesses who appear coached, or who have memorized their lines, won't impress. An occasional spontaneous question might do wonders. By and large, people do better answering questions than they do trying to recall previous answers.

Preparing for Cross

Knowing *what* is one thing, knowing *how* quite another.

> *"Listen to the question you are asked, be sure you understand it, answer only the question and don't volunteer information."*
>
> *"Sure. No problem."*

Roleplay!

Having another lawyer do it is probably best; it adds realism and allows you to observe what happens.

> Does the witness *listen carefully* to the question?
>
> *Pause* before answering?
>
> Answer *only* the question and not volunteer?

Deal with *why* a witness will be tempted to volunteer or to explain away. Remind your witnesses that the opposing lawyer is *not* their friend and will *never* be convinced by what they say. Warn of the *dangers* of volunteering and explaining away: the opposing lawyer will follow up with more questions and lawyers generally win. Finally, reassure the witness that you will have redirect and the witness can volunteer or explain away then if it's needed.

Dealing with routine attacks and methods.

Has the witness said anything, or written anything, inconsistent with current testimony? If so, warn the witness of impeachment on this basis, get an explanation of the inconsistency, and remember it is safer to have the explanation come on redirect, not during cross.

Along similar lines, discuss possible impeachment for bias and how to respond to it.

Advise as to the dangers of answering a series of questions yes or no: the opposition is out to confuse, and that it is perfectly proper for a witness to explain an answer if yes or no would be misleading.

Tell the witness that it is fine to pause and think before answering. Explain that, while it may feel like a long time, it won't seem that way to others.

Objections.

> *"If I object, stop talking. Sometimes I will object only to slow things down if I think you are getting in trouble. Think and slow down."*

Where to look.

Advise the witness *not to look at you* when asked a difficult question. It smacks of coaching. Conversely, if the witness feels that he is getting in trouble, the witness *should not look at the opposing lawyer*. Lawyers can be intimidating. Stress that cross-examination is *not* a *conversation* between the lawyer and the witness. Breaking eye contact breaks this mode and allows for reflection. As in direct, it is best to look at the jury; if not, at the back of the room.

CHAPTER 16

REFRESHING RECOLLECTION; EVASIVE WITNESSES; PRIOR STATEMENTS

This chapter basically lays out how to deal with problem witnesses, your witnesses who freeze up on the stand, and opposition witnesses who are evasive or change their testimony. The next chapter, on Objections, can provide a quick review of that topic.

Refreshing Recollection

Despite your efforts at preparing them, some of your witnesses simply go berserk. If so, break out of role, stop asking questions, and *talk* to the witness.

Nervous witness: "Now everyone gets nervous testifying for the first time. We all understand. Just take your time."

Cool witness: "Take off those sunglasses."

Unclear witness: "I think the jury is having a hard time following. Slow down."

Run-on witness (cutting off): "That's enough. I believe you answered my question." (Or, "Who asked you to testify anyway?")

If one of your witnesses forgets on the stand, one option is to *ask leading questions*. A generally recognized exception to the prohibition against leading on direct is in the case of the forgetful witness. You must lay a sufficient foundation showing that he does not recall by asking non-leading questions.

You should also be familiar with how to *refresh recollection* with a writing.

1. Lay a foundation that shows the witness cannot remember. Ask for the information several ways, concluding "Then I take it you cannot recall what happened on the 17th?"

2. Have the writing marked for purposes of identification. The writing can be anything: a deposition, a newspapers story, even a napkin. In fact, it need not be a writing at all; it can be an object, such as a toe.

3. You must show the item to your opponent before approaching the witness." Your Honor, let the record reflect that I am showing opposing counsel what is marked as plaintiff's number two for identification."

4. Ask permission to approach the witness.

5. *"Mr. Witness, I hand you plaintiff's number two for identification and ask you to read it to yourself to see if it refreshes your recollection of the events."*

Now you have two choices: the right way and the ever popular wrong way.

    6.   The *wrong* way:

> Q: *Tell us what happened on the 17th.* Or, even worse:

> Q: *Read what it says.*

The document is hearsay and, unless otherwise admissible, say as a business record, it is not admissible. The only reason the witness can *silently* read it is to help refresh recollection.

    6.   The *right* way:

> *Take* the writing from the witness.

> Q: *Having read that, do you now have a current recollection of what happened on the 17th?*

> A: *Yes.*

> Q: *Tell us what happened on the 17th.*

At this point your opponent can take the witness on *voir dire* to test whether the witness actually recalls the 17th or is about to merely testify as to what is written. If the latter, it is inadmissible hearsay.

To the chagrin of law professors everywhere, many judges simply let the witness read what is written. This is particularly true in the case of police officers. They are often allowed to keep their reports with them and refer to them during their testimony.

If this is happening to you, for shame! Object! Don't let the witness keep the document.

Evasive Witnesses

Like law students on exams, witnesses on cross like to answer *their* questions, not yours. Here is a quick review of your options.

The essential thing is to *look* at the witness and *listen* to the response. (Not look at your note pad and rehearse your next question.) Has the witness answered your question?

> Q: *Now isn't it a fact, Dish, that you ran away with the spoon?*
>
> A: *The times were out of joint. The cow had just jumped over the moon.*
>
> Q: *Your Honor, would you instruct the witness to answer "yes" or "no?"*

Remember that *you don't have to* control the evasive witness. Evasive witnesses lose credibility. Explanations confirm the need to explain and ducking questions suggests there is something to hide. Perhaps, instead of cutting the witness off, asking for admonishments, and pulling your hair, it might be best to let the witness explain, explain, explain.

Most judges will *not* instruct witnesses to answer "yes" or "no" and will allow them considerable leeway in explaining their answers. So leading questions don't always control the witness; they can pop out. What's to be done?

Repeat, and, if necessary, repeat your question.

> *Q: That wasn't what I asked you. I asked you*
> *if you ran away with the spoon.*

An alternative, *before* repeating the main question, is to pursue the deflection. Often the witness, sensing trouble, made it up on the run and will be unable to maintain it in the face of pursing questions.

If you anticipate evasion, you can try to deal with it before you get it. Some lawyers control evasive witnesses through fear. They begin their cross, cross. Win a few rounds early on and the witness will likely be less evasive and more willing to answer the questions. There are costs to instant aggressiveness. Jurors resent bullies. And, as one of your goals is to use adverse witnesses to develop good material for your case, if you have bloodied the witness early on, you might not get the time of day.

> *Q: What time of day is it?*
>
> *A: I know, but I wouldn't give it to you.*

Another approach is to *close the doors* on the witness. Basically you try to anticipate the possible escape routes and close them off before the witness realizes the need to flee.

Bluffs can work. Convince the witness that you can easily expose any fabrication or exaggeration. Your psychological state is key. Project confidence.

While mixing metaphors is frowned upon, changing children's stories is not, particularly if they have a common element, say the moon.

> *Q:*   *Isn't it a fact, that in the great green room, there is a picture of three little bears, sitting in chairs.*
>
> *A:*   *Yes*
>
> *Q:*   *And a comb and a brush and a bowl full of mush?*
>
> *A:*   *Yes.*
>
> *Q:*   *And a quiet old lady whispering?*
>
> *A:*   *Yes.*
>
> *Q:*   *Now, tell the jury, what was she whispering?*

The initial questions alert the witness: "I've been in that room. I love that room. I know what I'm talking about. Mess with me and it's Goodnight, Witness."

Impeaching with prior statements

Overrated.

Jurors realize, as we did before law school, that people describe events differently on different occasions and that memories are never constant. In fact, inconsistency can be argued as a test of truth:

> *Ladies and Gentlemen of the Jury, we know that the witness was telling the truth because he told it as he remembered it, even though he knew that he had made somewhat inconsistent statements before. If he was lying, he would have told you exactly what he said during his deposition.*

Impeach with inconsistencies *only* if it will help; don't do it simply because you know how. Generally the inconsistencies should be sharp and should be material.

A major problem is *retrieval*. In the heat of battle, don't count on remembering where you can find the inconsistent statement. For each witness you are to cross, make a list of the key points you want to develop and the key points they will hurt you with. Next to each point, indicate where you can find the statement you expect them to make.

When witnesses testify differently, don't assume they are lying. More likely they are confused or mistaken. A gentle, rather than accusatory approach, might result in "You're right. What I said before is correct. Sorry."

Tom Mauet, in *Fundamentals of Trial Advocacy*, suggests a three part approach: recommit, build up, and contrast.

Recommit:

> Q: *On direct you testified that the Joel Segielman did not attend the meeting of October 30, isn't that right?*

Build up:

> Q: *Do you recall giving a deposition in this matter at my office on August 3rd?*

> Q: *And, as that was closer in time, your memory of events would probably be better?*

> Q: *You swore to tell the truth at that deposition and you did tell the truth?*

Q: At the beginning of the deposition, didn't I
tell you if you didn't understand a question
not to answer it but ask me to explain?

Contrast:

Q: (aside to counsel): I am reading from page
20, the first several lines. Do you remember
my asking you (reading from transcript)
"Who was at the meeting on October 30?"

Q: Do you remember answering "Well, Kay
Kavanagh was there and Joel Segielman"?

It is better for you to read the inconsistent statement than having the witness do it. Likely they will
fumble around and muck it up.

Computers can play an impressive role in all of
this. First, you can download the transcripts of
depositions in your Notebook and access the prior
testimony with a search function. You can then
flash the exact testimony on the monitor. If you
have really big bucks, and have video taped the
deposition, you can have transcript calibrated with
the video so that, by highlighting the relevant portion of the transcript, you can play back the actual
witness statement.

Prior *oral* statements are more tricky. They are
more likely to be denied. You must still set them up
by reminding the witness of the time, place and
circumstances of the prior statement.

Q: Do you recall talking with Helen Doucet
about this matter on August 3rd?

> *Q: Didn't you tell her that Joel was at the meeting?*

If the witness *denies* the prior statement, then, as long as it is material, you can prove it up by calling Ms. Doucet.

If the witness *admits* the prior inconsistent statement, then that's pretty much it. You can't prove up the prior statement because it is admitted. Questions like "Are you lying now or were you lying then?" are clearly argumentative.

You might want to ask the witness to explain the inconsistency but this can be risky. Always remember that you have closing argument to argue its significance.

CHAPTER 17

OBJECTIONS

This chapter deals with when you should make objections, how to respond when your opponent does, and finally gives a quick overview of the most common ones. Before that, a quick point of admissibility versus weight.

An Aside: Admissibility v. weight

This is a key concept: the fact that evidence is admitted, does not mean that it is going to be believed. Say your opponent has called an expert who has questionable qualifications. Before the substance of the expert's testimony can be admitted, your opponent must lay the proper foundation: that the expert is qualified. If you wish, after your opponent has examined as to qualifications, you can ask to *take the witness on voir dire* in order to show that the person isn't that well qualified. If you prevail, the testimony will *not* be admitted. On the other hand, if you think the testimony will be admitted, you can wait until cross to attack the expert's qualifications, in essence showing that the testimony should not be believed.

When (and When Not) to Make Them

The worst reason to object is because you can.

The clearest case to object is when the evidence *hurts* you *and* you have a realistic chance of keeping it *out*. Testimony resting on hearsay and testimony that rests on speculation are the best examples. Win these objections, and the jury never hears the testimony.

Don't object just to make a nuisance of yourself. The evidence will eventually come in, probably in a stronger fashion, and the jury will conclude that it *must* be important because you fought to keep it out. That, and that you're a show-off.

Take *leading*. If you believe that your opponent is suggesting answers that he *cannot* get by proper questioning, object. However, if he *can* get the same answer by proper questioning and he is leading because he is sloppy, sit there. He's telling the story, not his witness. However, if you think the witness may mess up if left to testify without being lead, object.

Take *lack of foundation*. If you suspect that the witness' testimony relies on hearsay or speculation, object. If you know the witness has an adequate basis for the testimony, sit there. Object and your opponent builds a pyramid. Without an adequate foundation, testimony is suspect: "Sure, that's what the witness said, but how does she know?

Objections can serve purposes other than keeping out evidence. Sometimes they are a method of communicating with the jury.

"Your Honor, I object, counsel is being argumentative."

> *"Objection, your Honor, counsel is assuming facts not in evidence."*

> *"Your Honor, I object, counsel is misstating evidence."*

Sometimes objections are made in order to slow up your opponent in order to give the witness time to think.

> *"Your Honor, I fail to see the relevancy of this line of questioning."*

> *"Your Honor, would counsel allow the witness to answer the question?"*

In short, don't object because it is there; only object if you have a good reason. On the other hand, *don't fail to object* because you can't think of a category. The comedian Shelley Berman pointed out that, getting on a plane, most of us would like to ask what to do in the event of a crash. But we don't: "We would rather be dead than look foolish."

So it is with lawyers. Listening to their opponent examine the witness, in their bones they know that the opponent is doing something objectionable, indeed, something despicable. "But what is the category? What is the precise objection? And what if I am wrong?" Law school all over again.

My mentor, Gary Bellow, in his *first* trial, objected:

> *"I object, your Honor, I have never seen a lawyer do any such thing."*

> *"Neither have I. Sustained."*

There are two kinds of people: those who will not do anything unless they are sure it is permissible and those who will do anything unless they know it is prohibited. Gary was in the latter category and was the best lawyer I have known.

But I digress.

If you feel something is improper, object. What if you don't know the legal grounds? Tell the Judge what you find objectionable:

> *"Your Honor, I object, counsel is being overly dramatic."*

> *"Your Honor, I object, counsel is testifying."*

We are not dealing with precise legal categories at all. For example, the Federal Rules do not define nor mention such objections as "compound question," "asked and answered," "non-responsive," "argumentative." Rather, Rule 611 simply gives the judge the power:

> *"to exercise reasonable control over the mode and order of interrogating witnesses and presenting evidence so as to (1) make the interrogation and presentation effective for the ascertainment of the truth, (2) avoid needless consumption of time, and (3) protect witnesses from harassment or undue embarrassment."*

Traditional objections are justified under this broad language and they are not exhaustive. An overly dramatic attorney may be getting in the way of the "ascertainment of the truth."

Many lawyers find it useful to have a list of common objections at counsel table. Generally it is not enough to puff up like a peacock and shout "Objection!" To preserve your right to appeal an adverse ruling, you may have to state your grounds for objection.

Stand when you make an objection. This will endear you to the court at a time when you need it most. It will also divert the attention of the witness who might actually shut up.

Responding to Objections

Some lawyers assume that their opponent is correct and go on to the next question, often without awaiting a ruling by the judge. This stampede results in the omission of important testimony and forecloses any right to appeal. To preserve your right to appeal, you must first get the judge to rule on the objection. This may not be as easy as it seems. Your opponent objects and the judge nods. Nothing goes on the record. "Your Honor, are you sustaining my opponent's objection?" Experienced trial judges will, at this point, nod vigorously.

Once you have the ruling on the record, generally it is also required that you make an offer of proof as the substance of the excluded testimony.

Opponent: I object.

Court: Sustained.

You: Your Honor, I would like to make an offer of proof.

> *Court: Counsel for both sides, approach the bench.*
>
> *You:* (Softly so the jury won't hear) *Your Honor, this witness will testify to X.*

Don't be stampeded when your opponent objects. On the other hand, don't automatically assume that your opponent is wrong and begin to argue. (If you are to argue, remember, that the argument is *to* the judge, not *between* counsel; talk to the judge, not to your opponent.) When your opponent objects, it is best to rephrase the question if you can; if you can't, then argue the objection.

One common problem in rephrasing the question is that you may not understand the grounds for the objection. For example, you are merrily examining a witness when suddenly your opponent screams:

> *"Objection, lack of foundation."*
>
> *"Sustained."*

You have no idea what they are talking about. Before admitting ignorance, try smoking them out, "Your Honor, I think there is sufficient foundation. Would opposing counsel be more explicit in indicating in what ways the foundation is lacking?" If your opponent stonewalls it—"I'm not going to try your case for you"—you probably have no choice but to ask for a recess to go look up the law. Best for you to make a fool of yourself than let your client die.

Thirty Second Evidence Course

The most common objections are hearsay, irrelevant, lack of foundation, speculation and argumentative. You should have a good feel for these objections in addition to those that go to the form of the question, such as leading, calls for a narrative, or is compound.

Hearsay.

"I heard," "I read," "Everyone knows," "He said," and even "*I* said" should put you on alert. Hearsay is a statement (a) made out of court and (b) offered for the truth: If so, you need an exception. When your adversary's witnesses are testifying, ask yourself: "How do they *know*?" Did they see the sky was falling, or have they been talking to Chicken Little?

Irrelevant.

Does the testimony make more or less probable a fact at issue? Admitting irrelevant evidence is no great sin, it just takes time and perhaps creates confusion. The objection is often used as a ploy to alert a witness on cross that those innocent questions he is being asked aren't quite so innocent. The response: "Your Honor, I will tie up in a few more questions." If sustained: "Your Honor, I would like to make an offer of proof."

No foundation.

In the case of *regular witnesses*, before they can testify to what they saw, heard, touched, tasted or smelled, it must be shown that they were in a position to see, hear, touch, taste or smell. If he is to testify that the car ran the red light, you need to determine the following: was he at the scene? Did he see the car enter the intersection? Did he see the color of the light? If the witness is testifying to an *expert opinion*, the foundation required is his qualification and the need for expert opinion in the case. As to a *document*, has it been authenticated? *Miranda* is the foundation for criminal confessions. In responding to a "no foundation" objection, ask yourself, "What does the law require me to prove before I can get to where I am?"

Speculation.

From a lay witness, anything that begins "I think," "I feel," or "It seems to me" is suspect. Generally lay witnesses can testify only in the language of perception—"I saw, heard, felt, tasted and touched." Again, *lack of foundation* objection can flush out speculation: "The sky was falling because everyone was running."

There is one exception which allows lay witnesses to offer opinions:

> *If the witness is not testifying as an expert, his testimony in the form of opinions or inferences is limited to those opinions or inferences which are (a) rationally based on the perception of the witness and (b) helpful to a clear understanding of the witness' testimony or the determination of a fact in issue. Federal Rules of Evidence 701.*

In the case of experts, make sure the opinion to be offered is one which will "assist the trier of fact to understand the evidence or to determine a fact in issue." If the jurors can figure things out themselves, expert testimony is objectionable.

Argumentative.

    Q: You expect the jury to believe that?

    Q: Are you lying now or were you lying then?

    Q: Does your grandmother wear cowboy boots?

Asked and answered.

Your opponent can't ask the same question again and again to stress the answer. Of course, on cross you can ask questions already answered on direct and on direct you can repeat some questions in order to go back and pick up a line of inquiry.

"Disgusting."

Best to think of a better buzz word. The Federal Rule:

> *Although relevant, evidence may be excluded if its probative value is substantially outweighed by the danger of unfair prejudice, confusion of issues, or misleading the jury, or by considerations of undue delay, waste of time, or needless presentation of cumulative evidence." (Rule 403).*

Leading questions.

Does the question suggest to the witness how he should answer? This can occur by either a statement followed by "isn't that right?" or a question which supplies key facts with no explicit suggestion as to how to answer. The latter is leading as it suggests the key facts.

Questions calling for a narrative.

A question should be specific enough to tell the witness—and your opponent—the general contours of what you want.

"Immediately after the robbers entered the store, what did they do?" The idea is that your opponent should know enough about what's coming so that she can interpose an objection before it gets out.

Compound questions

Questions which put in play more than one fact.

"This chapter was a very helpful review of objections but you are happy to be done with it, isn't that correct?"

CHAPTER 18

A CHECKLIST AND REVIEW

In an ideal world (one where professors, *writing* about litigation, dwell) you will finish with your trial preparation a day or two ahead. This will give you time to get a sense of the forest and to take a close, critical look at some of the trees. This checklist will help.

You can also use this checklist to review some of the more important points we have covered. It doesn't include them all but it does include a lot of them.

Overall

Do you have a good *working* knowledge of *leading* questions and *non-leading*, yet not vague, questions? Are you familiar with the importance of silence in focusing attention? How will you make sure you listen to the answers?

Do you tell an effective story?

Will the jury identify with your client and see the events from that perspective?

Have you taken adequate steps to assure that the jury, who has no prior knowledge of the conflict, can follow it? Will you use repetition to aid memory?

Will your story be believed? Do you include enough detail? Things witnesses *did*?

Are there ways to make it more dramatic? Suspense? Confrontation?

Can demonstrative evidence (charts, documents, re-enactments, computer use) improve the clarity and believability of your case?

As to the order you are calling your witnesses and presenting your evidence, why? Do you effectively use primacy and recency?

Jury Selection

Have you thought about the kind of jurors you want?

Will you involve your client in deciding on the preempts?

Do you have voir dire questions that will flag things you don't want discussed in the jury room, *i.e.* "I don't believe in pain and suffering."

Opening Statement

Do you have a simple theme, perhaps employing the Rule of Three?

Do you have an effective opening riff and dynamite closing one?

Is your goal to give a clear road map or focus on specific key issues?

How do you handle the issue of clarity versus suspense?

Do you avoid promising too much and do you avoid argument?

Does anything you say risk "opening the doors?" (Opening the door is the advocate's worst nightmare, except, of course, the one about being eaten by a dinosaur.)

Could your opening be improved by charts or PowerPoint?

Will you direct your remarks to the entire panel or focus on who you think will be the key jurors?

Will you talk slow enough and avoid big words? Will your tone be conversational?

Will you try to "draw the sting?"

Your Witnesses

Have you met with them to discuss anxiety, the prohibitions against hearsay and speculation, the problems they may face on cross, and to warn them against being too partisan? Have you told them of the importance of redirect? Have you warned them against blurting something out that may trigger opening the doors or cause a mistrial?

Have your witnesses reviewed prior testimony or writings that they may be impeached with?

How are you going to get your witnesses comfortable on the stand? How will you step back in order to allow your witnesses to testify?

Do you know the correct procedure of refreshing recollection?

Does the order of your questions make the most sense? You need not go chronologically and your first and last questions are key.

Have you considered drama as well as clarity?

Do you effectively personalize your witnesses?

Do you lay adequate foundations for their testimony (even if you can get away with not doing so)?

Remember that details and beliefs confirmed by *actions* create belief.

Will you draw the sting?

Would demonstrative evidence help?

As to *each* witness, what objections do you anticipate that your opponent will make? How will your respond?

Do any evidence problems jump out? If so, write a memo in support of your position, *citing* a controlling *case* or *statute*. Don't wing it; be prepared with the law. Judges take their jobs seriously.

Does any of the testimony risk opening the doors?

As to your opponent's witnesses

While opposing a direct, your most common *objections* will be hearsay, speculation, lack of foundation, and leading. Do you know when you should, and when you should not, object?

If you think some of your opponent's evidence will trigger tricky evidence problems, do you have a memo supporting your position?

As to each, will you cross-examine? If so, why? What will be your tone, friendly, hostile, or both?

Do you think you opponent will try to draw the sting? If this happens, how will you respond?

Can you elicit information from the opposing witnesses that will help your case?

Can you limit the thrust of their testimony by underscoring what wasn't said?

If you are attacking the witness, is your theory mistake or perjury?

If you are attacking the story, will you try to establish inconsistent details, take on the testimony directly by seeking bedrock, or try to confuse the witness with slash and burn?

Can you give a good reason to justify the order of your questions?

As to each witness, what will be your tone, and why?

What will you do if the witness is evasive?

Have you read the prior statements and depositions given by the witness? Are you familiar with the procedure to impeach with a prior inconsistent statement?

Closing argument

Is your overall structure the best? Why do you discuss the points in the order you do?

Are you open to the possibility of changing the order in light of evidence you did not foresee or in light of what your opponent said during opening or closing?

Is your goal to marshal the evidence or to give the jurors a new way to think about it?

Do you focus on the key material and not waste time on minor details?

Have you considered the issue of leading with the conclusions you want the jury to reach as opposed to building towards them?

Are you being too candid? Too contentious?

Do you supply arguments, and stake out positions (sometimes in somewhat extreme form), so that your allies on the jury will have an easier time of it?

Do you make use of the *extremism bias*?

Will you direct your arguments to all the jurors or just a few?

Are you making arguments you don't believe in? Should you?

Are you anticipating attacks on your position? Should you?

Are you arguing specific facts or vague abstractions?

Are your metaphors fresh? Do your analogies work? Are your stock arguments flawed?

Do you use IRS transitions between your points so that the jury will understand the relationship between the points: "and" or "or"?

Are you clear on how each point fits? If you aren't being explicit in your argument, do you have a good reason not to be?

Can your argument be improved with visuals?

Consider charts, diagrams, exhibits, and computer devices such as Power Point. They will enliven your presentation and make it more effective. Remember what Alice said: *"What's the good of a book without pictures?"*

Do you run the risk of misstating evidence? Of putting yourself at issue? Is your argument overly emotional so as to draw an objection or alienate jurors?

Do you return to your theme? Do you have a great opening line?

"My client awoke to find himself turned into a giant cockroach."

Do you have a great closer?

"All my client wanted to be was a good dog."

Don't leave these critical moments, the first and last thing you say, to the creative moment. Without a clear and rehearsed exit, you will stumble around, waiting for a flash that never comes, and will ultimately limp off.

"That's all, folks!"

CHAPTER 19

CLIENT INTERVIEWING

"Hi, this is your lawyer. Got a few minutes? In our first interview, I forgot to ask you a few questions."

"Hi, this is your lawyer. Got a few minutes? In our first interview, I forgot to build rapport."

In all the things you want to accomplish in your first interview, don't forget rapport. You'll be working with this person for a long time, on important matters, and mutual trust and understanding will be central. You need to know at least a little of the person, as a person, in addition to as a client, and the client should know at least a little of you, as a person, in addition to as a lawyer.

While a "building rapport" segment is somewhat artificial, a little chatting, sometime during the interview, about common interests and backgrounds would be nice. Other ways to build rapport are showing empathy and understanding, being non-judgmental, maintaining eye contact, listening and being enthusiastic.

Keeping rapport means returning telephone calls, even if to say nothing is happening, and keeping the client updated.

One good way to think about the first interview is in terms of teaching. The client has things to teach you and you have things to teach the client. What are the lessons? What is the best way to teach them and what will get in the way?

What do you need to know about your clients' situation?

> What their problems are and how they affect their lives; what they think caused the situation and how they would like it resolved; and, finally, the bad stuff. How to get them to tell you all of this? Get them to narrate.

What do you have to teach your clients?

> Put yourself in their position. Will they have questions about the interview itself? They will surely have questions about their legal situation and what happens next. Here you face the dilemma of early (and, possibly, inaccurate) reassurance versus stony professional non-commitment.

Let's begin with the clients' side. First a further discussion of what you need to learn from them, then a discussion of the need of client narration, the things that can shut it down and the thing that can encourage it, active listening.

Clients as Teachers

Five Easy Questions

Doctors face a difficult time treating patients from other parts of the world. Concepts of disease, of cause, and of cure may not match. The result can be tragic: pills not taken, symptoms not revealed, and, surely as important, neither side forced to reconsider their assumptions and to rethink their methods. (For a terrific non-fiction book describing one such incident, see Anne Fadiman, *The Spirit Catches You and You Fall Down*.)

Doctors must adjust the treatment to the patient. Arthur Kleinman, a psychiatrist and medical anthropologist at the Harvard Medical School, developed a list of questions designed to allow patients to *educate* physicians as to how they view disease and treatment. These questions focus on four concerns: how the patient views the disease, what the patient believes caused the disease, how the patient thinks the disease should be treated, and, finally, what it means to be cured.

What does the plight of doctors in far-off jungles have to do with us in our spiffy offices? As a lawyer, you bring categories of thought (landlord/tenant, tort, due process), and a particular sense of relevancy, honed by three years of law school ("Mr. Lane, we really *don't* care what your grandmother said!"). "Thinking like a lawyer," you have a general approach to solving problems and a concept of a "good outcome." All of which is inevitable and fine; the only problem is that your categories and approaches might not match those of your client.

A divorced father living with his two small children in an apartment is served with an Eviction Notice. He comes to your office. It is obvious that his problem is the Eviction Notice; it is obvious that the solution is legal research and negotiation; and it is obvious that the best outcome is to defeat the eviction.

Obvious to *us*. But what about to *him*?

Drawing on the work done in the field of cross-cultural medicine, I recommend five kinds of questions that will help you represent your actual client rather than the client you assume you have.

1.   How does the client *define* the problem?

What do you see as your problem? How will it affect you? What do you fear most?

The fact that the problem fits neatly into one of our categories, doesn't mean that it is the root concern of our client. Maybe the response will be "Getting evicted," but maybe not: "I'm worried about the kids having to change schools," or "I'm worried if I lose the apartment I'll lose custody."

2. What does the client think *caused* the problem?

What do you think caused the problem? Why do you think it started when it did?

While we see "Nonpayment of rent," our client may see more fundamental causes: "I lost my job," or "One of the kid's needed braces," or "I lost the money at the casino."

Note that it might be important to distinguish between long-term causes and immediate triggering events.

3.   How does the client think the problem can be *solved?*

How do you think we can deal with this problem?

It is important to enlist the client in thinking of solutions. They may have better ideas than do you. (They aren't even *in* the box.)

4.   What are the client's *goals*?

What would be a good outcome?

Often clients will not have thought this through. Although goals might change during the course of the representation, get a good feel at the beginning where you want to go.

5.   What are the *weaknesses* in the client's position?

What will the other side say about this?

Clients aren't anxious to disclose unfavorable information, information that is critical. Rephrase: "In what ways are you a rat?" A similar question is *not* on the medical list: physicians, as opposed to medical researchers, really aren't interested in hearing bacteria's, or, indeed, the rat's, side.

Encourage your clients to teach you how they see the problem and how it impacts their life, let them talk to you about their take on causes and solutions, and help them consider their goals and to divulge harmful material. If you do, you will see their situation as do they and you won't end up treating the wrong disease, or prescribing the wrong pills.

Further you will be able to test the validly of your own assumptions and categories.

Of course, none of this will work if your clients clam up.

The Importance of Narration

Where's Poppa? a movie from the Vietnam War era, featured a criminal assault trial. The defendant was an anti-war activist and had confronted the victim, a general, on the beach at Santa Monica. The defendant's lawyer assumed that, after a few angry words about the war, at worst his client kicked some sand in the general's face.

> *Q:* *(by the prosecutor) Now, General, after the few angry words and after the sand-kicking incident, did the defendant do anything else?*

> *A:* *Yes. He bit off my toe.*

Shocked defense lawyer turns to his client and urgently whispers, *"Did you bite off his toe?"*

"Yes."

"Why didn't you tell me?"

"You didn't ask."

We can't fault the lawyer for not asking: "Did you happen to bite off his toe?" One could ask a thousand specific questions without thinking of that one. What we can fault the lawyer for, however, is not allowing the client to narrate:

"OK, you saw the general on the beach and walked over to him. Tell me everything that happened after that."

Ask too many *specific* questions, you'll *never* get the full story. The root problem is that, once you get a whiff of a legal issue, you will want to take command, like a doctor treating the first symptom. Specific questions are important *once* you know the client's concept of the problem. Checklists, on such topics as "Divorce," "Bankruptcy," "Impeachment," can help elicit significant facts that might otherwise go unnoticed; however, specific questions, asked too soon, sink the interview into a swamp of specifics, trees without forests.

Your goal is to get your client to talk, not to answer your insightful questions. *Make motivational statements* and then *shut up* and *listen*.

"During the first part of the interview, I won't ask many questions. It is important that you tell me all about your problem."

"Good, that's exactly the kind of information I need." "You're doing fine."

Obstacles to Narration

In addition to the urge to treat the first symptom mentioned, several factors contribute to premature questioning which cuts off narration. First, as professionals, we are supposed to "be in charge" and just sitting there sure doesn't feel like it. Asking questions makes us the ringmaster: we set the agenda and force the client into the subservient position of responding. Thinking that clients expect us to run things, we do. But do they?

Impatience plays a role. Clients tend to ramble; they even tell us what their grandmothers had to say. We like neat tales, not *Ulysses*. A landlord-tenant problem becomes a debtor-creditor problem, explodes into a domestic problem, and slowly filters down into an employment problem. Then, "My son was arrested last night."

Some clients seek help without a clear understanding of their problem. They require time and space to sort things out. "Rambling" is not insanity; it's problem development.

Discomfort with *silence* can trigger inappropriate questions. When a client falls silent, *think* before jumping in. Perhaps the client has nothing more to say on the topic, and if so, something from you is appropriate. However, the silence may mean that the client has seen a relationship between something just said and something else. Maybe the client is sorting this out and perhaps deciding whether or not to reveal further information. The compulsion to ask a question, to raise the noise level, may well destroy something important. (One way to avoid embarrassment is to position the chairs at a slight angle to allow graceful glances away.)

If the client remains silent, before asking the next question, "Was there anything else you wanted to say about that?"

Finally, there are some subtle factors at work, factors that may cause us to change the subject, either by asking a specific, diverting question, or by body language that suggests certain topics are inappropriate. Our *desire to win* might direct a narration away from unwanted materials, and our *fear of emotion* may abort a complete description of the problem.

Enough about you. What breaks the narrative flow on the *clients' side*?

Consider the *threatening nature of the material*. Not all injuries are "polite," and not all activities are "respectable." If this is the cause of hesitation, meet it head on:

> *"Many people feel uncomfortable talking about the extent and kind of their injuries. But it really is important that I get a total picture of what happened and I have heard it all."*

> *"I'm on your side, and I will stay on your side even if you have done something stupid."*

Active Listening

Several years ago there was an educational film designed to show differing counseling techniques. Four leading psychologists separately interviewed the same patient. The first three were very good and offered scads and scads of insight. Then came Carl Rogers, the founder of non-directive counseling. Carl just sat there. No insights. No advice. Every now and then, after the client said something like, "I'm concerned about my daughter," he would say, "You're concerned about your daughter."

Nothing easier. Nothing more powerful. Within a very short period of time the patient got to a much deeper level of personal insight than she had previously. Just sitting there, just keeping the ball in the client's court, just filling some silences by simply reflecting back what the client just said, Carl was able to do what the profound insights and good advice of the others could not. He allowed the patient to think through her situation, to have her own insights.

The technique is known as *active listening*. It is easy to describe but difficult to do. Thomas Shaffer in *Legal Interviewing and Counseling* describes it: when the other person pauses, you say *"You are saying THIS about THAT."*

> *"Let him correct you if your reflection is wrong. Try to get into the feeling behind what he says; make them your own. Make the words your own; reflect what he means, in your words."*

Reflecting back what the client said assures you understood it correctly. It becomes a test that is corrected immediately. What else can be said for the technique?

1. It prevents you from jumping in with a question and thus closing down or redirecting your client's thought development. It is akin to nonjudgmental, non-directive grunts, silences, and comments such as "I see," "Tell me more," and "Go ahead." But it is better than these devices that, unlike

active listening, can be done while sleeping (and it may seem that way to your client).

2. Active listening quickly builds rapport. It is overwhelming to be listened to: not replied to, not graded, not contradicted, not patted, just listened to.

3. Active listening can get you off the hot seat. We may panic when a client asks, "How will I take care of the kids?" I used to think that if I acknowledged the problem I had to solve it. I kept my head down and asked the next question. But there is no rule that you must solve every problem your client mentions; you can acknowledge problems without committing yourself to their solution. Simply reflect the problem back: "You are concerned about the children." Active listening allows you to acknowledge the problem while not taking responsibility for its solution. Responsibility stays with the client.

4. Active listening encourages feelings. By reflecting back feelings, you are telling the client that it is proper to discuss feelings in a law office.

Ay, there's the rub.

Some lawyers fear emotion. "I'm a hard-headed, nail-chewing problem-solver; none of that soft fluffy stuff for me."

As to the fear of the expression of emotion, take solace in the well-known fact that a tear does not lead to total breakdown and suicidal behavior. *Necessarily*. You can usually ride out tears and blood-oaths. As to the dichotomy between legal problems and emotional problems, of course there is none. Probably the most important things for you to know are how your client *feels* about the situation, how the client *feels* about the opponent, and how the client *feels* about various legal alternatives.

As I said at the top, active listening is easy to describe, hard to do. *Practice*.

An Exercise

Ask a friend to spend 15 minutes describing a family, school, or work problem. Just sit there. When the person pauses, just reflect back what was said. Don't offer judgment ("I agree with that"); don't ask specific questions ("What did he say then?"); and don't shift the flow to your liking ("On, that's interesting. Tell me more.").

"You are saying THIS about THAT."

Lawyer as Teacher

Before your client gets there, ask yourself two questions:

"What will this client want to know?"

"What should this client know?"

Opening Subjects

Assume the client is a first time caller.

1. How long will the interview last?

2. Will I have to pay for it?

3. Am I committing myself to hiring this lawyer?

4. Will the lawyer gossip?

5. Will there be an old *Time* magazine to read?

Address these concerns:

> *Let me tell you something about the interview before we begin. We have about 30 minutes and there is no charge for it. One of the things we will have to decide at the end is if you need a lawyer. If you do, you can hire me or go elsewhere. I encourage clients to shop around.* [This openness usually assures that the clients will not shop around.] *We will discuss fees if you decide to hire me.*
>
> *One thing I should tell you is that everything you tell me, even if you don't end up hiring me, is confidential. That means I can't, and won't, tell anyone what you tell me, unless you want me to. That includes other members of your family, your boss, and even the police.*
>
> *Do you have any questions?*

You might also want to set up the expectation of narration:

> *In the first part of the interview, I'll ask some general questions. It is important that you tell me as much as possible about the situation. I*

won't ask many specific questions until I get a good idea of your situation and what you want done about it. I may jot down some things while you talk. Don't let that distract you.

A personal quirk. I hate, "Tell me in your own words." Far better:

Q: *So tell me about your trip, let's say, in Middle English.*

A: *Whan that Aprille with his shoures soote, the droghte of March hath perced to the roote * * * Thanne longen folk to goon pilgrimages."*

Closing Subjects

Clients will need to know something of their legal position and something on the legal process.

Will there be a trial? When? What's going to happen before then? Will I be forced to talk to the other side? Will I be arrested?

Consider a brief overview. In a routine divorce case, for example, set out the relevant time frames (filing, hearing, interlocutory period, final decree), mention Conciliation Court, and touch upon the law concerning child support and custody. And, although you know that uncontested divorce hearings are a lark, your client probably doesn't (unless, of course, you practice in California).

The hearings will be held in about two months. No one will be there except maybe some other lawyers and their clients. The whole thing takes about three minutes.

At the end of the interview, be sure to cover: *who is to do what*. Discuss what you intend to do before the next appointment and what you expect the client to do (bring in papers, not talk to others about the case).

Make sure, by written agreement, the client understands the fee arrangement, what it covers and what it doesn't (appeals?), who is responsible for what costs, and when payments are due.

Special Problems

Getting used to it

Most people who consult lawyers don't come to pass the time of day. They need help and they are likely *scared*. C.K. Chesterton, the British novelist, has written:

> *The horrible thing about all legal officials, even the best, about all judges, magistrates, barristers, detectives, and policemen, is not that they are wicked, (some of them are good), not that they are stupid, (some of them are quite intelligent), it is simply that they have got used to it.*

Enough said

Giving Advice

You will want to say "Everything will work out fine." It is overpowering when someone treats you as a prophet. Many clients will be desperate and the urge to reassure them will be extremely strong. Be cautious.

Everything may not work out fine and then you are in a fine kettle of fish. Further easy reassurances to desperate clients may indicate to your client that you either don't understand the problem or don't care about it.

Make it clear you will be there for the client and that you will work zealously. That's all you can guarantee and all the client can expect.

Unlike law school, it's all right not to know all of the law:

> "This is an important case and I'm sure that you don't want something off the top of my head. I will have to do some research before I can fully advise you."

How can you be sure the client has understood your advice? Be aware that most clients will not raise their hand and risk the laughter of everyone in the room. If appropriate, you might want to ask the client to repeat your advice, just to see if you explained it properly. Be aware that once you get beyond legal jargon you still talk like a graduate student.

Getting the Truth

> One of my first cases involved a used car dealer. Under close, indeed insightful, questioning of my clients, I determined that the salesperson had engaged in misrepresentation, committed fraud, and violated a plethora of consumer protection laws. I spend the next weeks drafting a killer, indeed insightful, Complaint, big bucks for my clients and severe injunctions against the defendant.

A funny thing happened on my way to Court. My clients, despite repeated phone calls, never returned to sign the Complaint.

Getting the truth from your client, and all the "inconvenient facts" in the case, is critical. Without them you cannot adequately advise the client nor prepare to meet the negative material at trial or in negotiation.

But, when someone comes for help, you'll want things to work out well; you'll long to hear a winning story. Consciously or unconsciously, you might lead the client to a more agreeable version of the facts, to a killer Complaint.

Try a mind-game. In the initial stages of the interview, assume the role of *disinterested reporter*. And *expect rain*. There are few perfect cases. Only in comic books and faraway galaxies do the good and bad neatly divide for combat. Expect that the gentle princess sitting across from you did something mean and petty which triggered the forces of evil and darkness against her. (If the forces of evil and darkness are sitting across the desk, get your fee up front.)

Realize too that your client will not want to divulge harmful material. Like a good doctor, you must pry, even if your client resists.

Deal in Facts, Not Conclusions.

"Before I pulled the trigger, the victim was approaching me holding a meat ax in a threatening manner."

Such sloppiness cannot be tolerated. Was the victim walking or running? How far was he when you first saw him? When you fired? Where exactly were you standing and where was he? In which hand did he hold the meat ax? Was it raised or lowered? Which way was the blade pointing? Was anything said? Exactly what and at what point in time?

Inconvenient facts hide in vague conclusions.

In some cases specific fact configurations are key: self-defense, misrepresentation, the intersection collision. Take the necessary time to develop the facts. And it will take time. Probably the best way is to have the client relive the situation:

> *"You have just entered the store. I want you to see yourself walking in. What did you do right after you went in? Tell me as much as possible."*

Confront the Client

Clients *lie* and, to make matters worse, they aren't very good at it. This is an unpleasant fact of law practice. Get used to it. If you are to do a competent job, it may be necessary to confront your client. It gets easier, after you have been burned a time or two.

> *"What! You don't believe me?"*

> *"No, I don't."*

> *"You're not the only lawyer advertising on the late show."*

> *"Well, I believe you but it's a hard world out there and no jury will.*

The "complete truth" model has one exception. It is not necessary for the criminal defense lawyer to know if the client "did it." Under ethical rules, you cannot put on a witness if you know that witness will commit perjury. Some criminal defense lawyers "Mirandize" their clients, "If you tell me you are guilty, I will not let you get up on the stand and deny it. Now, what happened?"

Teaching Yourself

We all want to get on with the next task but, right after the client leaves, I suggest you do two things. The first is obvious: write up what was discussed. You will realize everything you forgot to ask.

Second, review the interview itself. As I have written elsewhere in this book, again and again, the best lawyer I know *always reviews.*

Ask yourself how the interview went. Was it a good interview? Why? What went well, what went badly? Why? Do you like and trust the client?

1. If you gave an overview, how did it go?

2. Did the client talk, or did you ask too many questions?

3. Did your desire to win cause you to over-look weaknesses? Did you lead the client into key factual characterizations?

4. Did you make clear what's to happen next? Does the client now have a good idea of the legal procedure of his case, such as time frames and the content of future hearings?

5. Did you feel pressured into giving advice off the top? Did the client seem to understand it?

You, an authority

One of the hardest things about becoming one is realizing it. No matter your age, no matter your accomplishments, you probably feel that you are the same person you always were. In my first years of teaching, I was shocked when my students wrote down what I said ("No, wait a minute. I'm really not that sure"). In high school, an elderly woman came to talk to us: "How does it feel to be old?"

"The same as it does to be a teenager."

Why am I telling you now that you are an authority? To end the chapter currying favor? No. To remind you that during an interview, you are not a neutral scribe, writing down what happened. What you say to your client, what you ask, what you seem interested in, *counts*. Clients will have a powerful incentive to conform to what they take to be your expectations. Your prejudices and values affect the outcome. The observer affects what is observed. We don't need quantum physics to tell us that.

If you enjoy conflict, probably the story you hear *and* the story the client tells will be one which lends itself to confrontation. If you dislike conflict, more likely the opposition's position will seem, both to you *and* your client, more reasonable.

No two lawyers will get the same story.

CHAPTER 20

COUNSELING

"Get at the client's problem immediately and stick to it. Don't bother to explain the reasoning processes by which you arrive at your advice. The client expects you to be an expert. This not only prolongs the interview, but generally confuses the client. The client will feel better and more secure if told what to do and how to do it, without an explanation of how you reached your conclusions."

* * *

A hiker, on his way to Bangor, came upon a fork in the road. One sign pointed left; "Bangor 3 miles." Another pointed right; "Bangor 3 miles." The hiker turned to an old farmer who was leaning on the fence.

"Does it make any difference which way I go to Bangor?"

"Not to me."

Counseling is an on-going process rather than a separate chapter. It begins in the initial interview, when you work with the client to identify needs, concerns, and possible solutions. As we will see in the chapters on negotiation, you will continue to work with the client in defining goals and priorities. This chapter assumes an end point: where there is a proposal on the table, to plead, to settle, to sign, and the question is whether to accept or reject it.

Who makes that call? Ultimately, of course, it is the client who must sign, say "I do," or "I did." But who should make the real decision, the lawyer or the client?

Who's in charge?

There are two approaches. The *traditional* model is exemplified by my first quote, advice once given to lawyers by the Wisconsin Bar Association. It puts the lawyer, as expert, in charge. The Bangor story captures the *participation* model, albeit in rather stark form. Clearly the decision is the hiker's, not the farmer's. In an ideal world the farmer would have told what he knew about the two forks, their grade, their scenery, and their general condition. He might have also helped the hiker sort out how the hiker felt about these variables but, if finally asked, "Does it make any difference which fork I take," his response was the correct one: "Not to me." It is, after all, the hiker's journey.

Of course, had our farmer been a retired Wisconsin lawyer, he would have said, "Take the one to your left; stop bothering me and get a move on!"

Let's tease out the assumptions of these approaches, not to adopt one for all times and all situations, but to help you consider which might work better, given the client and given the case.

The Traditional Model

The traditional model seems a tad old-fashioned, what with the current emphasis on such things as "patients' rights" and the general attack on professionals and on the very notion of expertise. No doubt, however, it is practiced in many law offices today and is perhaps the norm: clients are pretty much told "Take the one on the left." A lot can be said for that approach.

First, elitist or not, as a lawyer, you are smarter, better educated, and more knowledgeable than your average bear. One would assume you would make better decisions. Second, it saves time and money. The participation model calls for extended discussions: you explain why you are advising what you are advising and then the client evaluates and ruminates. Not only are these discussions costly, they may undermine client confidence and trust: "This lawyer bear doesn't know that much more than I do." There is surely something of a placebo effect in law: if the client has confidence in the lawyer's expertise, it is more likely that the outcome will be favorable. Finally, many clients *expect* to be told what they should do. That's why they hired you, that's why they didn't go to law school. The participation model demands of the client energy, intelligence, and judgment. Some would rather leave the driving to us.

If one wanted to be uncharitable, one could characterize the participation model as "shared existential angst." The anguish of making decisions, and all the insecurities and uncertainties involved, are shoved unto the client–of course, for the client's own good.

The Participation Model

This model acknowledges that lawyers have a lot to contribute to *help* clients make decisions, but rejects the notion that most decisions made in a law office are narrow matters of expertise. An analogy to medicine might be helpful. There the rule is "patient consent." Doctors, however, present us with the "right" decision: lose weight, take cholesterol-lowering medications. They don't ask our reactions; they don't tell us why. While legally we are free to ignore the advice, we feel guilty if we do, knowing that we are making a stupid decision because we crave chocolate or the bliss of denial.

Right decisions work in medicine because patients and doctors share the same goal: good health and long life. When that goal changes, as it often does in end-of-life decisions, when the *quality* of life may trump the *quantity* of life, doctors lose their expertise. Most legal decisions are like these decisions, where the goal, not the method, is up for grabs.

The participation model assumes that a client's decision will often be *better* than yours. This is because the decision involves so much more than, say, the proper application of the parol evidence rule. The decision rests on value judgments concerning such things as time, money, risk, and face. You cannot know, or rather, cannot experience, the life and values of your client.

The farmer cannot know how much the hiker enjoys beauty or dislikes hills. Let me give you a vivid, real-life, example, one to throw doubt forever on the easy assumption, "I know what's better for that person." In the prime of life, we look at individuals crippled by horrible diseases, living in wheel chairs and think, not me, I would rather be dead.

Nancy Mairs, author of *Waist High in the World*, lives in a wheelchair, unable to feed, bathe, or dress herself.

> *"There are readers who need, for a tangle of reasons, to be told that a life commonly held to be insufferable can be full and funny. I am living that life. I can tell them."*

Participation can lead to better problem solving. Clients can supplement the lawyer's specialized knowledge, fill in gaps, catch mistakes, and provide additional insight. Conversely, the collaborative task of having to explain and discuss the problem with the client can help the lawyer avoid mistakes and gain further insights.

Even if the client eventually decides on the course the lawyer would have initially recommended, the journey has likely not been a waste of time. My colleague, David Wexler, has made something of a cottage industry with his notion of *therapeutic juris- prudence*: lawyers should be concerned with the psychological well-being of their clients as well as their legal well-being.

It is therapeutic to allow clients to decide, even to insist that they do so. Being the captain of one's ship *matters*. So does competence. The participation model assures that the client learns about the situation and, with knowledge, comes control and confidence.

Decisions tend to pan out better with "I chose this" rather than with "I didn't have any choice." If things go badly, and they might, taking responsibility is critical. Our prisons are full of prisoners who are there, not because they committed a crime, but because their lawyers sold them down the river by "forcing" them to plead.

If you decide on the participation model, don't think you are off the hook. Before your client comes in, think how you would decide the issue. This will focus your thinking and provide a valuable ground for your discussions.

> *"I think this is a good offer because of X, Y, and Z. However, if you take it, you will be giving up A and B. It strikes me that X, Y, and Z are more important, but that's just my opinion. What do you think?"*

By giving your reasons, you allow the client to come to a different conclusion; the client may prefer A and B. The danger with this approach is that you might become wedded to your decision; then advice becomes argument. Realize your power; if you don't *invite* disagreement, your client might agree simply because, bumper stickers to the contrary, very few question authority.

As to your overall approach, you may wish to involve your client:

"I think you should take the left fork. If you wish, I can go over all of my reasoning and see if you agree with it. Some of the things I think are important, such as no trolls hiding under bridges, you may not think important. This approach will take some time but you might feel better about the decision once you know my thinking. How do you want me to proceed?"

These models, traditional and participation, are no doubt extremes. Even Wisconsin lawyers realize that they are not Oracles or Wizards, and must, when giving advice, at least allude to why their advice is sound. And, if any work at all is going to get done this afternoon, one cannot have full client participation in every decision. Rather than follow one approach consistently, you will tend to stress one or another depending on the nature of the decision, the role of expertise in making it, and the intelligence and interest of your client.

Rather than "models," which connote scripts, I think it more helpful to think of the two as basic orientations or attitudes. If you believe that as an expert you have a better sense of what your client should do, no amount of "What do you think?" will trigger client participation. Conversely, if you believe that your client has a lot to contribute to the decision, even a dogmatic "Go left" from you will likely trigger, "Tell me why."

This raises a very basic issue: how you view our profession, the role of authority, and the role of expertise. I will return to this issue at the end of the chapter. For now, some bread and butter issues: a counseling checklist, the role of Devil's Advocate, dealing with legal uncertainty and the problem of self-interest, and finally, when good clients go bad, either legally or morally.

Counseling Checklists

Checklists can never capture the necessary subtlety, but they can help by raising issues and approaches that might otherwise be overlooked.

One traditional device is to project outcomes into three categories:

— *Best outcome*

— *Worst outcome*

— *Most likely outcome*

Time frames are obviously important. A terrific short-term decision may eventually spell disaster. D–I–S–A–S–T–E–R.

Binder and Price, in their fine book, *Legal Interviewing and Counseling: A Client–Centered Approach,* suggests that major legal decisions have implications in several areas: *legal, economic, psychological, social,* and *societal* (impact on others).

These categories can frame discussions:

> *"If you were to sign this contract, what is the best result you see? What might go wrong, and what would the worst result be? What do you think is most likely to happen?*

"A good way to think about a decision is to break it down into various facets. So, should you accept their offer? First let's look at the pros and cons of the economic aspects, both in the short term and long term."

To save office time, consider sending a letter to your client:

Dear Client,

Next week we will meet to discuss whether you should accept the most recent proposal. To prepare for that meeting, I want you to write out some thoughts. Assume that it is two years from now, and you have accepted the proposal. How will it have affected you economically? How will it have affected you socially in terms of family and friends? How will it have affected the lives of others, such as suppliers, competitors, employees? How do you think you will feel about having accepted it, regret or satisfaction?

Don't just think about these questions. It has been my experience that if you write out your answers, you will learn a great deal more.

Your job is to help your client evaluate the choices from differing perspectives. Your client probably hasn't thought of the decision in these ways. Allow space, be non-judgmental, and use the *active listening* skills discussed in the last chapter. Feelings are important, and emotions are not to be feared.

My sense is that many lawyers adopt the traditional approach out of fear of where the participation model might lead: clients talking about difficult and personal issues that lawyers have not been trained to handle. But, again, difficult and personal issues are often at the root of legal problems and help illuminate their solutions.

During your office conference, you might want to make some notes on the various matters you discussed. A copy can be taken by the client for further reflection. To rush a client into a decision often is to take the decision from the client.

One final point. Even if an extended discussion on the various implications of a decision does *not* result in a decision that concludes the matter, it will prove invaluable in further *negotiations*. You will come away with a real sense of your client's needs and desires and will hence be better prepared to come up with creative proposals and solutions. More on this in the chapter on Negotiation.

Touchy Subjects

Playing the Devil's Advocate

No matter how much you are committed to client autonomy, to be an effective lawyer, you must probe and meddle. Your client may be resting a decision on inaccurate information or concerns.

> *"I don't want to take the settlement."*
>
> *"Why?"*

> *"Because I don't want to admit I did anything wrong."*

> *"I can draft around that."*

Beyond probing, as my colleague Andy Silverman says, you must occasionally play the part of Devil's Advocate.

> *"True, the right fork does have nicer scenery. But there are trolls."*

Max Weber had a great phrase, "inconvenient facts." It is the job of good teachers (and of good lawyers) to get those in our care to recognize them.

> *If you take such and such a stand, then you have to use such and such means in order to carry it out. Does the end justify the means? We can force the individual to give himself an account of the ultimate meaning of his own conduct. A teacher who succeeds in this stands in the service of "moral" forces by fulfilling the duty of bringing about self-clarification and a sense of responsibility.*

We all want sunshine and song, reassurance, support, and praise; no one wants "inconvenient facts." Well, as lawyers it is our joy to praise and support our clients; it is our *duty* to force them to be realistic and responsible.

> "Sure, we can sue the bastard. He deserves it. But litigation is a horrible thing to go through. It may take years and may become the most consuming thing in your life."

"Sure, we can lower our offer. Your supplier is on the ropes now. But if you drive the price down too far, what's going to happen in a couple of years?"

"Sure, it would be fun to be King, but witches have been wrong before. So don't Banquo on it."

Finally, as a good teacher, keep clear on what you actually know and what you suspect. Your advice will, of necessity, partially rest on hunches and guesses: what it is like to be in jail, to be in an automobile accident, to testify at a trial. Note the source of much of your information: your view of "Boys' Camp," will likely turn on whether you saw Disney's or Cagney's. Better still, take an afternoon and go visit. A friend of mine, a Juvenile Court Judge, used to require neglectful parents to attend parenting classes, *until* she decided to attend one herself.

One "down-home" point. Acquaint yourself with community resources—usually the United Way has published a booklet. Not all problems that walk in your door lend themselves to legal solution. Recall the very first case we had together, that of the dad with the eviction notice. Community resources would have been key.

Not knowing

Once upon a time, an English jurist wrote, "Certainty is the mother of Repose and thus the Law aims at Certainty." Then along came Justice Oliver

Wendell Holmes, who sat down beside him, and said:

> *"Certainty is illusion and repose is not the destiny of man."*

Even when all the alternatives are on the table, all of the pros and cons, all of the short-term and long-term implications, you're still not there. The decision will turn on the *client's* values, based in large part on *your* predictions: *"If I go to trial, what are my chances?"*

Predictions are the hardest part. There are extremes. At one end are lawyers who underplay the uncertainty of the law and make bold predictions. I think this extreme is triggered by the feeling that "professionals are supposed to know this stuff." At the other extreme are lawyers who overplay uncertainty, perhaps in fear of being wrong, perhaps as a way of avoiding the hard work involved in reducing uncertainty.

Be up front with your uncertainty as a way to encourage your client to be open about the extent to which judgments rest on estimates and good guesses. Remember that "good judgment" is not synonymous with "being sure."

Self-interest

"Teach, don't preach." Impossible for teachers, impossible for lawyers. Knowledge does not exist, out there, like a peach, ready to be brought in and examined. Teachers and lawyers must select, must order, must emphasize. All of this is well and good and is what we are paid to do. Realize, however, the power. Once we have shaped peoples' conception of the world, Jerome Bruner points out, "We can safely leave their actions to them—in the sense that, if they believe themselves standing before a precipice, they will not step over unless they intend suicide."

Your selection, ordering, and subtle clues should be designed to further your client's interest. The danger is that you might, consciously or unconsciously, use them to further your own. An additional deposition means more money for you, a guilty plea means no trial preparation for you, and a tougher stance on a negotiation might help your reputation.

The path taken *does* make a difference to you; avoid, for your own ends, turning hills into cliffs.

When advice is not taken

If a client insists on a bad *legal* decision, dictate a memo, for your client's signature, that you advised a different course of action.

What of bad *moral* decisions? "I want to pave Paradise and turn it into a Parking Lot."

This is the stuff of shrill law school debates.

"We aren't moral babysitters!"

"Well, yeah, but I didn't come to law school to do evil!"

"Softie!"

"Pig!"

Professor Thomas Shaffer offers a way out. He provides a provocative analogy. You are a druggist and someone comes in to buy a hypodermic needle. You believe he will use the needle to shoot heroin. What do you do?

You can sell him the needle.

> This is akin to the "hired gun" ethic of lawyering. It is not our job to be moral watchdogs.

You can claim you are out of needles.

> This is akin to the "lawyers are moral actors too" ethic. To solve the Parking Lot problem, the lawyer might fudge: "Paradise is on the endangered list; zoning won't allow paving," knowing full well that competent lawyering could easily change the result.

According to Shaffer, both solutions are flawed because they rely on power rather than principle. In the "hired gun" model, the client has it; in the other, the lawyer has it. The third way:

> *Tell the customer that you think that he will use the needle to shoot heroin and that you believe heroin is a bad idea.*

This will generate a discussion and opens the possibility that the conflict will be resolved upon reason and reflection, not by power. But as all parents know, discussions are often shams: "Okay, let's talk about your wanting a nose ring." The parent is planning to *use* reason to *compel* the desired decision.

The trick to making a discussion a discussion, rather than a slow burn, is that both sides must entertain the *possibility* of being convinced by the other. Customers, kids, and clients have to agree to listen. Druggists must be willing to be convinced that heroin is okay, parents must be willing to take a serious look at nose rings, and lawyers must be open to the possibility that the highest use is Parking Lot, not Paradise.

If your discussion results in a stalemate, then you have two choices. First, under most circumstances you can, and probably should, withdraw from representation. If you decide not to withdraw, your duty is to represent your client. Get a shovel.

On Care and Cure

When I was a Public Defender, I often felt as if I didn't *do* anything. Most of my clients pled or were convicted; very few walked.

For a long, long time, doctors didn't *do* anything either. Before the wide use of penicillin in the Second World War, usually a disease would run its course and the patient would either get better or die. Still, doctors were vital. They helped relieve the pain, and they helped relieve the fear. *They were bedside.*

As a public defender, entering pleas, losing cases, I too was bedside. I was with my clients as they passed through a strange and threatening process. Cures are great, but care is important too. Too great an emphasis on cure can short-change care.

With the advent of wonder drugs and new methods of surgery, doctors began to actually *cure* their patients. *Care* suffers. Medical treatment is now the five-minute consultation and a small bottle to take in the bathroom.

Be bedside for your clients. Take time to explain things, answer phones calls, and occasionally step out of role and ask how they are doing.

This chapter opened with what was really a discussion about how one views the profession. Under the traditional model, lawyers are experts. Clients come with legal problems; it is our job, and our sole job, to solve the problem, with the Devil taking the existential stuff.

I want to close by revisiting that issue, of course, not to preach, but to teach.

A great novel for lawyers is Trollope's *The Warden*. Set in England in the 1850s, the novel involves the kindly Mr. Harding, who, under the terms of a trust, runs a nursing home for about a dozen old men. Somehow the old men get it in their minds that Mr. Harding is abusing the trust and is cheating them. They file suit. Harding is devastated. Ultimately he is forced to hire a lawyer, Sir Abraham, who, through technical maneuvering succeeds in getting the old men's suit dismissed. There is never a hearing on the merits.

> *It was very clear that the justice of the old men's claim or the justice of Mr. Harding's defense were ideas that had never presented themselves to Sir Abraham. A legal victory over an oppos-*

ing party was the service for which Sir Abraham was, as he imagined, to be paid. Of the intense desire which Mr. Harding felt to be assured on fit authority that he had wronged no man, that he might sleep at night without the pangs of conscience, that he was no robber, no spoiler of the poor, of such longings Sir Abraham was entirely ignorant; nor indeed could it be looked upon on as part of his business to gratify such desires. Such was not the system on which his battles were fought, and victories gained. Success was his object, and he was generally successful. He conquered his enemies by their weakness rather than by his own strength.

How do you view *your* job?

CHAPTER 21

PLANNING YOUR INVESTIGATION

Humpty Dumpty sat on a wall,
Humpty Dumpty had a great fall.
Humpty Dumpty, well, he died.
Was it accident or suicide?

You represent the Widow Dumpty. Allprovidence Insurance, a Canadian company, has refused to pay on Humpty's life insurance policy on the basis that his death was not accidental, but suicide.

"He would never do that," the Widow Dumpty tearfully concluded. "He was always such a good egg."

"She'll make a very sympathetic witness," you think, making a mental note to keep anyone with high cholesterol off the jury.

Unfortunately, Allprovidence has an eyewitness, Pinocchio. He gave the following statement to Allprovidence:

I, with Humpty, sat on that wall,
Poor old Humpty, he did not fall,
He was sad, in a big dump,
All who knew him, knew he would jump!

What to do? Rewrite? No, I tried that, *several* times.

Make a plan.

Investigation doesn't seem tough. "Was Humpty depressed?" "Did he have financial worries?" "And who is the Pinocchio fellow, some kind of puppet?" You will be tempted to get going, to contact witnesses to see "what happened," to call Allprovidence to see what they have to say.

Not yet!

Common Errors: Starting Too Soon and Looking for Love

Starting without a plan can prove costly. First impressions are made just once: you don't want to call Allprovidence only to stutter "Well, that's not what *we* think!" As you will likely get only one shot at a witness; don't waste it with, "Well, what happened?" Even witnesses anxious to help you may not give you the most significant piece of information because they don't know what it is (and, at this point, you may not either).

That said, it is imperative to interview *incident* witnesses as soon as possible, not only because memories fade but also because conversations with others, newspaper stories, and Allprovidence investigators may cause memories to change.

Another obstacle to effective investigation is being too much of an advocate; being too committed to proving your client is right. Be open to the possibility that the case is weaker than you think and look for weaknesses in *your* case as much as you seek weaknesses in that of your opponent. Don't take your client's word for it; don't assume friendly witnesses are not biased; and don't stop asking questions because you think the answers might hurt.

Legal investigation is *not* moseying around. It is focused on what you have to prove (or disprove) at trial (even though most cases settle). Where to begin? Alas, the law library.

Legal Research (Great News!), and the Dangers of Computers

The best news in this book: *Legal research in practice is different than in law school!*

In law school, you spent hours and hours researching fake issues; in practice, issues matter and legal research is usually in a series of short bursts, 20 to 60 minutes, first to get a feel for the controlling law, later to draft pleadings, later still to write or respond to motions.

If you are new to an area of law, take some time to get an overview from *ALR*, treatises, or Nutshells. Then turn to controlling *statutes* or *regulations*. The case method in law school tends to down play the importance of these; in practice, you will find that almost always there is a controlling statute or regulation. *Skim* the annotations, not only to flesh out the law, but also to see the kinds of evidence others have used in similar situations.

Another good source of general information are *form jury instructions* used in many jurisdictions.

Do your *own* research. This is essential. Have someone else do the work, you will not understand the nuisances of the law and, more importantly, you will not know the roads not taken.

Computer assisted research is dangerous. First, it gives you the tree without the forest. You may find a legal principle that *seems* to apply to your case but, without understanding the surrounding and background law, you might not understand how the principle is applied or its limitations. Second, a broader search may trigger a realization that the problem may be approached somewhat differently. Third, computer research is too easy. You come across an applicable statute or case, push a button, print it out, file it away, and go home. If you force yourself to *take* notes, you will read much more closely and save forests. "Does this case *really* help me? With what specific language?

Looking Backwards: From Conclusions to Blood, Sweat, and Tears

Everything we do is backwards. From your legal research you will know what legal conclusions you will want the jury to reach. You will also pick up such critical matters as *burden of proof.* (In an action on a life insurance policy, does the claimant have to prove accidental death or must the Company prove suicide?)

Once you know the ultimate factual conclusions you want to argue to the jury, you are ready to leave the tidy law library and muck around in the raw data of the universe, those things that people see, hear, feel, taste, touch, and smell.

It might help, but probably won't, to categorize evidence into two types: *substantive* evidence, which bears directly on the conclusion (the Widow Dumpty's testimony that Humpty was happy), and *credibility* evidence, which goes to whether the substantive evidence should be believed (she is, after all, his widow). These two can be sub-divided into *positive* and *rebuttal* evidence.

What you need is *leads*, not categories. Here are three devices to get you beyond the obvious in looking for leads: the "If so, what else" question, the importance of time frames, and the search for what's not there.

"If so, what else?"

Let's assume we want to show Humpty committed suicide. *If so, what else* might be true? Again, I believe in writing things out; thoughts beget thoughts.

> — *He might have been depressed over an incident at work;*

> — *He might have had financial worries;*

> — *He might have had bad news from his doctor;*

> — *He might have had marital problems.*

> — *He might have grown weary of having a diminutive as a first name.*

The careful reader will note that all of the above are themselves conclusions: we still have not reached bedrock: specific witnesses, specific documents, specific exhibits attesting to specific raw facts.

> *If Humpty was depressed over work, what witnesses should I interview? What questions should I ask? What documents might be relevant? Could there be any physical evidence supporting it?*

Time frames

Look for evidence, not only at the time of the incident, but at times *before* and *after* the incident.

Recall that Pinocchio will testify that he saw Humpty jump, not fall. What you will have to do is convince the jury not to believe him. You can do this by showing that he is mistaken or that he is lying.

> *Ladies and Gentlemen of the Jury, the evidence showed that Pinocchio, in testifying that Humpty jumped, is not to be believed. This is because:*
>
> *A.   Pinocchio is mistaken (or)*
>
> *B.   Pinocchio is lying.*

At trial you will have to choose between these alternatives. Here we are investigating which is more likely.

Pursuing the mistake thesis, consider three variations of our basic *if so, what else* question:

1.   *If* Pinocchio is mistaken, *what else* might be true *at the time* of the incident?

2.   *If* Pinocchio is mistaken, *what else* might be true *before* the incident?

3.   *If* Pinocchio is mistaken, *what else* might be true *after* the incident?

Looking at the time of *incident*, you will generate investigative leads as to Pinocchio's ability to observe the incident. Did he have a good view? Was he distracted? Looking at the time *before* the incident, you will generate investigative leads which might pre-dispose him into making a mistake. Had he been to an eye doctor? Had there been a prior incident where he showed himself afraid of heights and hence likely to be distracted? Is there anything in his background that would predispose him to mistake an accident for a suicide? Something he knew about Humpty? About eggs? About life?

Looking *after* the incident, is there anything that will lend support to the thesis that he is mistaken in his belief that Humpty jumped? Knowing that the opinion of others can influence what we recall, did Pinocchio read about Humpty's death in the newspaper or discuss it with others? What information did he get from these sources?

Another time frame: the trial itself.

Ladies and Gentlemen of the Jury, think back to when Pinocchio was answering my questions on

cross-examination. He kept looking at my oppos-
ing counsel. Remember too how he stumbled on
several answers, and he kept his hand covering
his nose. And did you hear, or was it my
imagination, that, at least twice, he gave a little
whistle?

Thus far we have been looking for positive evidence, things that are (or were) there. Negative
evidence is important as well. How to find what's
not there?

Reverse the Propositions

Ever since grade school, we've been proving ourselves right ("Pinocchio wasn't looking!"). And calling our opponents names ("Pinocchio has sawdust
for brains!"). Consider something more subtle,
more *Zen*. Assume Pinocchio is *correct*: he saw
Humpty jump. *If* you saw a suicide, what would you
have done? Reminder the three time periods.

Ladies and Gentlemen of the Jury. Allprovi-
dence would have you believe that Pinocchio
saw a suicide. If you had seen a suicide, what
would you have noticed? Strange behavior. But
Pinocchio didn't see any. If you had seen a
suicide, what would you have done? Call out:
"Don't jump." There is no evidence that Pinoc-
chio called out. After the suicide, you would
have immediately reported what you saw to the
King's Officer. But no, Pinocchio went shop-
ping!

That's about it for planning your investigation.
Begin in the law library to discover the controlling

law, turn legal conclusions into factual conclusions, and then search for ways to turn factual conclusions into the grunts, sights, and smells of existence. One final thing, something interesting.

Circumstantial Evidence, Koch's Postulates and Angst

Assume that you had gone to Medical School and now, rather than reading Nutshells, you are a famous medical research scientist. You have come across a new virus and you suspect it causes a certain disease. How would you go about proving it? There are no eyewitnesses: even with the most powerful of microscopes, no one sees a virus cause a disease. Few viruses confess and those who do generally lie.

One approach to test whether virus X causes disease Y would be to test individuals who have Y to see if they carry X. Assuming they all did, have you proved the causal link?

Another approach would be to isolate the virus and insert it into unsuspecting (and unconsenting) mice. If all the mice came down with the disease, have you proved the causal link?

A German scientist, Robert Koch (1843–1910), established a set of postulates that must be satisfied to conclude that a particular micro-organism causes a particular disease.

> 1. The micro-organism must be found in all cases of the disease. By itself, this doesn't prove causation because there will likely be

several micro-organisms found in all cases of the disease.

2. The micro-organism must reproduce the disease when introduced into a healthy experimental animal. By itself, this doesn't prove causation unless the first postulate is satisfied: even if introducing the virus leads to the disease, unless all cases of the disease manifest the virus, then there may be another cause.

In one of the greatest moments in medical history, in 1882 Koch announced to a world that he had found the cause of the great killer of the age, tuberculosis, the white plague. Prior to his announcement, doctors believed it was caused by unsanitary conditions, such as bad air. Koch had discovered a certain bacillus and showed that it was present in all individuals with TB. Further he showed that, if injected into mice, the mice came down with TB.

Koch's discovery lead to different treatment routines and eventually control over this killer. However, a theoretical problem remained. Koch himself tested positive for the tubercle bacillus and yet he didn't have TB. In fact, only about 10% of those infected come down with an active and severe case of TB. For people to die from TB, additional factors must come into play. Bad air?

For a medical researcher these are important points. One doesn't want to spend one's career attacking the wrong virus and, even if the virus "causes" the disease in the sense that tubercle bacilli cause TB, if there are other factors at play, it might be easier to control those factors than to eliminate the virus. For lawyers these are important points as well.

Recall our case of the dad with the eviction notice; there were many ways to state the problem, some of which would lend themselves to easier solution. Koch's work also shows that circumstantial evidence is always suspect.

Can we ever be sure of anything? "Well, we found Humpty's suicide note."

> *"Now more than ever it seems rich to die,*
>
> *To cease upon the midnight with no pain,*
>
> *Fade far away, dissolve and quite forget,*
>
> *That tomorrow, I'm an omelet!"*

But it is possible to write a suicide note, sit upon a wall, change your mind, and, alas, slip.

There may never be *conclusive* evidence of anything. This may lead to a certain amount of anxiety. What should we do tomorrow? What if God came down and told us? As Sartre pointed out, we would still have to decide whether it was God talking to us or the Devil in disguise.

I'm going for a hike. You should too. (But who's talking?)

CHAPTER 22

INTERVIEWING WITNESSES

Scott Fitzgerald, to get better at his trade, would often ask himself: "How would I write that scene?" Don't think it is too much of a stretch to suggest that, after you witness an event, you ask yourself, "How would I prove what happened?" Besides witness testimony, is there anything that happened *before* or *after* the incident that would make it more likely to have occurred? Would there be any supporting documents or physical evidence?

Most of pretrial investigation consists of witness interviews. Many law offices use professional investigators. Consider doing some interviews yourself for the same reason you do your own legal research: you get a better feel for the case. Even if you aren't going to dirty your hands, this chapter will help you work with those that do.

This chapter deals with informally interviewing witnesses; the next deals with formal depositions.

Goals and Restrictions

Goals

1. *Finding out what the witness knows.*

This will often involve active listening and forcing the witness to break down conclusions ("Law school was hard") into supporting detail. It may also involve jogging memory ("Did it happen before or after the Big Bang?").

Don't duck the bad and the ugly; better to find it out now. Friendly witnesses might hesitate to disclose unfavorable information. Ask them to. "Are you aware of anything harmful to my client's case?" Some commentators suggest that you facilitate the impeachment of hostile witnesses by encouraging them to express bias against your client, to exaggerate, and to lie. Then, at trial, you can attack them as biased and their testimony as exaggerated and untruthful.

2. Finding out what the witness doesn't know.

This is to protect you from being surprised at trial by "new revelations."

3. Searching for leads.

Hearsay and speculation are fine. Does this witness know other witnesses? Know of any documents?

There are significant differences between formal depositions and informal interviews. Depositions are compulsory; witness interviews are not. Depositions are transcribed; witness interviews often are not. Depositions are taken with your opponent present; witness interviews are taken in dark alleys. Depositions can be taken of adverse parties; witness interviews cannot. Thus you will face four problems: getting the witness to talk to you, memorializing the conversation in such a fashion that you can use it, if necessary, at trial, being ethical and not encouraging false recollection, and, finally, making sure that the witness is fair game. Let's start with the last.

Restrictions on witness interviews

In some states, Victim Rights Legislation places restrictions on defense lawyers interviewing victims (but not other witnesses). Other than that, the only folks you *cannot* talk to are *parties* to the lawsuit. Are *employees* parties? Some are; it depends on the jurisdiction. Basically, the higher they are, the more likely they are included. Be sure to check the current status of the law in your jurisdiction: otherwise, big trouble. You can, of course, depose adverse parties.

What about *potential* adverse parties? Unless you know they are represented by counsel, you can contact them. Confirm that they don't have a lawyer. Don't be guilty of *Abuse of Letterhead*, hounding letters sent to unrepresented folks, threatening dire straits unless the person does your bidding. Be very leery of purporting to give legal advice to potential adverse parties ("The law requires you to do X").

As to your opponent's witnesses, the Federal Rules require that parties, without discovery request, disclose "the name and, if known, the address and telephone number of each individual likely to have discoverable information that the disclosing party *may* use to support its claims and defenses, unless solely for impeachment, identifying the *subjects* of information". (Rule 26). If your state does not have a comparable provision, the names of witnesses your opponent plans to use are probably obtainable by interrogatory.

Note that no one owns a witness and you are free to interview (and depose) your opponent's witnesses. While a witness can refuse to be interviewed, you can point out to that witness that the refusal will look bad at trial.

> *Q: Now isn't it a fact that you refused to talk to me or my investigator before trial?*

Planning Issues

As with formal discovery, there are interesting timing issues: You want to strike while the iron is hot, but you want to be prepared.

Interview *incident* witnesses as soon as possible; time is of the essence. Some commentators say a matter of weeks, or even days, can make all the difference. Not only can memory be corrupted by conversations with others, your opponents will have a significant advantage if they are able to get the witness first.

Another priority is to visit the scene: stop signs get moved, stores go out of business, and trees fall without making a sound. A rough diagram and photos will help down the road. Visiting the scene at the same time of the event can also help you find additional witnesses.

Learn the basic "facts" of the case from friendly and neutral witnesses. Approach hostile witnesses with knowledge and confidence. To the degree they are aware of your knowledge, to the degree you seem to be confirming rather than discovering the facts, the less likely they will be tempted to withhold or falsify information. One reason to visit the scene is to be able to stun the witness with "That must mean you were standing next to the elephant."

Two minor issues: where to interview and interviewing by phone.

Be solicitous of neutral witnesses as they can make or break your case. As to hostile witnesses, commentators generally advise showing up at their homes or work, unannounced, the theory being that they will generally not agree to an appointment and that surprise prevents them from getting "steeled." On the other hand, I do not advise routinely abusing people if, for no other reason, that hostility generated now may come back to bite you at trial. In this game, everyone is a repeat player.

It is common to do some investigation by telephone. Three items of advice. First, consider a follow-up letter to the other party embodying what was said and asking if your understanding of the conversation is correct. Second, note all telephone calls in the case file with a brief description of what was said. Third, if the person at the other end does not believe you are a lawyer, tell him the page your telephone number appears in the phonebook and ask him to phone you back at that number. Either that or offer to explain "per stirpes."

Realize that, from an evidentiary standpoint, what you get by telephone is fairly worthless. You will not be able to testify as to what was said and, if an investigator made the call, there may be problems with authenticating that the person on the other end was the person the investigator thought.

Getting witnesses to talk and sign

Witnesses are not *obligated* to talk to you. Nor are they obligated to talk to reporters or, for that matter, to buy used cars. A lot of creative thought has gone into solving these problems.

First, the *strategy of identification*. We are all more comfortable talking with people we identify with: older folks are more comfortable talking to older doctors; women, discussing personal matters, are more comfortable with other women; men, discussing personal matters, are never more comfortable.

In addition to age, sex, and race, there are common interests and backgrounds. If you think identification will be critical, and you don't match, consider getting someone else to conduct it or at least to accompany you.

"I don't want to get involved." You'll hear that a lot. Start gingerly, appealing to their sense of fairness, pointing out that, depending on how the interview goes, they may not have to get involved. The Big One is the threat to depose them.

Some won't want to talk because they fear that what they will say will get back to other people.

While you cannot guarantee confidentiality (you are not their lawyer), you can address this concern with the reassurance that you will do what you can to protect the confidences.

Consider the role of self-fulfilling prophecy in all of this. Act as if there is no question but that the witnesses will speak with you. If you are unsure, the witness will sense it. Does interviewing witnesses with the goal of finding ways to discredit them make you queasy? It shouldn't. Maybe you will discover that your case should not be pursued. Beyond that, if the story of your client and that of the witness conflict, the adversary role dictates that you attempt to show why the witness's version is incorrect. You won't get too far into the interview if you begin, "I'm not going to believe what you will tell me and I am here to find ways to discredit you." Some lack of candor is inherent in the nature of the adversary role.

> *Malt does more than the Canons can,*
> *To justify our ways to Man*

Never ask, "Will you talk with me?" Used car salespeople *never* ask if you want to buy the car. Rather they project the belief that you will. Writing up the contract ("Just to see how it looks on paper"), they ask you to sign so they can see if they can get the "super deal past the manager." The net result is that you become convinced that you have already agreed to buy the car; it's just that you can't remember when. To say "No" at this point would be like breaking your promise. The devices:

self-fulfilling prophecy and never asking the person to decide.

Reporter and TV anchorman Jim Lehrer, in his book, *The Last Debate*, recounts some reporter's tricks. Bob Woodward, of Watergate fame, would approach a potential source with:

"Others have told me the whole story, I just want to confirm some details."

A variation of "Woodwardizing" is to say something outrageous, forcing the source to correct it and, while doing so, reveal what you are really trying to find out.

It is much easier *to refuse to begin* a conversation than it is *to end it*. Get the witness talking. Make small talk before moving to threatening material. If the person refuses to talk with you shift from confrontation to explanation; ask the witness why. Finally, don't increase reluctance by taking notes. Take out the yellow pad (or tape recorder) only after the interview is going well, "Just to make sure I get it all right."

Note: While it is appropriate and, in some kinds of cases, routine to advise your *client* not talk to anyone about the case, it is inappropriate to advise a witness not to talk to the other side. However, you can remind a witness that they are not legally obligated to talk with the other side except in a formal deposition or in court.

Getting a signed statement

Signed witness statements are important at trial in terms of possible impeachment. However, they are more important in negotiation: "Here are five witness statements supporting my client's version of the facts. Want to settle?"

Should you include the bad stuff? The downside is that your opponent may read it, either as part of a negotiation package you prepare or during trial. (If you show the statement to the witness to refresh her recollection, your opponent may have the right to read all of it.) However, your opponent may get the bad stuff anyway and it might not even be admissible at trial.

Including negative information increases the likelihood that the witness will sign and will come away with the impression that you are a fair person. Again, everyone is a repeat player.

How do you get the witness to sign? Self-fulfilling prophecy will play a role as will trying to discover the witness' reluctance and addressing those concerns. Your major concern, however, is not so much getting the witness to sign as it is to get some proof that what the statement says is accurate. If the story changes at trial, confronted with the statement, the witness will likely deny reading it or understanding it. Hence, the "tricks" are aimed at *closing these doors* by getting the witness to read the statement and indicate its truthfulness.

— Make minor errors in the statement, for example, misspell the witness's name. When the witness reads it, the errors will be corrected, thus foreclosing "I didn't read it."

— Read the statement to the witness in front of other witnesses.

— One writer in the field of investigation, with obvious good will, recommends the following signature clause:

I have read the foregoing statement and it is correct. However, I refuse to sign it because I do not wish to get involved.

_____

Signed

If the witness *refuses* to sign, not all is lost. You know what the witness has to say and can prepare to meet it at trial. If necessary, you can take the person's deposition. But, because you cannot testify in a trial you are handling, you will be unable to testify as to what was said during the interview. You would have avoided this problem had you taken another person with you to the interview. This might be a good idea, particularly in cases where you run the risk of being accused of impropriety, such as defense counsel interviewing a crime victim.

Ethical temptations

Your opponent's not there. Temptation!

There is nothing wrong with convincing the witness that your client is okay.

> *"I represent Allprovidence insurance, which is owned by people like you. We get a lot of false claims filed. Not only are these people cheats, but it means that we have to raise rates for everyone."*

And there is nothing wrong with confronting the witness with statements from others or with documents that contradict what the witness says. The witness might have misspoken and will correct the statement (If you don't think the witness will change the statement, you may want to save the material to confront the witness at trial).

However, some commentators suggest you go further and essentially lead the witness to your version of events.

> Do not say, *"Was M driving about 55 m.p.h.?"* Instead say, *"Wasn't M driving at about 55 m.p.h.?"*

The outer limit of this is the subornation of perjury. Well short of that line, however, are considerations of individual conscience and witness backlash. (At trial: "Yes, that's what I said. But you tricked me into saying it." Again, everyone is a repeat player.)

Time for an illustration and review.

An instructive transcript, with irritating editorial interruptions

Jones is facing eviction, allegedly for nonpayment of rent. The theory of the defense is that the landlord is evicting in retaliation for Jones complaining to the Health Department concerning conditions at the apartment house. Here his lawyer is interviewing a neighbor. Let's pick it up at the top.

> Attorney: *(Attorney knocks and witness opens the door). Hello there. My name is W. Mitty. I work for NBC television and we are doing a special on apartment living. May I have a few minutes of your time?*

Cut!

Why is our first instinct deception? Why is our first impulse to dress up like a plumber and secrete recording devices about our person? There may be times where deception is necessary. However, as Ellen Goodman once wrote about *60 Minutes*, deception should be our painful last choice, not our easy first choice. With hard work, you can generally get the truth. Look for a disgruntled employee.

Okay. Let's take it from the top.

> Attorney: *(Attorney knocks, witness opens the door). Hello there, my name is W. Mitty and I represent your next door neighbor in the legal proceeding with the landlord. I would like to ask you a few questions.*

Witness: *Go away.*

Attorney: *Please.*

Witness: *No.*

Attorney: *Do you like my hat?*

Witness: No, I do not like your hat.

Attorney: Goodbye.

Curtains!

What's wrong with this? Nothing wrong with the pleasing reference to *Do You Like My Hat?* by Dr. Seuss. But don't jump right in; a little small talk is fine, perhaps to get the witness to identify with either the lawyer or with the client. You might want to give the witness some idea of the controversy and your theory of the case. That may trigger information that specific questions never would.

Attorney: (*Attorney knocks, witness opens the door*). *Hello there, my name is W. Mitty and I represent your next door neighbor. The landlord is trying to evict him, claiming he didn't pay rent. We think he's being evicted because he complained to the Health Department. You know if he gets evicted, it will be real harmful to him, and his children. And landlords shouldn't get away with this.*

Witness: *Go away.*

Attorney: *This will take only a few minutes. If you don't have time now, when can I come back?* (The lawyer's attitude— "Of course you will talk to me, the only question is when.")

Witness: *Look, I don't want to get involved. This is a fight between the landlord and Jones.*

Attorney: *You feel that it really isn't your concern and you feel getting involved would just be a hassle.* (A dynamite "active listening" response. When people feel understood, they tend to open up. Watch this!)

Witness: *Yeah, that's exactly right. I already don't get along with Jones and all I need is to have the landlord after me.*

Attorney: *No use just looking for trouble.*

Witness: *Right. What happens if the landlord gives me the boot?*

Attorney: *Moving and finding a new place is a real pain. That's a worry. How long have you lived here?*

Witness: *About a year.*

Attorney: *New to the area?*

Witness: *Yeah. From out of state.*

Attorney: *Me too. Where from?*

The attorney is doing great, expressing understanding of the witness' concerns, subtly shifting the conversation to neutral topics and even getting in some common points of identification, both being from out of state. The witness will believe she agreed to talk, it's just that she can't remember when.

Attorney: *What's Jones like as a neighbor?* (As in the case of client interviewing, begin with broad, open ended questions.

This allows the person to narrate what he deems important and will generally unearth details which specific questions never would. Use specific questions only after you have a good overview).

Witness: *Not good. Wild parties. Wakes up my baby.*

Attorney: *That must be hard on you.* (Here the lawyer faces two choices, first, to shift the conversation away from this unfavorable information but this would be a mistake. It is important to learn, early-on, the negatives. The second choice is to either pursue the details supporting "Wild parties," or to defer that and ask if there are other items in the category of objectionable behavior.)

Attorney: *Other than the parties, any other things about Jones as a neighbor?*

Witness: *No, not really.*

Attorney: *So, other than the parties, Jones is a good neighbor.*

Witness: *I didn't say that. I only said I didn't like the parties.* (So much for trying to lead the witness.)

Attorney: *That's fair. But in terms of being a bad neighbor, the only thing you can think of is the parties. Right?*

Witness: Yeah. (Here the attorney has *closed the door* on the witness. If she signs a statement reading "I have one complaints about Jones as a neighbor, wild parties," she can be impeached if she adds to her list of complaints.)

Attorney: *I would like to know more about the parties. How often are they?* (Bravo, don't shy away from the "bad" stuff. Pursue—the parties may be nightly or may be monthly. You need to know).

Witness: *About every weekend.*

Attorney: *Well, let's see. Today's Wednesday, was there one last weekend?* (Again, pursue the details).

Witness: *I don't think so.*

Attorney: *Do you recall when the first party was?*

Witness: *No, I can't remember.*

Attorney: *Was it before or after Christmas?*

Trial lawyers, listening to answers, always have two background concerns:

1. How does the witness know that?

2. Has the witness answered my question?

As to the latter, you hear a lot of deflections, half-answers, and "I'm not sure," "Maybe," and "I can't remember." Once you recognize a non-answer, pursue:

> *Attorney:* Did the landlord ever tell you Jones
> was late with his rent?
>
> *Witness.* I'm not sure.
>
> *Attorney:* Well, if you're not sure, then you can't
> say that the landlord did tell you that.
> Correct?

End Game

Some of the practice is tedium. The thrill of finding the case "on all fours" is soon replaced by the wearisomeness of briefing and shepardizing. So too with investigation. It is critical for you to spend the long boring hours in preparing investigation reports and witness statements. Why? Often trial will be far in the future. (The doctrine of past recollection recorded is more than a condescending concession to senior citizens). Writing down the results of your investigation also serves as a check on its inclusiveness. As you write you will likely realize areas that need further investigation. Finally written reports thicken the file. During negotiation this will help convince your opponent of your seriousness and competence.

After each of your investigative efforts, write a summary. As to areas to cover, consider the five "W's"—who, what, when, where, and why—plus how.

CHAPTER 23

DISCOVERY: *THE HOSTILE DEPOSITION*

Discovery is boring.

That's my basic insight. The rest is filler.

Discovery's image is not the youthful and vibrant David challenging giants; it is the tottering English judge, nodding off. When drafting interrogatories your concern is not with grace, insight or zing; it is with quibbles and nitpicks. And the deposition scene is not the stately courtroom where inspired questions flash; it is a lawyer's stuffy conference room where little questions nibble.

Pretentious filler.

Depositions are taken in someone's office, usually a lawyer's.

You laugh? When I was a law student, a survivor of a rigorous Civil Procedure course, I could spot "work-product" at fifty paces but, alas, when it came to where depositions were taken, and who was there, and whether there would be bagels, I hadn't a clue. Writing a book, *or* preparing a witness, assume *nothing*.

Who will be in the room? Not the judge. If there is a dispute, the lawyers will have to go to court.

303

There will be a court reporter, who swears the "deponent" and transcribes the hearing. After a few weeks, the deponent will receive a copy of the transcript to read, correct, and sign. While you can't cross out what was said, additions and qualifications can be put at the end: "The Devil made me say it!"

Parties can attend. Bring your client to watch, to learn about the process, to help with follow up questions, and to get a sense of how the opposition views the conflict, occasionally a real impetus to settlement. Also, if there are differing accounts, it will be harder to lie with the other party sitting there.

In the 1970's, when the War on Poverty was burning bright, Gary Bellow, of California Rural Legal Assistance, deposed a county's chief housing official in front of a room filled with his clients, migrant farm workers living in rat-infected county labor camps. His goal was community organizing; a smart lawyer knows you can use legal devices to achieve nontraditional ends.

Usually depositions are informal but expensive: client time, lawyers' fees, and the bill from the court reporter. The party calling the deposition pays for the court reporter and the original transcript; the other party must pay for a copy. Transcripts are protected by copyright and cannot be shared outside one's office. The prevailing party usually is able to recover these costs.

This chapter is written with the Federal Rules in mind. Many state discovery statutes parallel these Rules. If yours don't, there is still much in the chapter that will help you.

There are essentially two kinds of depositions: those taken of the adverse party and hostile witnesses, and those taken of friendly witnesses. They are day and night in terms of the goals and techniques. Most depositions are taken of adverse parties and of witnesses aligned with them. They are "hostile" in a strategic sense, not, necessarily, in the nasty stare sense. Often the atmosphere is friendly and relaxed. In this chapter we'll look at hostile depositions from both sides: taking it and defending or opposing it. In the next chapter we'll look at friendly depositions and other discovery devices. But first, some quick, general points.

Scope of Discovery and General Planning Matters

The scope of discovery is wide. Rule 26 of the Federal Rules of Civil Procedure, provides:

> *Unless otherwise limited by order of the court ... parties may obtain discovery regarding any matter, not privileged, that is relevant to the claim or defense of any party, including the existence, description, nature, custody, condition, and location of any books, documents, or other tangible things and the identity and location of persons having knowledge of any discoverable matter.... Relevant information need not be admissible at the trial if the discovery*

> *appears reasonably calculated to lead to the discovery of admissible evidence.*

And "relevant evidence," is evidence

> *"having any tendency to make the existence of any fact that is of consequence to the determination of the action more probable or less probable than it would be without the evidence."* Evidence Rule 401.

Due to widespread discovery abuse, the Federal Rules were amended in 2000 to limit discovery. First, the scope was somewhat reduced, with the old rule allowing for discovery of information relevant to the "subject matter" of the litigation, not just claims and defenses. Second, no discovery is available until after the parties have met and conferred, thus preventing filing a suit along with a notice of deposition. Third, the number of interrogatory questions has been limited to 25. Fourth, depositions are limited to one 7 hour day. While all of these limitations are subject to override by court order, they have a major impact on discovery planning.

There is always a conflict between speed and preparation. Getting the jump in discovery can pay dividends. Your opponent will realize that you are serious and that the litigation is going to be expensive. Settlement looks better. Further, an early deposition commits your opponent to a version of the facts, and gives you time to explore leads and check the dubious aspects of your opponent's yarn.

But there is a case to be made for the turtle. The more you know before you take a deposition, the more effective you will be in focusing inquiry. The limit of seven hours means that depositions can no longer meander leisurely toward the coast. Second, discovery is always a two-way street; your opponent is learning something of your case from the questions you ask. Finally, early activity on your part forces your opponent to get busy. Do you want to make hay while your opponent sleeps? Consider the virtues of informal investigation.

Another overall planning issue is the order in which you depose the witnesses. Who goes first? Traditionally, at trial, you call your client *after* your other witnesses have testified, thus avoiding a lot of silly inconsistencies and contradictions. Turning this ploy around, consider deposing the adverse party *before* you depose the henchmen. For the same reason, it might be well to depose the adverse party *before* your opponent deposes your client. If you do, invite your client.

Two other rules of thumb on deposition order:

1. Depose neutral witnesses before hostile ones;

2. Depose collateral witnesses before central ones.

Both will give you a strong factual understanding of the case before moving to more difficult encounters.

Should a set of interrogatories precede the deposition? They are vastly less expensive and will, by clearing up the basics, allow for better and more focused depositions. On the other hand, in considering and answering your interrogatories, your opponent will be learning about your case. Consciously or not, the deposition testimony may be tailored in light of this knowledge.

Note that you no longer need to waste interrogatories to obtain the names of your opponent's witnesses. These must be disclosed without formal discovery. Rule 26.

Preparing to take a "Hostile" Deposition

Planning

Prepare as if *you* were on trial. You are. Consciously or unconsciously the opposing lawyer is taking your measure. Are you taking the case seriously? Are you putting time and effort into it? Do you know how to handle yourself? Settlement value will soar or crash on these assessments.

Prepare as you would prepare for trial. What are your objectives? What areas do you wish to explore? In what order do you want to explore them? What specific questions will you ask? All of this will result in a list of questions or general topics that you will pursue in the deposition.

Even though you will have a list of questions, *don't* be wed to it! This is, after all, *discovery.*

During *trial,* uncharted waters can be dangerous. The risk is considerably less in the discovery stage. If you are to run aground on unexpected and harmful answers, better now than at trial; you have time to right the ship. This metaphor is getting me nowhere. At the discovery stage, your general goal is to find out as much as possible; as you go through your list of questions, be sensitive to *hints*, *clues*, and *half-answers* and be prepared to take profitable detours. If they lead to material harmful to your case, better now than later.

In planning, don't think exclusively in terms of trial. A deposition might be used primarily to set up pretrial motions. More often, they play a central role in negotiation and settlement: how can I use this deposition to further my settlement goals?

Obnoxious adversaries

As my colleague Ana Maria Merico–Stephens points out, sometimes an "obnoxious litigator, smelling blood, will try to scare you into early retirement at your first deposition." Unwarranted objections, speaking clarifications, and shameless uncivility are the weapons. If you know your stuff, not to worry.

> *Any objection during a deposition must be stated concisely and in a non-argumentative and non-suggestive manner.* Rule 30.

Remain calm and focused. If the behavior continues, consider halting the deposition and call the judge or bring in a video camera. This usually works.

Note that there is a critical distinction between your opponent objecting to your questions and instructing the witness not to answer. If your oppo-

nent objects as to the form of your questions, you
can either:

1. Rephrase the question, or

2. Instruct the witness to answer

The latter choice simply means that the objection
as to form can be raised again at trial *if* the transcript is being used at trial.

The *only time* your opponent can instruct a witness not to answer is to protect a privilege, enforce
a prior court sanctioned limitation, or to bring a
motion to the effect that you are conducting the
deposition in bad faith or abusing the witness. So
says Rule 30.

Irrelevant objections. The test is whether your
questions are "reasonable calculated" to lead to the
discovery of admissible evidence that is "relevant to
the claim or defense of any party." If your opponent
objects on these grounds, you can choose to ignore
the objection with "Objection noted. Now, Mr. Witness, answer the question." This puts the ball back
into the court of your opponent whose only alternative is to adjourn the deposition and seek a protective order. This is a very risky route as your opponent, if wrong, faces sanctions.

Note, however, that this objection is most likely
made in order to signal the witness to think before
answering: while the answer may not seem relevant
to the witness, upon reflection, it will. Of course, if
you explain the question's relevance, the cat will be
out of the bag.

One final planning thought, of the "Oh no, I forgot to have children!" variety. Subpoena the witness or eat the bagel alone.

Goals of the hostile deposition

Possible, and somewhat conflicting, goals:

1. Developing new leads.

2. Developing favorable material.

3. Discovering how bad things are.

4. Committing the witness to specifics.

5. Testing the witness and looking for impeachment material.

How you conduct the deposition will depend on which of these goals you are pursuing. Let's take a look at each.

Goal: Developing new leads.

"Is there anything this witness knows that might lead me to other witnesses or documents?"

"Who else was there?"

"Were there any photographs or recordings?"

"What exactly did your grandmother tell you?"

Many people keep diaries and journals that they may review before the deposition. Ask. If they have, then you can seek it by filing a Request for Production. (Always ask your witnesses if they have such documents and ask to review them before the deposition.)

You can, by appropriate subpoena or agreement with opposing counsel, require the witness to bring books, documents and other tangible evidence to the deposition for your inspection.

Don't worry about admissibility. You can ask questions that call for *hearsay* and *speculation*. You may not be able to get the answers in at trial but they may lead to other evidence. As all good gossips know, hearsay is simply a wonderful source of information; speculation, even better.

Goal: Developing favorable material.

Is there any way this witness can help you? Even the most hostile of witnesses can, if in no other way than taking certain issues out of contention:

> Q: *Now you admit the defendant didn't come out of the house until 10 minutes after the explosion?*

Favorable material from a hostile witness is quite impressive to a jury. "Even my adversary's star witness agrees with our contention X."

You should be friendly and, where appropriate, use leading questions. If you also intend to attack parts of the person's testimony, better to save the attack until after you have explored developing favorable material.

Goal: Discovering how bad things are.

Pursue the bad and *ask "Why?"* You don't want to first learn of damaging material at trial. Learn it early, when you can prepare for it or when you can settle. The downside of "take no prisoners" is that you might uncover some devastating evidence that your opponent otherwise would not have. If your opponent is competent, this is unlikely.

Here your questioning style is open, hoping for narration. "Anything else?" and "Why?" will pepper the transcript.

One time you may consider *not* pursuing the bad is where the witness may be *unavailable* for trial. You might want to stick with using the deposition to search for leads and perhaps impeachment material and pretty much avoid the substance of their testimony. If the witness does not appear at trial, then the transcript will appear, like the ghost of Christmas Past or Hamlet's dad. And, as we have learned from those two, the less said, the better. You won't have a ghost of a chance to rebut; when did Hamlet's uncle get to tell his side?

Goal: Committing the witness to specifics.

If the witness's testimony changes at trial, you can seek solace in the doctrine of *prior inconsistent statements*. For impeachment to work, however, you cannot have a sloppy deposition transcript filled with vague questions and unclear answers. When you are trying to commit a witness to specifics, your style will be much more controlling (not necessarily hostile) and leading questions will be common.

Even if you get a clear answer, witnesses weasel. When confronted with a prior inconsistent statement, expect: "I may have said that at the deposition but I didn't understand your question," or "I was tired," or "That was on a Monday morning and

Monday mornings are particularly bad in terms of existential angst." (As my editor Stephen Golden reminds me, Bob Hope might say, "Angst for the memories." That's why Stephen's the editor.)

Begin the deposition closing doors:

> Q: *Now I am only interested in what you know. Don't guess. There are two kinds of guessing. Number one, you cannot understand my question and guess at what the question means. The second type of guessing is where you can understand my question perfectly well, but do not know the answer and guess at it. I do not want you to do either; okay?*

> A: *Okay.*

> Q: *Thus, if you answer a question, it means you understood the question and that you know the answer, unless you have told me otherwise; all right?*

> A: *All right.*

> Q: *And if you don't know, just tell us you don't know, or you don't understand, and I will either rephrase it or in some way make it understandable; okay?*

> A: *Okay.*

> Q: *Is there anything preventing you in any way from giving accurate testimony today? Spiritually, how you doin'? Do you realize Sartre wasn't even an American?*

In order to get a clear transcript, one suitable for impeachment:

> *Q: Before you answer a question, let me finish asking it, even though you might know what it will be. And answer with "yes" or "no," not "uh-huh" or "unh-uh."*

Goal: Testing the witness and looking for impeachment material.

How will this witness perform at trial? Will the witness be believable? Will the witness enlist the sympathy of the jury? To see how the witness stands up, consider a riff of hostile cross. If you are evaluating the witness, *watch* the witness, don't keep your head down taking notes. Although you'll be taking notes, there will be times you put down your pen and concentrate fully on the Q's and A's. Note-taking can interfere with the flow of the deposition and the pause can give the witness time to regroup.

Everything in life is reversible (except for my belt, which claims to be). *The witness will also be getting a feel for you and what it is like to be examined.* To avoid this byproduct, some lawyers suggest that you present different demeanor in the two activities, lamb followed by tiger. These clever lawyers anticipate everything, except other lawyers advising witnesses to change *their* demeanor.

Should you confront the witness? This is a difficult issue. During the deposition, the deponent may say contradictory things, may contradict a prior statement or say something that is easily refutable by a document you have in your file. You will be tempted to go for it. But if you confront the witness during the deposition, even if he or she can't think of an explanation just then, by the time trial rolls around, you can expect a very fine one. Confrontations are usually more profitable at trial.

On the other hand, if you save the confrontation for trial, there is always the chance that the witness has a good explanation and you might look rather silly. Further, you will not have time to check its truth. Realize too that a substantial attack on the testimony during the deposition may cause your opponent to rethink the case and settle it. That said, most advise to save impeachment for trial, even if you believe the case will probably settle.

The only time you should *definitely* confront the witness is when it is likely that the witness will not testify at trial and the deposition will be introduced. Wait in that case and you will not be able to confront the witness.

Conducting the deposition

Should you be a jerk?

Because there is no jury, the risks are less and perhaps the "Formidable You" might convince the other side to settle. On the other hand, you may be able to accomplish more of your goals by affecting a more agreeable persona. Before you get there, decide upon your demeanor. Your demeanor may change during the deposition as you move from one area to another or in light of the witness.

Listening to answers.

Working from a list of questions, the danger is that you will be thinking of your next question rather than carefully listening to the current answers. Focus on the answer, and pause before asking the next, and ask yourself:

   1. How does the witness know?

This question raises possibilities that the witness is relying on hearsay or on faulty conclusions based on observed data.

   2. Has the witness answered my question?

Don't interrupt witnesses who are going off on frolics of their own; allow them sufficient rope and learn important things. However, when the witness stops, ask yourself "Has the witness answered my question?" If not, repeat it. This cannot be stated too strongly. *Be sure the question you asked was answered.* Slick witnesses are very good at dancing around a question without specifically answering it. Your heart will sink when you read the transcript to find that your killer question simply wasn't answered.

Dealing with objections

If your opponent objects to the *form* of the question ("Leading," "Vague," "Compound"), you might want to rephrase it. If you don't, and if the objection is good, then it can be renewed at trial *if* you're going to use the transcript at trial. If you don't care about that, simply tell the witness "Go ahead and answer."

As we have seen, there are very few times your opponent can properly instruct a witness not to answer, basically, only to protect attorney/client privilege. Even in these situations, ask the witness to answer the question. As it is the client's privilege, the client can waive it and, indeed, some do.

Enough of taking a hostile deposition. What if you are on the other side?

Defending a hostile deposition

Prepare thyself

Put yourself in your opponent's shoes:

> *"If I was taking this deposition, what areas would I explore? What documents would I seek?"*

Spend some serious time preparing the deposition that you would take.

1. This will allow you to better prepare your witness for the deposition.

2. This will provide a ground upon which your opponent's thinking will jump out. What was your opponent's goal in exploring areas you did not anticipate? Why didn't your opponent explore areas you would have?

Consider pre-deposition motions

Unless your opponent is going bananas, the only thing you can really protect *during* the deposition is *privilege*. There may be other areas you wish to put off limits, such a *work product*. Documents and tangible things prepared *in anticipation of litigation* are considered work product. If you fear that some of this might be disclosed during the deposition, seek a pre-deposition protective order. It will be protected unless your opponent has a substantial need for it. Of course, by bringing such a motion, you alert your opponent to the existence of such a document and may lose it at the hearing.

Note, however, that if you gamble and your opponent unearths work product during the deposition, you can still object to its introduction at trial. The only objections you waive are those that go to the form of the question.

Prepare and educate your witness

Lawyers would never allow their clients to testify at *trial* without first going over their testimony; far too many just have their witnesses *show up* for their deposition.

Most cases settle and a major factor on the settlement is how well your clients and witnesses do during their depositions. Realize too that a case might be lost if the witness doesn't know what to expect.

Educate as to the setting: no judge, court reporter, maybe the adverse party, and, yes, in someone's office but, no, probably no bagels.

Prepare the witness with a practice run. Refresh recollection as to key points if you don't want "I don't know" or "I don't recall."

There is no need to educate the witness as to everything—"I don't know" is a legitimate response to a deposition question (unlike that in an interrogatory where there is a duty to investigate). Will "I don't know" from this witness hurt you at trial? If not, no need to educate.

Caution

Anything you show your client or your witness to refresh their recollection *may be* subject to disclosure. The law is somewhat tangled in this area. There are considerations of work-product and attorney/client privilege. Nonetheless, a routine question is: "Did you review any documents or other writing in preparation for this deposition?" What you *tell your client* in preparation for the deposition is protected by "attorney/client," but what you tell *other witnesses* in preparation is not.

Caution the witness

You will tell everyone, "Tell the truth." Beyond that the traditional advice is *just answer the question and don't volunteer*. That's fine but you need to go further and address *why* the witness will want to volunteer.

> *"You'll want to volunteer information to tell your side of the story. Don't. There is no way you are going to convince the other lawyer you are in the right. And the lawyer will likely be friendly but the lawyer is not your friend. Remember. The lawyer is being paid to go after you."*

Tell witnesses that they will get the chance to tell their side at trial. Tell them it is fine to admit to "inconvenient facts" and warn them that trying to explain hurtful facts away just makes things worse.

> *"Depositions are not conversations; you are dictating a court document. To avoid getting into a conversation, look at the court reporter, not the lawyer."*

Another traditional piece of advice: *Pause and think before answering.* While long pauses look bad at trial, they will not show on a written transcript. You may also want to warn witnesses, by way of illustration, of leading questions and rapid fire questioning which can confuse the honest as well as the dishonest.

On the other hand, you don't want to scare the wits out of the witness. Reassure the witness that, although depositions are serious and critical, they are not as scary as trials. The public is not invited. Mistakes can be rectified when it comes time to sign the transcript (although the original answer will stay in the transcript).

Being there

> *A minister sees God in the first pew and, in panic, phones his Bishop. The Bishop is skeptical and advises a vacation. The minister insists and eventually the Bishop agrees to come to see for himself. There, in the first pew, sits God.*
>
> *"Over there," whispers the minister. "I see," replies the Bishop. "What should we do?"*
>
> *"Look busy."*

Resist the temptation. Yours is a mostly passive role.

1. Object when necessary to protect privileged material.

2. Object if your opponent is cutting off the witness, arguing with the witness or otherwise acting improperly. If your opponent is going far afield, object as to relevancy and thus set the stage for an argument that your opponent is acting in bad faith. Note that this objection signals the witness to think before answering: the opponent may be sneaking up, closing doors, and laying traps.

Should you object as to matters of form? Unless this is confusing the witness, probably not. Often the only result of an objection as to the form of a question is that your adversary will ask a better one, thus resulting in a clearer transcript. Opposing a hostile deposition, the more confused the transcript, the better; chaos caused by a sloppy opponent rocks.

To keep yourself occupied, focus on your adversary's questions. Why is the lawyer interested in that topic? How will that point be used at trial?

At the end of the deposition, *you can question the witness.* Other than clearing up obvious misstatements or mistakes of the witness, don't. It just tips your hand. You'll have your day at trial. One exception: if your opponent is deposing your *expert* and has not gone over the expert's qualifications, you should. If the expert unexpectedly splits, without the qualifications on record, you may have a hard time getting the testimony in and, even if you do, it will be weakened by the omission.

Back at the office

After a week or so, you'll get the transcript but don't close up shop until then. Write a memo to the file covering two topics:

1.   What did my opponent learn of my case?

2.   What did *I* learn about my *opponent's* case?

Write the memo *now*; resist the Siren's Song of getting on with the rest of your life and surely never, not once, stop to smell the flowers. (If you've smelled one, you've smelled them all.)

CHAPTER 24

FRIENDLY DEPOSITIONS AND OTHER DISCOVERY DEVICES

A cartoon shows several bee hives, one of which has a shingle over the door. A beekeeper explains:

"Those are the attorney bees. They represent the killer bees."

This has really nothing to do with discovery but it *might* lead to something relevant. Dare you object?

"Friendly" Depositions

The major reason to take the deposition of a friendly witness is to *preserve testimony*. Occasionally they are taken as part of a *negotiation strategy* ("Look how strong my witness is"), or to set up Motions for Summary Judgment which can be supported by deposition transcripts.

It is one of the great ironies, in a field marked with so few, that "hostile" depositions often aren't, and "friendly" depositions seldom are. They are one-person trials, with the proponent of the deposition conducting the direct and with the opponent conducting the cross. Both sides know that the transcript will likely be used at trial in lieu of live witness testimony.

To prepare for such depositions reread the chapters on Direct and Cross earlier in this book. There are some additional specific points to be made.

As proponent:

1.   If you use the transcript at trial, your opponent cannot then object to the *form* of the questions you asked (leading, compound, etc.), but can object on substantive grounds (hearsay, speculation, lack of foundation). Objections such as lack of foundation can be fatal at this point because, as the witness is not in the courtroom, you can't back up and lay a proper one. Therefore make sure you lay the proper foundations during the deposition.

2.   Having a deposition read into the record is Dullsville. If possible, lead with a joke. Consider video. Video depositions of out of town experts are becoming more common as a method of cutting litigation costs.

As opponent:

1.   You have to treat the deposition as a trial and be prepared to cross-examine. How can you prepare for it if you don't know what the witness will say? Of course, when giants walked the earth, they *never* knew; but enough of the good old days, the days before killer bees. While you cannot interview adverse parties, you can interview any witness who will talk with you or you can take a

taped statement. If the witness is key, and won't agree to an informal interview, consider having a *discovery* deposition before what in effect is the *trial* deposition.

2. You must make, or waive, objections as to form: leading, compound, vague, calls for a narrative. This is because your adversary can correct the questions during the deposition but cannot at the trial, the witness not being there. Just because you have an objection as to form, doesn't mean you should take it. Often it simply allows your opponent to be more focused.

Interrogatories

Interrogatories have definite limitations. They lack spontaneity and answers are calculated. You have no follow-up questions for evasive answers. Interrogatories can be served only on *parties*. To gain information from *witnesses* you must do so informally or use depositions.

Nevertheless, interrogatories can be quite helpful in obtaining specific information and narrowing issues:

— *How many employees do you have?*

— *How many years have you been so employed?*

— *How many angels can sit on the head of a pin?*

Interrogatories are better than depositions in that "Beats me" is not an adequate response. There is a duty to take reasonable steps to find out, such as thumbing though old philosophy notes. And an interrogatory reaches not only the *personal* knowledge of the party but also the information *available* to the party, such as information stored somewhere in the corporation.

Under a recent revision of the Federal Rules, you only get, without court order, only 25 questions (including your first: "Is it animal, vegetable or mineral?"). This means that probably most of the old form books, which listed hundreds of questions and were sold by the word, are hopelessly out of date. However, consult them for general ideas in different kinds of cases.

Although the new amendments limit the number of interrogatories, they also require your opponent to turn over such things as witness names, documents which may be introduced to support claims, unless for impeachment, and other items. Rule 26. Before the amendments, interrogatories had to be used to get at this information and, in some state jurisdictions, still do.

 1. *Describe and indicate the location of each record and document kept by you concerning "X."*

Be as specific as possible, otherwise your opponent may object that the question is so broad as to be unduly burdensome, or worse still, send you a list of documents so long as to be essentially meaningless.

2. *State the name and location of each and every person who has knowledge concerning "X."*

Even though your opponent spent three weeks searching for the only eyewitness, the name and location are not work product. Compare the statement your opponent took from the witness.

3. *Identify each person you expect to call as an expert witness at trial and state the substance of the facts and opinions to which she is expected to testify and a summary of the grounds for each opinion.*

You cannot demand to know the names of the experts your opponent has *interviewed* but has decided not to call at trial. This allows lawyers to seek expert advice without getting stung.

4. *List all of the witnesses you intend to call in support of your allegation that the sky was falling. Indicate the substance of the testimony of each.*

Consider combining discovery devices:

Request for Admission: Admit that the sky was not falling.

Interrogatory: If you deny this assertion, list the witnesses you intend to call in support of your denial and indicate the substance of the testimony of each.

Request for Production of Documents: If you deny the assertion, attach copies of all documents you intend to introduce into evidence as support of that denial.

Admissions and other discovery devices

Admissions can be used to take uncontested facts out of a case:

> *You are requested to admit the truth of the following statements pursuant to Federal Rule 36, which provides that these matters will be deemed admitted unless, as to each, you serve within 30 days an answer, or an objection thereto, stating the reasons why you cannot truthfully admit or deny the matter.*
>
> *You may not give lack of information or knowledge as a reason for failure to admit or deny unless you state you have made reasonable inquiry and that you still lack sufficient information to admit or deny. The statements are as follows:*
>
> *That, during the period alleged in the complaint herein, you were a resident of New York City.*
>
> *That, during the period alleged in the complaint, King Kong was on a frolic of his own.*

As the example indicates, it is possible to request admission of propositions involving mixed questions of law and fact.

Other Discovery Devices

The Federal Rules provide for two other main discovery devices:

> *Rule 34: Production of Documents and Things and Entry Upon Land for Inspection and Other Purposes*

Years ago, when I was burning bright, I brought an action to close, as a public nuisance, a large cattle feedlot, owned by a pillar of the community. It was next to a small and very poor community lived in by migrant workers and their families. I was able to get my expert onto the feedlot to collect samples to prove that indeed the zillions of flies that tormented my clients came from the feedlot, not, as the defendant claimed, from them.

Rule 35: Physical and Mental Examination of Persons

These are extremely important in the defense of personal injury cases. A doctor of the defense lawyer's choosing examines the plaintiff and the medical records and then gives an opinion as to the cause and extent of injuries.

Corrections and Sanctions

Rule 26(e) requires you to supplement discovery disclosures if you learn that in some material respect the information disclosed is incomplete or incorrect.

Courts are getting much more serious with discovery abuse. If you are thinking of playing fast and loose, read Rule 37. There is real sting in it.

"Buzz," says the killer bee. "That was a self-defense buzz," quickly adds the attorney bee.

CHAPTER 25

NEGOTIATION: HARDBALL AND PROBLEM–SOLVING

"He killed himself."
"Did not. It was an accident."
"Was not."
"Was too."

Law students were negotiating. If accident, Widow collects $1 million insurance, if suicide, $500,000. Things were going pretty much as expected, "We have a great case; yours sucks!" "Not so! Our case is terrific; yours sucks!" Finally, the students representing the company gave their last offer: "$600,000 and that's it!" Something unexpected happened. Rather than responding, the student representing the widow said: "Given her other sources of income, how much does she need to live comfortably?"

The shouting stopped; the students moved to the same side of the table and started making lists of income and expenses.

Not all negotiations are the same. Context matters. One critical variable is whether litigation looms if settlement is not reached: it does in personal injury and criminal cases; it does not in negotiating transactions where disappointed parties walk away. Another important variable is whether there are significant long-term concerns: are the parties one time players or will they be together for the long haul? Other variables include the emotional charge on the parties and the personalities of the lawyers.

Not all negotiation styles, approaches, and ploys work equally well in all contexts. Always keep context in mind. This introductory chapter covers some general matters, such as the two basic approaches to negotiation and the limits of machismo. In the next chapter, we'll go into the trenches to explore nasty ploys and the choices you will have to make. In the final three chapters, I will look at specific negotiating contexts: negotiating a personal injury case, negotiating a transaction, and, finally, negotiating a dispute concerning an on-going transaction.

Styles: Hardball v. Problem Solving

"There are two kinds of people," wrote Robert Benchly, "Those who believe there are two kinds of people and those who don't." Surprisingly, there are also two basic negotiation styles: hardball and problem-solving.

Hardball

Hardball views negotiation as a game to be *won*. Like prose, it comes naturally and is what we usually think of when we think "negotiation." It is also called "positional bargaining" in that the two parties stake out initial positions and slowly come together on a solution. ("I will be back by midnight." "No, you get home by 9.") It is marked by zero-sum thinking (what I get, you lose), puffing one's position while attacking the opposition, and keeping secrets while gathering "intelligence." A typical hardball ploy is a very high demand (or very low offer), followed by small and painful concessions, accompanied with threats of walkout.

Problem Solving

This approach views negotiation as a problem to be *solved*. It *rejects* zero-sum thinking: pies can be expanded, not just divided. It *rejects* secrecy: needs and goals are to be shared in search of a better resolution. Lawyers make lists, not threats, and brainstorming is common. See Chapter 1, *Legal Problem Solving*

Suppose a buyer and seller are negotiating a long term contract. The buyer has critical short-term needs. A hardballer would *not* disclose those needs in fear that the seller would jack up the price. A problem-solver would disclose. It may be that the seller has a large inventory that sits in storage, running up bills, or the seller may have other problems that, if disclosed, could be dealt with in a way that both sides would profit. Another reason favoring buyer disclosure would be to take the seller's measure: if the seller exploits this weakness, perhaps it is better for the buyer to walk away.

Because it builds trust and cooperation, problem-solving works well in situations where the parties will be in a long-term relationship. It also works well in situations where there are many issues on the table. Behind each issue lie differing needs and values and from this rich mix, creative solutions are quite promising. This does not mean, however, that one cannot play hardball in complicated and long-term contract negotiations; many lawyers negotiate long-term transactions in this fashion. Conversely, problem solving can work in cases where there are only one-time players and the dispute looks zero-sum as was the case with our widow.

One-time players and the matter of money

The concept of "one-time players" can be harmful as it suggests that the short-term is the only relevant time frame. But in all negotiations, the future should be considered. What one does today will impact the parties tomorrow and tomorrow and tomorrow. This is obviously true in the case of the widow, an archetypical "one-time player." As William Faulkner has written: "The past is never dead. It's not even past."

As to money, the dispute that walks into your office will often be about it. Realize that money can represent many things: respect, recognition, love, or, in the case of our widow, fear of hunger and homelessness. My favorite "money is more than money" story involves Michael Milken, the bond dealer who made, in the 1980's, over $400 million in *one year*. Two friends were talking about him.

"If it were me, I would quit after $25 million."

"That's why it will never *be* you."

By recognizing that dollars can be symbols, it is often possible to turn a zero-sum dispute over dollars into something more amenable to problem-solving.

Problem-solving strategies are becoming popular, thanks to books such as Fisher's *Getting to Yes,* and Mnookin, *Beyond Winning,* both deserving your attention. Both books show how the approach can create value and lead to happier clients. Another reason for the growing popularity is that many lawyers, having grown weary of chasing each other around the table, have embraced the approach as a more human and more satisfying way to practice. Opponents become collaborators and empathy replaces manipulation. A very attractive promise. Why doesn't it come naturally?

Partly because collaboration is at odds with our world view, "Us versus them". We fail to disclose our needs because we know they can become our vulnerabilities; we know this because *we* turn the needs of others into *their* vulnerabilities. Perhaps we learned this dark view from playground encounters, perhaps from Darwin's "survival of the fittest."

Is nature as "red in tooth and claw" as we fear? Probably not. It's just that we tend to see competition and overlook cooperation. In *The Lives of a Cell* Dr. Lewis Thomas argues that an impartial look at nature will disclose a great amount of symbiosis: species cooperating to assure joint survival. If we look at our own lives and families, cooperation frequently trumps competition; and yet we still act in the belief that exploitation is the norm.

Another factor undermining the wide use of cooperative models is the fear that we might be selling out our client.

> *"I understand your needs concerning this issue. They are more pressing than those of my client. I am sure I can convince my client to concede this issue."*

"Have I just sold out my client?" thinks the lawyer. "Perhaps instead I should have increased my demand."

I think we all carry some form of the hard/soft dichotomy, with hard being aggressive and dogmatic, with soft being cooperative and understanding. Despite our protestations to the contrary, it seems we are on safer grounds when we snarl.

Another reason hardball continues as the norm is that it seems easier, less complicated, and more in line with lawyer expertise. Problem-solving envisions lengthy discussions in areas that often lie outside of our expertise. Given these concerns, hardball probably will remain the norm in routine matters, such as smaller personal injury cases and minor crimes.

Then there is the problem of unilateral disarmament. If the buyer discloses its needs, what's to say the seller won't play hardball and keep its needs secret?

For problem solving to work, the lawyers and the clients must all be committed to it. If you want to try the approach, first discuss it with your client and then with your opponent. Explain how needs negotiation and creative problem-solving can benefit the short term and long term needs of both parties. Hammer out ground rules:

> *"We will take turns disclosing our clients' interests, needs and goals, and agree not to exploit them by changing demands in light of the disclosed material."*

> *"When we make proposals, we will disclose how they help meet the needs of our clients and will justify them in terms of fairness rather than by the threat of deadlock."*

> *"If we deadlock, we have failed."*

Even then, a major theoretical problem with the problem-solving approach remains. Clients may be compelled to sacrifice what the law would otherwise award them in order to solve the "mutual" problem. An analogy is to the treatment of juvenile offenders. In one of the great reform movements of the early 20th century, juveniles were not to be treated like adults and punished for their crimes. Rather, the goal was helping young offenders cope with their underlying "problems." Jerome Carlin, in a brilliant book, *Civil Justice and the Poor*, argued that this mentality leads to a total erosion of the legal rights of juveniles. They were locked up, not so much because they committed crimes, but because they needed help. Often they were in custody longer than they would have been had they been adults at the time they committed the crime.

The great reforms in juvenile law near the end of the 20th century have been to make juvenile court more like adult court. Adults have the right to make their own decisions, even ones bad for themselves, and even bad ones for others.

Recall our widow. Maybe she had the stronger case. If so, the better approach for her lawyers would have been hardball: to demand the $1 million, with the insurance company saving litigation costs as well as avoiding a possible bad faith claim. To adopt a problem-solving approach will probably result in a settlement of less that $1 million.

To cope with this problem, even if you are committed to the problem-solving approach, do the hard work of preparing for the negotiation as if you were going to play hardball. Figure out the strengths and weakness of your case and those of your opponent. Ask yourself, to get a benchmark, if the matter were litigated, what would be the likely result?

Don't let problem-solving become a Siren's Song for the Slothful: "I'll just show up and we'll be able to work things out."

All of this does not mean that problem-solving is a flawed approach. Compare the alternative. Almost by definition, hardball negotiation will *not* come to an optimum agreement from the standpoint of *both* parties: it conceals, frequently misstates, information. Economists teach that ideal solutions, again from the perspectives of both parties, simply *cannot* be reached under these circumstances.

In the real world, of course, there are *three* kinds of people, those who think there are two kinds of people, those who don't, and those who, like me, see strong arguments on both sides. And, in the real world, most negotiations are a mixture of the styles. Even the Godfather would inquire into the opponent's needs and to try address them in his offer that "cannot be refused." And, even in the ideal world of problem-solving, no matter how big the pie becomes, at some point, it will have to be divided. As human beings, we are always convinced that we are entitled to the bigger share, not necessarily because we are selfish, but because we *feel* our own hunger, while that of others, no matter our empathy, remains abstract. Expect some hardball, even among the best of friends, but always remember the costs of secrecy and exploitation.

Your negotiation style will no doubt depend on the nature of the negotiations, the personalities of the players and, in large degree, who you are. Do you trust people, perhaps to a fault? Do you enjoy risk, bluffs and threats? Can you tolerate uncertainty? Do you avoid conflict? Seek compromise? Relish competition?

The good news is that there is no "preferred" approach in terms of effectiveness. Gerald Williams, in his fine work on negotiation, *Legal Negotiation and Settlement,* concluded that both hardballers and problem-solvers can be highly successful, and both can fall on their face. That said, there may be a *best style* for a given situation. Self-knowledge assures you that you are adopting a particular style, and pursuing particular objectives, because they are the *best* in the particular circumstances, not because "that's the way you are."

The really good news, however, is that the most important attribute of the effective negotiator is totally within your control: a good reputation for *honesty*. If your opponent trusts you, you are on your way.

Bad Reputations

Many a good dog has been given a bad name. To protect yourself, first realize the contentious nature of negotiations. To advance the interests of your client you will be tempted to be less than totally candid, relishing the haunting question as to what the meaning of "is" is. You will be a tad obtuse to leave yourself wiggle room. On the other side of the table, your adversaries will be hearing what they want to hear. All of this can add up to "You just can't trust this person."

This cautions *clarity*, even if it means disagreement. Don't leave a meeting smirking "They probably thought I agreed to that" because, alas, they probably did.

I want to close with machismo.

Machismo

One often hears "If I agree to that, it will be a bad precedent; others will want the same thing."

"If I don't get that, I'll never have lunch in this town again." One often fears, "If I agree to that, I'm just being a wimp." At the root of all of these lies machismo. It starts young.

> *After a California earthquake, a girl, about 6, and her brother, around 4, were being interviewed for the 6 o'clock news. "It was very scary," the girl said, "we were in the house and it started to shake and things started falling and we both started crying."*

> *Her brother, who frankly wasn't paying much attention to the interview, suddenly raised his head and gave his sister a sharp look. "I wasn't crying," he said indignantly. "I was screaming."*

Soon machismo grows into the feeling, particularly among men, that if you back down once, that's *it*. We're not talking chopped liver and even failed negotiations; we're talking street murders and wars.

Does it always make sense to hang tough?

In the old days, before Health Clubs and Home Gyms, Charles Atlas would advertise weights on the back of comic books. The first frame would show a bully kicking sand in the face of a skinny kid; the next, beautiful maiden leaving skinny kid for bully. Then we watch skinny kid sending away for the Atlas Program, and a couple of frames devoted to his workouts. In the final frame, well ... you know the rest of the story.

Let's return to those simpler days. Again, in frame one, we see Bully kicking sand. But this time we see a "thought bubble" above Skinny's head. "If I don't stand up and fight, it's sand in my face forever!"

Is he right? If Skinny takes it like a weakling, can Bully now stroll down the beach, confident that Skinny will always do so.

Not if Bully has a brain. "Skinny has been humiliated and has lost the girl, next time, he might fight like a dog. I'm going to a different beach."

Let's assume that Skinny follows Bully, fights like a dog, and wins. Has Bully been taught a valuable lesson? Will he now pick on folks his own size?

Not necessarily. Bully knows that Skinny got hurt in the last bout and he can figure that Skinny, even though victorious, will not pay that price again.

Does it always make sense to hang tough?

If you fight, next time you might be so exhausted you will refuse to answer the bell. If you don't fight, next time you might hear the music, the roar of the crowd, and it's goodbye Rocky.

My point? Life is more complicated than it seems, and while it may be important to teach lessons, we are never sure what lesson we have taught. Rather than drawing lines in the sands, consider love letters.

CHAPTER 26

IN THE TRENCHES

Before you go into a negotiation, you should have a fairly good idea of your goals, of the problems you might encounter, of how to deal with nasty negotiation ploys, and how to resolve issues likely to come up in the negotiation, such as whether you want to make the first offer and how to avoid deadlock.

Planning

One of the first things to realize is that you have some flexibility in defining the controversy. Assume that an American surveillance plane off the coast of China collides with a Chinese military jet, the jet crashing with loss of life and the American plane landing safely on Chinese soil. (Stranger things have happened.) You can correctly characterize the ensuing dispute as:

1. Between the crews of the two airplanes;

2. Between the respective air forces;

3. Between the respective militaries;

4. Between the United States and China; or

5. Between the "West" and "East."

Recall our widow. That conflict can be characterized as

1. Between her and the individual insurance adjuster;

2. Between her and the company (or the entire insurance industry);

3. Between a woman and the company;

4. Between an elderly person and the company; or

5. Between a vulnerable person and a powerful company.

Don't take an initial characterization as given. Play around. How the dispute is characterized opens up, or shuts down, certain issues and opens up, or shuts down, possible solutions. There is no "correct" characterization.

As to planning, never go into a negotiation to "test the waters" or to "see what they have in mind." Roger Fisher, one of the founders of the Harvard Negotiation Project, recommends, before negotiations, the Full Monty: write out a complete settlement proposal, something that your opponent need only say "Yes" to. This specificity will trigger focus.

Another key piece of planning is determining what is known in negotiation literature as BATNA: Best Alternative to Negotiated Agreement. What are your client's alternatives if agreement is not reached? Knowing these alternatives, not only will you have a good idea of your deadlock position, but you will have a lot more confidence during the negotiation.

Involve your client in formulating your goals and BATNA. Law school presents a cartoon version of human nature: defendants always want to escape liability and, if that's not possible, to put off the day of reckoning as long as possible, and, as for plaintiffs, they simply want more, and the sooner the better. Get your clients involved so that you can seek what they want, not what you think they should want.

Once you know what your client wants, consider how to sell it. While threats lurk in all negotiations, few of us like to wake up, look in the mirror and see "coward." We want to see someone brave but reasonable. As your opponents must sell their clients on the settlement, supply them with good arguments, something better than, "Well, the other lawyer scared me."

It is also a good idea to consider the controversy from the opposition's viewpoint. What might its goals be? What problems might it face? What will it risk from stalemate?

To aid your planning, the chapters that follow raise points specific to various negotiation contexts: torts, transactions, and disputes about transactions.

Nasty Ploys

The Used Car Dealer

Once it seems you have an agreement, your opponent claims to lack authority to settle and, just like the used car salesperson, has to run the deal by the manager. Guess what? If you suspect your opponent might do this, before you get underway, ask "Do you have authority to settle this right now?"

A related ploy is to spring an additional demand at the last minute, hoping that, having come this far, you will be likely to give in. Smoke out this ploy: "Before I give you my reaction to this proposal, I want to know if there are other matters it does not include?"

The Black Box

A foot soldier in Stephan Crane's *The Red Badge of Courage*, announced to his Civil War comrades that they were going to launch an attack the next day. Challenged as to how he knew, he responded: "Well, yeh kin b'lieve me or not, jest as yeh like. I don't care a hang." Crane commented:

> *There was much food for thought in the manner in which he replied. He came near to convincing them by disdaining to produce proofs.*

Negotiators exploit the black box. They claim to have additional evidence but refuse, for a plethora of reasons, to disclose it. Undisclosed weak evidence is more threatening than disclosed strong evidence.

Variations of the black box include rejecting an offer without comment, thus disclosing nothing, or demanding an initial concession on one matter even before discussing any of the others. Wanting to peek in the black box, we often agree.

Remember what curiosity did to the cat. Insist on dialogue.

Dissing

Some negotiators engage in subtle "dissing," such as being a tad late, mispronouncing the opponent's name or, in the case of Charlie Chaplin's *The Great Dictator,* Mussolini lighting his cigar by striking a match on Hitler's bust. Once you recognize these ploys as calculated, they become pathetic.

Necessary Choices

During a negotiation, you will likely have to make a lot of tactical decisions. It is far better to consider them before you start than it is to make them on the fly.

Student or Samurai?

Initial attitude is important. Unless you have a very strong position or really don't care about deadlock, it is probably not a good idea to be simmering samurai, saying little, shaking your head often. A more profitable role is that of student, viewing your first job to learn as much as you can about your opponent and your opponent's case.

Listen, not to find fault, not to contradict: "Not so, not so, not so," seldom is productive. Listen to learn. How does your opponent view the situation? What does your opponent need and want out of the agreement? Hear the other side out before you get into specific disputes.

Ask questions:

— *Why do you think that is a fair proposal?*

— *Why don't you think your client will agree to mine?*

> — *Tell me more about why you don't think my witness will be believed?*

It will be hard for you to sit there, not responding. There is a sense that if you don't *dispute* arguments, if you don't *contest* facts, you *accept* them. You will be tempted to jump in and cut off your opponent:

> *"Not so fast there. That argument simply ignores . . . ."*

> *"Stop right there. That simply isn't true."*

Don't brandish your sword; keep your opponent talking:

> *"I don't necessarily agree with that, but keep going."*

> *"I'm listening."*

> *"We'll get back to that but tell me more."*

A delightful book is *"Yes" is Better than "No."* Many Native Americans follow this as rule of thumb in answering the questions of government officials. "No" always lands them in trouble. This would be a good rule of thumb for you. What happens when someone actually agrees with us? The clouds part, the sun shines, and we're ready to spill our guts. Even in the most contested of negotiations, there will be many things you can say "Yes" to.

If "Yes" sticks in your throat, consider "Yes, but." This allows you to acknowledge the point without conceding where it leads: *"Yes,* my case does have those weaknesses, *but* I think that I can overcome them by . . . . ''

Try *active listening*. You do not comment or respond, you simply acknowledge what you have heard and reflect it back, thus encouraging the person to continue.

"You are saying THIS about THAT."

If you had been listening, I described *active listening* in the chapter on *Interviewing*, where the quest is to get your client to narrate without our interrupting.

Pre-conditions

Insisting on agreement as to one issue before others are discussed can be effective. Often these deal with collateral matters, such as "No publicity" or "No attorney fees." The danger is that you risk deadlock if your opponent refuses to agree. You surely don't want to start a negotiation with a firm demand and then, in the face of resistance, give it up.

Should you make the first offer?

Your *fear* is that you have grossly miscalculated the worth of your case. Your *hope* is that your opponent has.

Having the other side go first solves both problems. You won't be struck with your ill conceived offer, and you may get one better than your wildest dream. However, the more experienced you and your opponent are, the less likely either of you has grossly miscalculated and letting your opponent go first has a definite cost. The first offer becomes the base–you will have to force concessions rather than be convinced to make concessions.

If you decide you want the other side to go first, give some thought to how to make this happen. How will you respond if you opponent asks, "What do you think is fair?"

How realistic should your initial position be?

"Let's split the difference" is a traditional mind set and one that leads parties to take extreme initial positions. Your initial position, however, shouldn't be so extreme that your opponent will not take it seriously. You should be able to defend it as being fair and reasonable. Remember that one of you opponent's fears is that, in the end, an offer that should have been accepted was rejected and that things went worse at trial. A ridiculous offer removes this pressure: your opponent will surely do better at trial.

That said, convention dictates that you build in some fat, dollars or issues, for trading purposes.

Some negotiators make one take-it-or-leave it offer. This is known as *Boulwareism* (after a chief proponent of the technique, Lemal Boulware of G.E.). If the offer is a fair one, it might save a lot of haggle time; the downside is that it forces the opposition to "surrender." The common expectation is that we "get something" in negotiation, either that or we feel foolish.

As a side note, to counteract extremism triggered by "splitting the difference" thinking, baseball arbitration requires both the player and the team to make one offer: the arbitrator must pick one of them and not something in-between. You may find the approach being used in other kinds of arbitrations as well.

Finally, your initial position should include everything you want; it is bad form to hold back additional demands until later in the process.

Secrets

There are three kinds of matters that you might want to keep secret: your client's needs, your trial evidence, and your eagerness to settle. Let's take them in reverse order.

Do *not* disclose your *eagerness* to settle. When a couple is dating, the one who is less committed to the relationship gets to pick the movie. Don't disclose, at least initially, your minimum agreement position, that point where you would rather deadlock than go further.

As to *evidence*, should you save the ace of trumps to play at trial? Disclose it and your opponent can prepare for it at trial. Generally, however, it is a bad idea to hold back. One of your goals is to convince your opponent of the strength of your case. Holding back key evidence won't help you achieve that goal. Besides, with discovery, secrets are very hard to keep in any event. If you fear the other side will resort to perjury and falsification, then secrets on your part make more sense.

Some personal injury lawyers prepare *settlement brochures* for the insurance company. The brochure lays out the claims and theories in great detail.

Finally, the difficult issue of *needs*. Creative problem-solving can lead to better settlements and more satisfied participants, both clients and lawyers. Secrecy is the enemy of problem-solving. If both sides are committed to the approach, if both are trustworthy and both value long term relationships, then disclosure will work beautifully. However, if your opponent (or her client) is committed to hardball, go slowly.

If you decide to disclose certain things, consider at what point in the negotiation you will disclose them. If you decide to keep some matters secret, realize that your opponent will be watching for subtle signs, such as how you react to some proposals but not others. Does your body language suggest that you are not anxious to try the case? Or that your client has critical widget needs and no alternatives? Does the tone of your voice betray that you are unsure of a point?

What if your opponent asks? Don't lie. Practice graceful ways of not responding:

> *"Good question. Before I answer that, let's discuss...."*
>
> *"You know I'm not going to answer that."*
>
> *"How about them Bulls?"*

Concessions

Make one concession and the next thing you know your opponent demands Omaha. To avoid the appearance of rout, *give reasons* for your concessions. Don't just come down $8,000. "Listen, we may have some difficulty in making out the case for punitive damages; we'll come down $8,000." "If we settle now, we'll save about that amount in attorney's fees." "Just to get the ball rolling, I will consider dropping the demand by that amount."

It helps to ask your opponent just why it is fair to cut $8,000 from your claim. If the reason is a good one, use it to justify your concession.

Another graceful way to make concessions is to *link* them. "I will come down $8,000 *if* you agree to call your dog off."

Threats

A creditable "last offer" engenders tremendous psychological pressure. Accept it or stalemate. Stalemate, with all its traumas and uncertainties, becomes your opponent's responsibility. Acceptance, on the other hand, means certainty, finality and, of course, no more work.

"But, hey, come on. That *really* wasn't your last offer. I'm waiting."

The philosopher Robert Nozick defined the perfect philosophical argument as one which, if rejected, kills. Something similar is needed in our profession, perhaps a "Nozick Pill," which, once swallowed, would lead to instant death if a further concession was made.

Short of the threat of suicide, how can you make your threats believable?

First *mean it*. Don't make "last offers" as a puffing device. If you and your client are clear on your *stalemate position*, then meaning it won't be a problem. "We feel that further concessions make us worse off than not settling."

Second, take *steps*. Actions speak louder than words. If you are really willing to break off negotiations, what would you do? Set depositions. Look for alternative suppliers.

But what if your opponent threatens stalemate before you do? What if your opponent begins painting itself in a corner before you can even get your brushes out?

Avoiding Deadlock

If your opponent has really made a last offer, this means stalemate has been considered and accepted. Further threats along these lines will not be successful. Recall what the student lawyer did in the example I used in the last chapter, that of the widow and the insurance company. Faced with a final offer, the student *changed* the subject, from money to needs.

Rejecting an offer takes time and energy. If an offer of yours is rejected, don't simply rehash your arguments; *change your proposal* by adding, deleting or rewriting a term. This will force your opponent to reassess and come, once again, to the painful decision to risk deadlock.

Another possibility is to change the players. Perhaps the problem is with personalities. Ask the other lawyer if there is someone else that could step in or if there is someone else in the corporation that should be involved. Consider stepping aside yourself.

Negotiation by mail

Many lawyers open and often conclude negotiation by mail. Some criminal defense lawyers write lengthy letters proposing pleas which detail their client's past and point to weaknesses in the State's case. These letters might include copies of letters from character witnesses.

A major advantage of negotiating by mail is that it invites a considered response, a response that is often difficult in face-to-face negotiations. During a face-to-face negotiation, when you make a point, likely your adversary will deny it just to keep the matter open because it seems like that *unless it is denied, it is admitted.* Knee-jerk "nots" lead to stalemate. Having your arguments in written form, your adversary will have time to consider them without immediately reacting to them.

Written proposals can save time. Even when they do not resolve the matter, they will likely narrow the issues. Consider at least starting negotiation by mail as a well-thought-out and documented letter can impress your adversary with your competence and commitment. Writing is far preferable to negotiation by phone, which usually begins with an exchange of opening offers. There is a certain flipness to this approach. If your opponent calls and asks you for an offer, best to say, "I'll send you a letter."

Back Home

Write the agreement

Once you have negotiated the matter, volunteer to draft the agreement. There will be gaps and ambiguities in what was hashed out. Without violating the spirit of the agreement, you can fill omissions and resolve ambiguities so as to protect your client. It is only in writing up the agreement that the omissions will be seen. Because you are writing it from the perspective of your client, you will see omissions that your opponent probably would not. If she writes up the agreement, likely she won't see the omissions and ambiguities which harm your client. The others, she'll see.

The only downside to drafting is the rule of interpretation which holds that, in the event of ambiguity, agreements are read against the drafter. This rule makes sense; given the psychological viewpoint, the drafter should be more sensitive to ambiguities that go against him. If he does not clear them up, then it is reasonable to assume that the language was intended to go against him.

If you are settling a case that would otherwise be litigated, be sure to cover what happens if the other side refuses to carry out the settlement. Are you stuck with a suit on the settlement or can you reinstate the main lawsuit?

Learning from your experience

Consistent with what by now has become something of a whine, learn from your experience, don't just go on with the rest of your life. *Review your performance*. What went well? What went badly? What went as expected? What was surprising? What would you do the same? What would you do differently? You may wish to make your own review list. Probably it would be a good idea to do so *before* the negotiation. "Was I able to resist making the first offer?" "Was I able to learn X during the negotiation?" By listing criteria for judgment, you will be making your goals explicit and that should help in achieving them.

No gloating

Finally, be sensitive to your opponent's need to sell the agreement to her client. Give her material and arguments that would help her. Always congratulate your opponent on a fine job and give the lion share of the credit to her.

The easiest thing to give up is credit.

Gary Bellow told me that.

CHAPTER 27

TORTS

The time's, they are a'changin'.

Based on impressions drawn from visits to my son's elementary school's playground, "I'll tell my big brother and you'll be sorry" is quickly losing ground to "I'll sue!" This no doubt augers well for the financial future of our profession, and represents an encouraging step toward "Let's talk this out." Nonetheless, Ben and his friends are in for some rude awakenings.

A friend recently sat on a malpractice jury in a case against a hospital. The jury awarded the plaintiff what she asked for, $75,000. My friend thought that the plaintiff would be delighted but, leaving the courthouse, she overheard the plaintiff crying into her cell phone.

"It was horrible. I had to sit there for three days, listening to their lawyer say horrible things about me."

In assessing the worth of a settlement, your client, plaintiff or defendant, should know that litigation is consuming, hurtful, and not soon forgotten.

Flight insurance promises grim certainty: "Loss of one arm and an eye, $250,000." How much is it worth in our system?

Case Evaluation

Case evaluations are projections of how the case would fare before a jury. Two pieces of advice:

1. Your case is *worse* than you think. Your adversarial stance has made it appear better than it is.

2. To get a good feel for the actual strengths and weaknesses of your case, step out of role and view it as would a judge or jury. Talk to lawyers, bailiffs, court reporters, and make a nuisance of yourself at parties, remembering, of course, not to disclose names or identifying information.

It is possible to make case evaluation *sound* like science (and thus get tenure). The outcome of litigation rests on two variables—the likelihood of prevailing on the merits and, having prevailed, on the amount of judgment. Probability theory reduces it to a mathematical formula. If you have a 75 percent chance of winning, and winning brings you $100, the settlement worth of the case is $75. (Over 100 cases, you will average winning $75.) The smart money grabs $76, spurns $74.

But people don't behave the way they should. Some, loving the spin of the wheel, won't settle for less than $90; others, having heard "Double zero" too often in their lives, would take $60. Nonetheless this model, like most models, can help both you and your client think through the worth of the case.

The variables will be something of a bear. The likelihood of prevailing is an assessment resting on all of your legal training and your common sense. As to estimating the *amount* of judgment, there are two general approaches. In many locales, there are *jury services* which report the facts of recent cases and the amount of verdict. These may help in individual cases but probably are more helpful to get a sense of overall trends. In my neck of the woods, juries, at least on smaller cases, have been less generous to plaintiffs than have mediators.

The other method is by formula. A *rule of thumb*, followed by many practitioners, is that a personal injury case is worth *three or four times the specials,* the provable losses such as doctor's bills, medication, lost pay. The specials to be multiplied do not, however, include property damage. (Beats me!)

Specials:	
	$2750 (Hospital and drugs)
	$2600 (Doctor's fees)
	$4050 (Lost wages)
	$9400 times 4 = $37,600

Now just add property damage.

I wouldn't put too much stock in either approach. Jurors don't read jury reporting services and they aren't instructed as to the formula. Nonetheless, *what we think is real takes on substance.* To the degree that the players in the personal injury field believe in the approaches, they can be used in negotiation.

And there is something special about specials. They are "real," whereas pain and suffering are speculative. It seems probable that the higher the "real" losses, the higher the speculative ones. Jurors, knowing from TV advertising that lawyers take a third, may figure out what the plaintiff deserves and then add the amount the lawyer will get. Clearly the worthy plaintiff deserves compensation for medical bills and lost wages. With this in mind, work hard on establishing them, and, at trial, spend the time necessary to prove them. It is better to have the employer testify as to the lost wages than to rely on what may appear to be the self-serving testimony of the plaintiff.

The Curious Impact of Attorney Fees and Litigation Costs

Unlike many legal systems, ours does not allow the victor to recover the amounts paid in *attorney fees*, absent some contractual or statutory provision to the contrary. This curious little rule has had its impact on our society, witness the problem of the *small screw*: "Sure, we can get your $200 back, but my bill will be $500."

The rule has tremendous impact on negotiation. In fact negotiation is often really about avoiding additional attorney fees. Assume a breach of contract action; both parties project a jury award of $100,000. To litigate will cost each side an additional $10,000 in attorney fees. If the case is *settled* at the projected figure, the defendant pays $100,000, and the plaintiff receives $100,000. If the case is litigated and the jury returns the expected verdict, defendant pays $110,000, plaintiff nets $90,000.

Dickens vindicated! *Bleak House* renovated!

Note the *concept of negotiating range*. Plaintiff is looking at a litigation win of $90,000 while the defendant is looking at a litigation loss of $110,000. *Any* settlement between $90,000 and $110,000 leaves *both parties better off* than would litigation.

While *costs* of litigation (discovery costs, etc.) are generally shifted to the losing party, they too have an impact. Assume that the costs to each side of continuing to prepare for litigation will be $15,000. If the plaintiff wins, these costs can likely be thrown on the defendant *but* if the plaintiff loses then he will have to absorb his own costs *and* pay those of the defendant. If the chances of victory (and defeat) are 50/50, game theory instructs that both sides, by insisting on litigation, lose $15,000.

To show you how all of this might come together, consider the following opening offer:

> "We think $200,000 is a fair offer. We have special damages in the amount of $47,000. I can go over the list in a minute. We think that, given the gross negligence of your client, the jury will come in at about four times that amount or $188,000. I have looked at some recent jury awards with basically the same kinds of damages and the awards have come in at $150,000, $210,000 and $225,000. We can go over those if you like."

"If we go to trial, we expect a verdict in the neighborhood of $190,000. If we add to that the probable $15,000 your client will have to pay you, and maybe $5,000 in costs, that's $210,000. Add to that our $5,000 in additional costs we will likely incur, your client is looking at a trial loss of $215,000. That' s why our offer of $200,000 is fair."

"As for the law, this is a routine case and I can't see any tricky legal problems. Do you?"

Once you have discussed your case with others, played around with the jury reports, the formula and projected likely continuing (and thus savable) attorney fees and costs, there are a few other variables to consider.

Other Variables

Your adversary

If you don't know your adversary, call around. Good trial lawyer? Good negotiator? Hardball or problem-solver? Experienced in the field? Push hard for clients or a "high volume/low quality" provider?

Risk

To some, the preference is the bird in the hand. Others, even though they may like to gamble, cannot afford to. They cannot take the chance, even if minimal, of walking away empty-handed. Does one side have pressing economic reasons to settle? Is one side judgment proof or likely to go bankrupt?

Vindication

Clients and lawyers who see important principles at stake are formidable. Recall that you have some flexibility in defining the conflict: "Widow v. Insurance Company" good, "Vulnerable Elder v. Insurance Company" better.

Precedent and face

Is one party particularly vulnerable to an adverse litigation result because it will set a bad precedent? Does one side fear publicity? (Before phoning the press, consult the ethical rules on trial publicity.) If a party is a large organization, does the person making settlement decisions have any "face" concerns with superiors such as the desire to cover up an error or the desire to look competent by settling? Will a party lose reputation or self-respect if the matter is litigated?

Adversary's fee arrangement

If there is a *retainer*, likely the lawyer will favor minimizing the time spent; if there is a *contingent fee*, unless additional lawyer time means additional recovery, the preference will be to minimize lawyer time. A similar preference will be found when the lawyer is working for *no fee*; if there is an hourly rate, the lawyer will probably see Western Civilization threatened by settlement.

On philosophers and the arrogance of the living

At other times, and indeed in other countries, this chapter would be quite puzzling and, if you step back, it should be.

> *Due to another's fault, you lose one arm and one eye. Can it really be that the amount you will be compensated for those injuries turns upon postures, ploys and the skill of the lawyer?*

Apparently so. Gerald Williams, in his study of negotiation, gave identical files to leading P.I. and defense lawyers in many cities. He found a very large range in the dollar amounts of negotiated settlements. But, as philosophers teach us, the mere fact that this is the way things are does not mean that they have to be the way they are.

It is possible to believe that there is a just amount of compensation for the loss of an arm and eye; that it need not turn on negotiation technique. For example, St. Thomas Aquinas believed in "just value." An object's value does not depend upon market demand, its "just price" is that which covers the value of the material and labor which went into producing it.

Thomas Hobbes, in the *Leviathan*, forcibly rejected that notion and has, at least until recently, carried the day:

> *[The] value of all things contracted for, is measured by the Appetite of the Contractors: and, therefore, the just value is that which they are contended to give.*

Distant philosophical doctrines impact our lives. The philosophical doctrine of subjective value plays itself out in the office. With no objective standard by which to measure just compensation, we think in terms of lawyer's cunning. Sure we talk about the extent of damages, but often how much a person receives turns on his current need for cash and the extent he fears testifying, and on his opponent's vulnerability to publicity and the extent she can tolerate risk. Curious.

Another philosophical doctrine playing its part in negotiation is that of legal and factual *indeterminacy*. If the doctrine of subjective value makes it hard to guess how *much* you will win if you win; the doctrine of indeterminacy makes it next to impossible to predict *if* you will win.

Will the judge follow the maxim which reads, "Interpret a statute *broadly* to achieve its purpose," or the maxim that reads, "Interpret *narrowly* to follow the statutory language?" Cases are won and lost on such calls. As to the facts, what the jury will find to be true, will they, to borrow from Richard Pryor, believe you or their own lying eyes?

Of course, if you have read the realists or the crits, you know all of this already. The "blackletter" of that tedious discourse is that no case is as bad as it may seem and creative thought and diligent effort will disclose some saving loophole or nitpick. (People who actually *practice law*, however, often have a different view: most cases are *worse* than they seem).

The notion that law is indeterminate is not *compelled* by the universe. Just as people have believed in objective value, countless judges, lawyers and academics have believed that law is certain. The very first casebook was compiled by Christopher

Columbus Langdell, who was named Dean of the Harvard Law School in 1875. Recently Professor Grant Gilmore studied that casebook and found that it had nothing to do with teaching "how to think like a lawyer." It was very much concerned with teaching the "correct" law.

Legal formalism, the notion that there are correct answers, was overthrown by legal realism, the notion that there are only good, helpful, arguments. Like the formalists, and like everyone else, we believe what we are taught, and most of our teachers were the students of the legal realists. Day after day, for three years, we study cases that "could have gone either way."

Perhaps things are changing. Courts now strike price clauses as "unconscionable" and this seems like "just price" thinking to me. Courts are also developing "bright line" rules to avoid endless argument. But heady trends, fortunately, are not the stuff of Nutshells.

My point is simply this. Realize that we are all captives of our times. Never, not once, think that those who have gone before were stupid, never, not once, be intellectually smug.

CHAPTER 28

DEALS

"Doers" *do*; lawyers *caution*.

Folks embarking on a new relationship are usually optimistic and part of your job is to be the bearer of possible bad news. But don't make too many dour predictions as parties are always free to walk. But once they sign, they are stuck. You are, in effect, writing a *law* that the courts will enforce, with damages, injunctions, and, ultimately, the sheriff. What you write may be interpreted by judges not yet in law school.

Previously I dealt with the general negotiation techniques; here I will focus on special concerns in negotiating and drafting transactions. This kind of work promises the most for problem-solving techniques as both sides will want to make the pie as large as possible, and usually both are committed to long-range goals.

Essential Topics

"Deals" include real estate transactions, licensing of intellectual property licenses, loan agreements, requirement contracts, partnerships, employment contracts, corporate charters, and, indeed, Constitutions. Only a very foolish Nutshell would offer specific advice. However, Professor Stewart Macaulay, who has studied business practices for many years, points out that most agreements cover three basic areas:

1. *Duties*: Who is to do what, when, and for what price?

2. *Contingencies*: What effect will they have on respective duties?

3. *Failures and disputes*: What happens if one side doesn't perform? How will disputes be handled?

In this chapter, I'll first offer some tips on learning the ropes of a specific endeavor, then I'll give you some questions to ask your client, warn you of some of the distortions of legal education, give you a check list of hidden issues to consider, and finally close with issues surrounding drafting agreements which will be imposed, rather than negotiated.

Learning the ropes

If you are new to an area, first learn the ropes. Spend time with your client learning about the activity; visit the plant, the studio, or the practice field. Talk to lawyers who practice in the area. What are the pitfalls? The contingencies? The norms concerning allocation of risk and dispute resolution?

When it comes to drafting an agreement, *form books* and *checklists* for particular kinds of deals will be quite helpful. Reading a form contract, focus on each term and ask yourself, "Do I need some-

thing like that?" There is a problem with intellectual plagiarism however. There may be aspects particular to your case that the form doesn't address. It is
very *difficult to see what's not there.* Before consult-
ing form books, list everything you think the agreement should cover. This will help you see what's
not there.

What to Ask Your Client

Drawing on Macaulay's list, with one addition,
you should explore four areas.

    *1. "What will you do if an agreement isn't
       reached?"*

Knowledge of alternatives greatly strengthens
your bargaining position. Your alternatives will suggest the point at which to walk away from negotiations and will bring clarity about the objectives.
Without contrasts, we are blind.

    *2. "What do you want to accomplish and for
       what price?"*

The more specific your client is about goals, the
better. As to duties, disputes might arise as to
performance: how should they be evaluated? Price
should not be set without a clear understanding of
what risks one is assuming. A job that can be done
today for $10,000 should not be promised at that
price if there is a substantial possibility that costs
will increase tomorrow.

    3. "What can go wrong?"

"It's two years from now. What could have gone
wrong?" Increased costs? Strikes? Acquisitions? Re-
tirements? Pro wrestling discovered to be real?

As we will see, it is not necessary to cover every contingency in the agreement nor is it even necessary to mention them all to the other side. However, there is no excuse to *assume* that the world will forever stay the same. On the other hand, predicting the future is the stuff of Greek tragedy.

Once all the reasonable contingencies are accounted for, the price adjustments can be considered in light of which party will assume the risk, either under the agreement or under default legal rules.

4. "How should disputes be resolved?"

Parties may have a hard time performing and disputes about language can arise. A lot of creative work is being done in the area of dispute resolution: terms requiring cooling off periods, mediation or arbitration. All of these deserve a serious look. Consider carefully, however, the interplay of the formal and informal methods of dispute resolution. In many enterprises there is a strong tradition of informal dispute resolution, *i.e.* the telephone. If this fails, perhaps quick termination and litigation are appropriate, rather than forcing the parties to stay together, jumping additional hurdles.

Draft a "Yes" Proposal

As I indicated previously, Roger Fisher of the Harvard Negotiation Project recommends that, once you have a good understanding of your client's goals and concerns, consider drafting a proposal specific enough that, if the other side says "yes," that would be that. Even if you never show this proposal to the other side, writing it will do wonders to focus your thinking.

Overcoming Law School

I'm a cheerleader for legal education, and yet all that is taught is not necessarily correct: the belief that parties want legally enforceable deals; the view that if something can go wrong, it will go wrong; and, finally, the conviction that salvation lies in precise drafting. Or, to put it in a more succinct form, the lesson of law school is to *commit everyone, then overdraft, but with great precision!* Not so fast.

The Problem of Legal Commitment

Sometimes the parties *don't* want an enforceable deal and will be satisfied with a handshake. A great deal of the nation's business is conducted on the basis of informal, unenforceable deals. Get used to it. There are good reasons *not* to have the threat of lawyers and lawsuits hanging over your head and instead rely on goodwill and community reputation.

Ask your client: "Do you want an enforceable deal?" If the parties don't, make sure they are clear about that; otherwise one might later claim that the handshake sealed an enforceable oral agreement.

The Problem of Contingencies

In law school, no one ever lives happily ever after. All marriages end in divorce, all contracts, in breach, and all trips to the liquor store, in robberies or slips and falls, or both. After three years of this, no doubt you are something of a downer.

One rap on the legal profession is that we are deal-killers. Once we point out all that can go wrong, thus successfully spotting *all* the issues, no one wants to risk it. This is a real concern: parties don't have to enter contracts.

Let's say you *don't* bring a contingency to the table. What might happen? Maybe it won't happen, then nothing happens. If it does happen, and it is not covered in the contract, the world does not end. The parties either will work it out or go to court. Note that at the time the contingency arises, the parties will have more information and their agreement *then* might make more sense than their agreement *now*.

Of course, if it does arise, your client might get stuck. However, if you bring the contingency to the table, you might still be forced to assume the risk due to your relative bargaining strength. Or the parties might deadlock over the issue (and thus the agreement fails over something that may never happen).

One way to prevent deadlock in this situation is to agree not to agree, if it happens, we'll see. Or you can agree to negotiate "in good faith" or arbitrate the issue when, and if, it arises.

Of course, if the contingency does arise, and the other side has agreed to assume the risk, then your client will be glad that you raised the issue.

All of this does *not* mean that you should be *sloppy*. It is meant to remind you of the calamitous bent of your legal education, three years of "disasters *not* averted." Your job is to alert clients to the things that may go bump in the night. It is their decision whether these matters should become part of the negotiations.

However, if a client is taking a foolish risk, write a letter to the client so advising or you may be blamed later.

The Problem of Precision

> *Early statutes defined "theft" as a "felonious taking." What did that mean? Reformers were uncomfortable (they always are). Redrafted, theft became "to take an object of value from another with the intent to deprive said owner of said object permanently." In the old days, mothers, who stole food for starving babies, walked free: whatever a "felonious taking" was, that wasn't. But it surely was permanently depriving said owner, with intent no less!*

One problem with precision is that it is verbose: compare "felonious taking" with the mouthful that came after. Verbose means boring, pedantic, and, worst of all, costly.

Another problem with precision is that, while it controls discretion, it controls discretion. It is folly to believe that we can anticipate the future with such clarity that we know exactly what should be done in all situations. And yet we try and mothers go to jail.

Finally precision may be the enemy of compromise. In China, around the time of Confucius, there was a debate about whether the laws should be written down. The argument *against* this was that once the law was written, people would insist upon their rights, whereas in a just society people compromise.

Vagueness encourages compromise and vagueness allows for flexibility.

Again, I am not advocating sloppiness. But realize the costs of lengthy documents, drafted with precision. Perhaps you better serve your client with a (cheap) short and vague memorandum of understanding that will allow for compromise down the road. Do I make myself clear?

Hidden Problems

Here are a few things to worry about you might not have thought of.

Pre-contract liability

If you are engaged in lengthy negotiations and one of the parties is spending considerable time and funds in the expectation that an agreement will be reached, beware! Agree, early on, who pays for these preparations if the deal falls though. You can no longer rest assured that your client will incur no liability, until and unless, a contract is signed. Using doctrines such as promissory estoppel, some courts have shifted the costs of preparation to the other side.

Uninvited guests

Will third parties benefit or be harmed by the agreement? Consider that injured third parties might base claims on "third party beneficiary" or negligence analysis. You can draft around "third party beneficiary" problems by explicitly stating no such beneficiaries are intended.

Another potential disaster is the tort of interference with contract, third parties suing your client for entering into a contract with someone they had been dealing with.

Integration

Over the course of long negotiations, parties will come to agreements as to some issues. When the final agreement is drafted, be sure those issues are either included or were meant to be excluded. If a court finds that the agreement was "integrated," all else is likely lost.

Parol evidence

Make sure that the parties are using words in the same way. "Table for one" means one thing to a waiter, quite another to a mortician. (Okay, maybe parol evidence *isn't* that much of a problem, but I love the joke.)

Ethics and Contracts of Adhesion

Warm zeal and the defense of the unpopular are our grandest traditions. But they were forged in the hot fire of the adversary system. There, every move is scrutinized by the opposition. But lawyers are often asked to draft agreements that will *not* be negotiated or scrutinized, but will be *imposed*: form sales contracts, form leases, and form software licenses.

When the context has shifted, when there is no adversary, should our ethics change?

I would draft the agreement as I would an opening offer, one that gives my client maximum benefit and protection. Then I would assume the role of opposing counsel and try to hammer out something a tad more fair. Then I would discuss the matter with my client.

Balanced contracts can reassure customers; often bad things never happen and, if they don't, grand defensive clauses only offend. If bad things do happen? Not every landlord, every store, and every software company wants to get away with it. "You know, if I or one of my employees cause someone injury, I think we should pay up."

Don't assume the worst of your client. Ask. While the choice is ultimately the client's, it is proper for you to share your opinions, and, almost always, to quit.

Finally the more one-sided the agreement, the more likely it will be thrown out as unconscionable or as against public policy. Woe to the client who, relying on your well-drafted exculpatory clause, failed to obtain liability insurance.

Worse yet, woe to you.

CHAPTER 29

DISPUTES ABOUT DEALS

I put the following to my Contracts class; "Buyer and Seller are in a long term widget contract. Seller makes late deliveries and Buyer cancels. If you are the seller, what would you say?"

I was looking to review of contract doctrines: "Seller would say 'My late deliveries were immaterial breaches and, besides, Buyer has waived the time requirement by accepting late deliveries in the past. By canceling Buyer has breached! Let's crush Buyer!' "

After hearing my question, the students suddenly took a great interest in their shoes. One hand waved, however, that of the eight year old son of one of my students, condemned to contracts by a defaulting babysitter.

"Okay," I asked, "If you were seller, what would you say?"

"I'm sorry."

Although not taught in law school, "I'm sorry" can go a long ways. At bottom many disputes are not about "material breaches," or "waivers," or even widgets or dollars; they are often about hurt feelings and a sense of betrayal.

Here we focus on the situation where there has *not* been a total breakdown in the relationship. If there has been, then the negotiation is similar to that of a tort negotiation, casting blame and picking up pieces. Here we deal with the situation where things aren't going so well and the client needs advice. These are tough cases.

The dilemma is this. If your client *stays* in the relationship, problems may continue and even get worse; staying might simply delay the eventual. But if your client *leaves* the relationship, the potential benefits are lost and litigation becomes possible. We can say three things about litigation: it is expensive, it is hurtful, and one can always lose.

Your goal is either to help repair the relationship or help terminate it gracefully. This must be done with an eye to your client's litigation posture. To help you think about this tangle, we'll consider three topics: the emotional context, the legal context, and the negotiation context.

The Emotional Context

Unlike the case in most torts, when the parties are strangers, parties to contract disputes know one another and had, at one point, a valuable relationship. Then things started to go sour, phone calls were made, voices raised, performances suspended and law suits threatened. By the time you get involved, most likely the parties are mad and seek revenge. Even the boring, rational, list-making, economically maximizing business person will sulk at the sting of "being taken advantage of" or of being "harassed by unreasonable demands."

The surface complaint may conceal the real hurt. When Abraham Lincoln took office, several southern states were already leaving. In his Inaugural Address, he said:

> *"[I]f the United States [is] an association of States in the nature of contract merely, can it, as a contract, be peaceably unmade, by less than all the parties who made it? One party to a contract may violate it — break it, so to speak; but does it not require all to lawfully rescind it?"*

If taken at his word, it would seem that the Civil War was simply a contract dispute, admittedly, a tad more intense than most.

Probe to discover the root causes of hostilities. A successful settlement, one that will work, needs to address the root causes. The surface conflict will often be a zero sum conflict, where what one side wins, the other side loses. Getting beneath the surface and discovering the conflicting needs and goals can lead to a more creative way of dealing with the conflict, perhaps a win/win solution. Recall my discussion of "Hardball" and "Problem Solving" strategies.

Should you try to get your client to understand the other side's position? Tough call. During your first interview, allow the client to vent and don't urge "be reasonable." The client will be in no mood and will read your advice as insensitive or as betrayal.

Against these concerns is the notion that, if an amicable settlement is to be reached, one with a good chance of succeeding, mutual understanding is important, grumbling or not. First convince your clients that you are on their side and that you will fight tooth and nail for them. Once you have their trust, somewhere down the road, "Let's be reasonable; it improves our litigation posture."

On some occasions, however, your job will be just the opposite: to pour oil. Where clients face powerful foes, they may be all too willing to give up their rights and even, in some cases, their safety. The archetypical case is the battered spouse: "Let's just forget it. It was my fault and it won't happened again, and, if I go to court, it will seem like admitting I can't handle my own life." While these are valid concerns, you should point out that no one deserves to be beaten and that usually it does happen again. This kind of guilt, fear, and insecurity is not restricted to battered spouses.

Once, as I told you previously, I represented a community of farm workers who lived next to a feedlot. We filed suit on the basis of "nuisance." The powerful owner made a ridiculous offer, something along the lines of not increasing the number of cows on the lot. As required, I relayed the offer and, to my dismay, many of my clients wanted to take it. They were happy simply to be acknowledged and felt queasy about suing in the first place.

"Sure, we can settle the case right now. By the way, the owner told me that his cows didn't cause the flies, you did."

Oil works. Six months later, the cows, and the flies, were gone.

The Legal Context

If you don't do the hard work of assessing your client's legal position, forget the rest.

With all due respect to my wonderful colleagues who teach torts, the law of contracts, at least in terms of client counseling, is vastly more difficult and interesting.

1. In torts, *one* of the parties is liable or not. In contracts, often *either* of the parties may be liable. The Seller may be liable for breaching by making late deliveries *or* the buyer might be liable for canceling the contract in the face of an immaterial breach.

2. The damage rules in torts are fairly straightforward, except, strangely, in cases involving trains, either where someone drops fireworks at a station or where a vintage locomotive sets the Midwest ablaze. In contracts, there are tricky problems in proving damages, such as lost profits, and in recovering for such things as emotional upset.

3. In torts, the past is past; whether there was or wasn't a tort is set in time. In contracts the story is continuing: whether there is or isn't a breach may turn on the next telephone call. Except in nightmares, torts are

dead; contract disputes are alive and unfold under your direction.

Without a review of contract law (another Nutshell), to assess your client's legal position, you will have to predict, if the case is tried, who will be liable for what.

Damages

Contract damages are notorious for undercompensating injuries, given the tough rules about foreseeability and proving such things as lost profits. On some occasions, of course, contract remedies overcompensate for injury, when the expectancy damages exceed the reliance costs.

Consider how clever lawyers can up the stakes, by claiming a contract breach is also a tort or a RICO violation, and by bringing a class action.

Breach

The matter of breach is complicated. Read the agreement and don't be satisfied with your client's view. Precise wording can be critical. I tend to remember points that have been captured in powerful quotes and I am always in the market for a good one.

A Man for All Seasons, by Robert Bolt, is a marvelous play for lawyers to read. It deals with personal integrity and the importance of law. Why not cut down the law to get at the Devil?

> *"And when the last law was down, and the Devil turned round on you—where would you hide, the laws all being flat? . . . . d'you think*

> *you could stand upright in the winds that*
> *would blow then?"*

King Henry VIII has broken with the Pope in order to marry Anne Boleyn. He demands that all of his subjects approve the marriage. Sir Thomas More, as a Catholic, cannot. At one point he is asked, upon the pain of treason, to sign an oath.

> *More: What is the oath?*
> *Roper: It's about the marriage, sir.*
> *More: But what is the wording?*
> *Roper: We don't need to know the wording—we know what it will mean.*
> *More: It will mean what the words say. An oath is made of words!*

Contracts are made of words. A contract means, not what your client "knows" it does, but *what the words say.*

Of course, by the words I have selected, I don't want to be misunderstood as meaning that words mean what they say. Where have I been?

Words, legal scholars point out, are as slippery as fish and don't always mean what they seem to say. A lot of people have gotten into real difficulty by reading things too literally. "Says here time is of the essence and you're 15 minutes late!"

Putting aside parol evidence and trendy theories that meaning resides in the reader, not in the words, your first step is to read the documents carefully. Then, and only then, argue black means white. Hopefully you won't have to.

Assuming that one of the parties didn't do as promised, the next question is what the other party can do about it. Almost always the innocent party can hold the other to the promise in terms of damages; the critical question, however, is whether the innocent can cancel the contract. Here we come to the difficult issue of material breach. To get a handle on how serious the breach, either your client's or the other party's, consider the following questions, drawn roughly from the factors listed by the Restatement of Contracts as those to be considered in determining materiality.

— *To what degree has the breach harmed the other party?*

— *Can that harm be adequately compensated for?*

— *What will happen to breaching party if the contract is terminated? Will it suffer forfeiture, a warehouse of specially manufactured goods?*

— *Does it look like the breacher will shape up and perform?*

— *Has the breacher generally shown good faith and fair dealing?*

— *If this matter is delayed too long, will the innocent party have a hard time making substitute arrangements?*

The Negotiation Context

In your discussion with your client, break the dispute into three areas: the *cause* of the problem;

possible *solutions* to the problem; and business *alternatives* if agreement isn't reached.

> — *What went wrong? What would the other side say*
> *as to what went wrong?*

> — *How can the agreement be made to work? What*
> *would the other side say to these suggestions?*

> — *If the agreement is terminated, what are your alternatives? What would be the other side's alternatives?*

Before beginning negotiations, know your goal. To focus your thinking, with your client's input, draft a settlement proposal, one which, if the opposition agrees, would end the matter.

Once you know what you want to accomplish in negotiations, what should be your basic negotiation strategy? As we have seen previously, there are two basic approaches: Hardball and Problem Solving.

In terms of compelling settlement, hardball might work well. Hardball is not necessarily hostile, just firm. It is marked by high demands, begrudging concessions, and frequent threats of deadlock. However, if a settlement isn't reached, these things may come back to bite you. Judges and juries like reasonable folks and, if the matter is at all close, hotheads lose. Looking only toward litigation, initial proposals would be reasonable and would include concessions. If it comes to trial, your client should appear to be the one who has walked the extra mile.

Another reason to avoid hardball is that the problem-solving approach might work better. Problem-solving attempts to address needs, rather than exploit them, and tries to increase the pie, rather than merely divide it. Further, hardball can increase hurt feelings and, when people have been in a relationship, they are likely to remain in a relationship, even if it is legally ended.

Finally, an settlement based on hardball may not last the night. "I'll sign under compulsion but you better watch out!"

The U.C.C. has codified an interesting device, the Right to Adequate Assurance.

> *When reasonable ground for insecurity arise with respect to the performance of either party the other party may in writing demand adequate assurance of due performance and until he receives such assurances may if commercially reasonable suspend any performance for which he has not already received the agreed return. (U.C.C. 2–609)*

A mouthful, but a helpful mouthful. Consider such letters even in situations not covered by the U.C.C. Lay out, in non-confrontational language, why you are unsure of continuing performance and then propose a reasonable solution to the problem. It might be good to add that it is the hope of your client that things can be worked out so the relationship can continue. You hope this approach will lead

388   *DISPUTES ABOUT DEALS*   Ch. 29

to a solution; if not, then you have walked the extra mile and have a paper trail to prove it. Note that under the U.C.C. the failure to respond to such a letter, if reasonable, becomes a repudiation of the contract that allows you to terminate.

Finally, of course, never forget the power of "I'm sorry."

EPILOGUE: THE ISSUE IS US

"Hey, look at me!"

Soon you'll be walking. It is a marvelous thing, it is a joyous thing, to struggle with the basic skills, to break through, to fall, to dust yourself off, to totter and to take another step.

As you begin your journey, I'll run after you, shouting:

"Learn from your experiences!"

> After you have completed a task, be it an interview, a deposition, or a trial, take ten or fifteen minutes: What did I learned? What went well? What went badly? What can I do better?

"Learn from the experiences of others!"

> Read widely. Attend workshops. Try out different approaches.

"Write!"

> Only then will you slow down enough to access the depth of your insights.

This is a long book and together we have ridden many miles. Don't worry if you didn't "get" everything I had to say. Writing it, I have read a lot of other authors and I surely didn't get everything they had to say. Some of it I already knew, some of it I found tedious and garbled, but, every now and then, something would jump out. Suddenly I would see an old problem in a new way; suddenly there would be clarity instead of fog.

Lawyer friends occasionally ask me, "How can you stand teaching *Hadley v. Baxendale*, again, and again, and again?"

"Because *Hadley* is my *Galileo*, my *Fern Hill*, my *Pride and Prejudice*. Every time I read it, I see something new and exciting, not because I was dumb before, and before, and before, but because I have moved beyond old problems and now see new ones."

This is your career. As you move along, solving problems only to face others, reread parts of this book. Knowing more, you'll learn more: "That I already know, that point is tedious (but not garbled, oh no, never garbled!), but, wow, that one helps me understand cross examination in a slightly different way."

Read what others have to say. Go to trial workshops. Try different styles and approaches. If you are naturally quiet, try loud; if you are naturally aggressive, try passive. You may surprise yourself that what "could never be you" fits you like a glove.

There is always some new angle to explore and some new approach to consider. You will never be bored. Remember, however, that what worked for others, or what worked for me, may not work for you. Running your insights, your personality, against ours, eventually you will emerge as your own unique lawyer.

Law practice is only partly about law. Although I am reluctant to tell my first year students this, there are only two times *most* lawyers need to know *Hadley,* on the day of the final and on the woeful days of the July Bar.

What do you need to know, day in, day out? People. What skill do you need the most? The ability to solve problems. How do you learn people and common sense? By throwing yourself into endeavors that involve people making hard decisions: politics, board memberships, coaching.

And read widely. Daily, lawyers face the classic issues of truth and justice, death and injury, revenge, pride, sacrifice, forgiveness, despair and hope. Reading novels, histories, and biographies, you'll be there as heroes, villains, and ordinary folk face life's problems, sometimes grandly, sometimes badly. Great legal training, that.

In some ways, we covered the easy parts: how to plan cross-examination, how to play hardball, and how to write Greek tragedy. To continue with the opening metaphor, these are the things you need to know in order to walk; now the question becomes, *"Where will you go?"*

Gary Bellow and Bea Moulton introduced their great work on clinical education, *The Lawyering Process*, with this quote from Robert Coles:

> *In this life we prepare for things, for moments and events and situations. We worry about things, think about injustices, read what Tolstoy has to say. Then, all of a sudden, the issue*

> *is not whether we agree with what we have*
> *heard and read and studied. The issue is us,*
> *and what we have become.*

Don't expect big, sharp moments, a John Adams
risking his legal career, risking his political future,
and, indeed, risking the well-being of his family,
standing before an angry Boston jury, arguing that
his clients, British troops, acted in self-defense in
gunning down five unarmed patriots in the Boston
Massacre:

> *"Facts are stubborn things, and whatever may*
> *be our wishes, our inclinations, or the dictums*
> *of our passions, they cannot alter the state of*
> *facts and evidence."*

Facts are stubborn things. Most of our lives are
not the stuff of grand heroic moments; most are the
sum of little decisions, daily decisions: of short cuts
taken or declined, of secretaries and cab drivers
diminished or respected; of little lapses, and of
random kindnesses.

Little things. At a trial advocacy workshop, a new
lawyer listened to an experienced trial lawyer talk
about witness preparation. "Everyone tells them
what to wear, so I don't see what's wrong with
dressing up their testimony."

"I thought the analogy wasn't quite right," she
told me later. "But I didn't say anything; I didn't
want to come across as a moral softie."

You've chosen a tough profession.

Resist the expectations of others. In *War and Peace*, Tolstoy wrote of a wounded soldier regaining consciousness on the bloody field. There is destruction, smoke, and pain everywhere. The absurdity of it all hits him: "I am willing to die for the good opinion of people I don't even know."

Actually, it's not so much the *opinion* of others that runs our lives; it is our *opinion* of what the opinion of others might be. Usually we assume the worst. A torts professor gives his students the gruesome hypothetical: their client has committed some horrendous tort, severely injuring many. But legal research has discovered a loophole that will allow the client to walk and force the victims to suffer in silence.

"What would you do?"

"I won't feel good, but I would assert the loophole!"

"Do you first discuss it with your supervising lawyer or with the client?"

"No. If you show you have qualms, you'll never make partner."

These students have *never* been inside a law office, and yet they allow nonexistent partners to dictate the kind of person they will become. Maybe *real* partners and *real* clients would welcome an ethical discussion. "You know, I hadn't thought of that wrinkle. Now I know why I pay you the big bucks."

Don't project the worst unto others and then conform your life to meet "their" expectations. Ask them first. You owe at least that to the person you will become.

George Orwell was a police officer in Burma. An elephant had escaped and it was his job to track it down. Although the elephant had killed someone, by the time Orwell found it, it was standing peacefully. There was no reason to shoot it; nonetheless, Orwell shot it. Why? The onlookers expected him to; he was afraid "the crowd would laugh at me;" he shot it "solely to avoid looking a fool." Sound familiar?

While it may look like the colonial ruler is in charge, he is trapped; his role turns him into a "sort of hollow posing dummy."

> *For it is a condition of his rule that he shall spend his life trying to impress the "natives," and so in every crisis he has got to do what the "natives" expect of him. He wears a mask, and his face grows to fit it.*

In ten years, will your face be your own?

Always remember the power you have over others. One of my favorite quotes, which I used earlier, is from the British writer C.K. Chesterton:

> *The horrible thing about all legal officials, even the best, about all judges, magistrates, barristers, detectives, and policemen, is not that they are wicked, (some of them are good), not that*

they are stupid, (some of them are quite intelli-gent), it is simply that they have got used to it.

In ten years, will you still see your clients as individuals who bleed if you do prick them, or will they be the ones wearing masks, the masks "typical case" or "billable hours?"

Then there are the big three: alcohol, drugs, and bets. At first there is the rush of power, of money, and of Palm Pilots. Some become intoxicated and end up neglecting cases and stealing from clients. Almost all Bar Associations have confidential programs that help.

You have chosen a tough profession; you have chosen a wonderful profession.

The intellectual challenges are invigorating. We don't see 40 cases of flu each day and write the same prescription. A good friend, a lawyer, is married to a doctor. "Lawyer parties are better," she tells me. "Doctors just talk about their investments; lawyers talk about their cases."

But the intellectual challenges are not the best part. The best part is the people. Lawyers can be jerks but they are usually bright and they are seldom bored or boring. As for the clients, you will be involved in their varied lives at critical times. They come for help. Caring for others is a deeply satisfying endeavor; it is more than a job, it is a privilege.

In the Prologue, I quoted Holmes and will do so now again: "It is possible to live greatly within the law." Perhaps you will argue cases that shape our times, or perhaps you will be the trusted advisor of powerful groups, huge corporations, or even Presidents. Or perhaps you will never make the front page and will be simply another lawyer in the yellow pages, helping people with everyday problems. There is greatness in that as well.

Earlier I quoted "Facts are stubborn things." John Adams was our first Vice President and our second President. More importantly, he was a prime mover, perhaps the prime mover, behind the American Revolution. No John Adams, no American Revolution, and all of our lives would be quite different. John Adam's first love was practicing law:

> *Now to what higher object, to what greater character, can any mortal aspire than to be possessed of all this knowledge, well digested and ready at command, to assist the feeble and friendless, to discountenance the haughty and lawless, to procure the redress of wrongs, the advancement of right, to assert and maintain liberty and virtue, to discourage and abolish tyranny and vice?*

Indeed, there is no higher object. After three hard years, you possess all this knowledge, well digested and ready at command.

Go.

INDEX

References are to Pages

---

402   *INDEX*
References are to Pages

†